Managing the IT Services Process

Managing the IT Services Process

Noel Bruton

AMSTERDAM BOSTON HEIDELBERG LONDON NEW YORK OXFORD
PARIS SAN DIEGO SAN FRANCISCO SINGAPORE SYDNEY TOKYO

Butterworth-Heinemann
An imprint of Elsevier
Linacre House, Jordan Hill, Oxford OX2 8DP
200 Wheeler Road, Burlington, MA 01803

First published 2004

British Library Cataloguing in Publication Data
A catalogue record for this book is available from the British Library

ISBN 0 7506 57235

For information on all Butterworth-Heinemann publications visit
our website at: www.bh.com

Composition by Charon Tec Pvt. Ltd, Chennai, India
Printed and bound in Great Britain

Contents

Contents

Computer Weekly Professional Series

There are few professions which require as much continuous updating as that of the IS executive. Not only does the hardware and software scene change relentlessly, but also ideas about the actual management of the IS function are being continuously modified, updated and changed. Thus keeping abreast of what is going on is really a major task.

The Butterworth-Heinemann – *Computer Weekly* Professional Series has been created to assist IS executives keep up-to-date with the management ideas and issues of which they need to be aware.

One of the key objectives of the series is to reduce the time it takes for leading edge management ideas to move from the academic and consulting environments into the hands of the IT practitioner. Thus this series employs appropriate technology to speed up the publishing process. Where appropriate some books are supported by CD-ROM or by additional information or templates located on the Web.

This series provides IT professionals with an opportunity to build up a bookcase of easily accessible, but detailed information on the important issues that they need to be aware of to successfully perform their jobs.

Aspiring or already established authors are invited to get in touch with me directly if they would like to be published in this series.

Dr Dan Remenyi
Series Editor
dan.remenyi@mcil.co.uk

Series Editor
Dan Remenyi, Visiting Professor, Trinity College Dublin

Advisory Board
Frank Bannister, Trinity College Dublin
Ross Bentley, Management Editor, *Computer Weekly*
Egon Berghout, University of Groningen, The Netherland
Ann Brown, City University Business School, London
Roger Clark, The Australian National University
Reet Cronk, Harding University, Arkansas, USA
Arthur Money, Henley Management College, UK
Sue Nugus, MCIL, UK
David Taylor, CERTUS, UK
Terry White, Bentley West, Johannesburg

Other titles in the Series
Corporate politics for IT managers: how to get streetwise
Delivering IT and e-business value
eBusiness inplementation
eBusiness strategies for virtual organizations
The effective measurement and management of IT costs and benefits
ERP: the implementation cycle
A hacker's guide to project management
How to become a successful IT consultant
How to manage the IT helpdesk
Information warfare: corporate attack and defence in a digital world
IT investment – making a business case
Knowledge management – a blueprint for delivery
Make or break issues in IT management
Making IT count
Network security
Prince 2: a practical handbook
The project manager's toolkit
Reinventing the IT department
Understanding the Internet

About the author

Noel Bruton joined the UK computer industry in 1979, as a pre-sales support assistant for a mainframe manufacturer. He tried his hand at selling computer terminals for a couple of years, before returning to technical support. He likes to boast that he was 'there' when desktop computer networking started, travelling round the world in the early 1980s training technical teams on how to support this new technology.

In his first support management role, he ran a large and international group of support teams for a computer distributor, which supplied large network systems to major corporations. This was in the early days of helpdesking, and he found he was using techniques and producing levels of productivity that far outstripped the performance of many of the company's clients.

A press award for 'Best Helpdesk' followed. Wanting to understand his job better, he looked around for a book on the topic – there was none – so he wrote *Effective User Support*, eventually retitled *How to Manage the IT Helpdesk – A Guide for User Support and Call Centre Managers*, and now in its second edition with Elsevier of Oxford, England.

He started his IT support management consultancy and training practice in 1991. He now has a global clientele and writes frequently for the IT press and broadcast media.

In addition to his books and press articles, he produces a Website for the IT service management industry located at http://www.noelbruton.com.

He is also the author of the techno-political thriller *The Virus Doctors* (Starborn Books, Wales, ISBN 1 899 530 X). See http://www.thevirusdoctors.info.

Noel Bruton lives with his wife and son in West Wales.

About this book

This book is the product of the change the author has noted in the industry. The once-lowly and slightly chaotic helpdesk has matured into a highly sophisticated and professional function. Instead of being a separate and sometimes disregarded wing of the information technology department, the helpdesk has come to be a cog in an integrated IT service mechanism – indeed even the hub of that mechanism. The work is not an academic study of that phenomenon, but the views of an independent practitioner.

This book is not about helpdesks. It is about the overall IT service process, of which the helpdesk is only part.

I would offer a warning to the reader. This is not an academic work, merely studying options for running IT services. It is a set of occasionally furiously worded arguments for the why and how of doing things in a certain way.

All trademarks duly acknowledged.

Preface

A bit of history...

I joined the computer industry at a time when a multi-million dollar installation had a massive two and a half megabytes of memory and you needed forearms like Popeye to change a disk pack. Two hundred megs of online storage provided by a drive unit the size of a chest freezer, sitting with so many other similarly enormous, noisy and tastefully coloured boxes all housed in a refrigerator as big as a basketball court.

There was no such concept as 'information technology' then – what we did was called 'electronic' or 'automated data processing' (EDP, ADP or just DP). And clearly, if we had not yet begun to call ourselves 'IT', then we were still a very long way from 'IT services'.

There was precious little scope for a service ethos in computing at the beginning of the 1980s. These machines were hugely complex, designed and operated by engineers. Service provision was limited to drilling data and machine instructions into punched cards, writing programs in esoteric languages to present users with phosphorescent green forms and dropping reams of printout into groaning in-trays.

There was a strict, political hierarchy associated with computers in those days. Because only the engineers understood the beasts, and because school education limited the user's comprehension of 'computing' to a questionably relevant delving into binary arithmetic[1], the data processing department was a world unto itself. The company knew it needed computers, but its executives could not begin to grasp how the devices worked, so they left the computers to the DP manager and his egghead staff. And among that staff, the more one understood the technology, the more valuable one was deemed to be. At the top were the programmers – some of them drove to work in Porsches. At the bottom were the 'punch-girls', who wore Band-Aids on their fingertips and had to use three digits to enter a single character. Somewhere in the middle were the operators, who had to suffer the social inconvenience of shift-work. In 1979, when Liverpool Polytechnic languages faculty spat me into the lap of Britain's ICL (they of the orange, rather than blue chest freezers), formal user support was still six years away.

It was the computer, not the users, which took priority. Hardware or systems engineering prowess was the mark of human usefulness in the industry at that time. And if your work was in any way associated with the mainframe, you were considered to be in the computer industry, even if the company whose computer you programmed or operated was owned by a shoe manufacturer. The gap between computing and business was extensive. Only the 'systems analysts' could begin to cross it, and only then to convert a complex business need into even more complex machine instructions.

The DP department, in all its esoteric distance from commercialism, did not recognize the significance of the 'microcomputer' when it first emerged in the early 1980s. To the computing purists, these were mere toys, downloading data from the mainframe to calculate new totals in isolated spreadsheets. But gradually, the data began to be created first in the spreadsheets, then uploaded back into the mainframe, and 'distributed computing' was born. Suddenly, the mainframe could not fully function without the desktop computer, and the power gradually began to shift from the computer room to the user's desk. Then groups of users began to compile their collective data on a network server and suddenly the mainframe had an upstart rival.

---

[1] Special note to the maths teacher who chided my youthful and disrespectful enquiry into the usefulness of learning binary arithmetic with 'If you go into computers, you'll need it.' Well, Mike, I did go into computers and, yah boo, I didn't need it. Perhaps we could have spent that time learning something more relevant. ☺

By the time Microsoft™ Windows™ arrived, we even had a name for this technological shift. It was called 'downsizing', and it led to the world we now live in, where local area network servers have proliferated to such an extent that the mainframe has essentially become little more than a larger one of their number.

Computing is now done on the desktop. We have no more need for the massive printouts, because the personal computer can collate the data and present them in a form from which business people can take useful and immediate decisions without having to pore through pages of figures. Previously ancillary technologies like word processing have also been subsumed into the multi-function personal computer and mobile communications mean that physical proximity to the mainframe is no longer a necessity – a salesperson can check stock levels and file orders from a hotel room or an airport departure lounge. Finally, the computers have come to serve the business.

As a result of this, the data processing department had to rethink its purpose and establish new approaches to how it delivers the technology. Some of these philosophical shifts led to clumsy temporary outcomes, like the gauche marketing-think fad for calling users 'customers'[2]. Another of these shifts came with the use of the term 'information technology' rather than 'computing'. We came to realize that the purpose of our processing machinery was ultimately to provide the business with the information it needed to make decisions and take astute commercial action.

In more enlightened organizations, a further maturation of that shift has led to a deft restructuring of the way computing-associated services are delivered, to reflect the computer's true place as a mere tool, like a telephone. We now put the user of the tool into his rightful place at the pinnacle of a service delivery process.

It's not all rosy and mature, however. Some of the old mental boundaries remain with us. Even though program developers rarely drive Porsches any more, even though 'lights-out' computing has automated much of the overnight composition of job control language scripts and manual intervention associated

---

[2] In *How to Manage the IT Helpdesk – A Guide for User Support and Call Centre Managers*, I argued that a user is only one type of customer – others include 'anybody who consumes anything they perceive a service provider to have produced, whether or not they're right, and whether or not the provider realized he was producing it.' It is a misnomer to call a subset by the name of the master set.

with batch computing, some computer departments still tend to hang on to some of the old technocratic hierarchy. The IT architects look down on the programmers, who look down on the network engineers, who look down on the desktop support technicians, who look down on the helpdesk operatives, who look down on the hardware repairers, who look down on the call centre, who looks down on the procurement staff. With all this cascading kicking going on, from an animal welfare point of view, it's perhaps a good thing that IT departments tend not to keep cats.

For a number of years now, we have played with the halfway house of separating information technology and information services. In that model, the technocrats in information technology can remain largely oblivious of the organizationally and culturally distant computer user, and those who understand users well but computers apparently less well can work for information services. It should not be a question of which department is more valuable. Information technology provides the rails and the point-switching, information services provides the rolling stock, stations and ticketing. True, if we didn't have the rails, there would be nothing for the trains to run on – but if we didn't have the ticketing, we would have no means of financing the rails in the first place because the paying customer accesses the system through the services, not through the technology.

Where this book deals with computers, it does so only as they really are – as a respectable and useful range of machinery we deploy only as a means to an end, and not as an end in itself. Our machinery is meaningless unless we can offer its function in terms of a range of business-oriented services, which truly reflect the goals the business wants to achieve. And to that end, we make the technology transparent to the business. So we build what in today's jargon has come to be called the 'end-to-end' service process. At one end, a user may enter an expectation. He remains oblivious of the organizational and mechanical strategies we use to process that expectation. All he knows is that a desired and satisfying business result will drop out of the other end.

Information technology is only a component of a larger perspective. In the end, that perspective is of the strategy by which we choose to publish our services, the integrated process by which we manufacture them and the structure that enables that to happen, in a way that enables accurate and apposite service management decision-making.

It is in arriving at that perspective that so many companies are removing the last vestiges of technocratic hierarchy and linking technology and delivery together in a more appropriate manner. You'll know these companies when you see them. They have a department called 'IT services' or something similar. And that department has an organized and mechanistic process. This book is about designing, implementing and managing that process.

A few words about ITIL

There is already in the world a framework for designing, implementing services in an IT context.

The Information Technology Infrastructure Library (ITIL) is a collection of methodologies and pre-written processes for running an IT department, of which services is a necessary part. Published in the UK by Her Majesty's Stationery Office, ITIL is comprehensive, has a long history and has been adopted by public and private organizations all over the world. The books that constitute ITIL have been written by industry experts, some of whom I know personally and whose legacies of IT services theory and practice I hold in considerable esteem. The processes are cemented by considerable documentation and the availability of training courses for managers and staff in the ITIL-oriented company.

In my view, ITIL has become a victim of its own considerable marketing success. It is widely held to be a 'standard' for running IT services. By their own words, the professors of ITIL make no such claim, stating clearly on their website, 'ITIL is not intended to be prescriptive'. In other words, ITIL proponents make no insistence that ITIL should be adopted in its entirety, and they allow for the organization to tailor the implementation to suit policies and culture. This means that there may be as many interpretations of ITIL as there are companies adopting it, and this is of course the antithesis of a standard.

ITIL is scant in how it deals with customer relationships, which should in my view be at the heart of any services-based function. It is also indecisive in regards to staff, stating that bringing people into the ITIL implementation is a question for the adopting company, not for ITIL itself. As delivering IT services is largely a labour-intensive activity, for me this is a serious omission.

ITIL offers no benchmarks of performance, fiscal or operational, so any illusion of conformity between ITIL-based enterprises is further dashed. They have nothing against which to compare themselves.

Furthermore, ITIL manuals will tell the reader what needs to be done, but not how to do it. One of my favourite allegories is that of the use of a car. ITIL may suggest that to get from London to Oxford, one may get in a car and head for the M40 – but although there is a de facto standard for the use of a gearbox, ITIL will make little mention of the gear lever, so the non-driver will be none the wiser for commencing the journey.

This book addresses all those areas and more, as well as providing the basic advice on designing an IT services department that in my view, ITIL leaves out. I particularly go into the detail of how to design the processes ITIL says you (may) need. ITIL spreads its scope across the whole of IT – whereas I focus on services. This book only refers to the development and production sides of IT where there is a need to interface the processes in those departments with those of IT services.

This work will focus much more on staffing, business justification, service measurement, reporting and several other issues, which in my view are not yet fully developed in ITIL. That methodology, laudable though it is, says a lot about what you should do but too little about how you should go about it. On the other hand, I will be taking a much more practical approach.

So this work is not intended to be an alternative to ITIL. That methodology is non-prescriptive, so there is nothing to prevent you from making use of both ITIL and this book. Indeed, your IT services department may be richer for adopting both approaches.

Noel Bruton
Cardigan, January 2004

List of Figures

List of Case studies

Introduction

1.1 Why this book: causal factors

I wrote this book because IT is changing. It is becoming more service-oriented and talking with increasing sincerity in terms of 'customers' of IT. Ten years ago that sort of thinking would have been rare, but now it is commonplace.

It is safe to say that the vanguard of the new service ethos in IT was the helpdesk. I feel I have to admit my bias here, having been in user support for the better part of a quarter of a century, but I do not recall any other part of IT wearing sackcloth and ashes for most of the 1990s because it felt so guilty about its failure to provide adequate customer service. Alone in IT, it was the helpdesk that insisted on and acquired purpose-built software tools to better control its service process. The Helpdesk Institute, Helpdesk User Group (as was) and other professional bodies came to the fore and bleated persistently about the urgent necessity to improve service management.

Then in 2001, that striving reached a new maturity. Here in the UK, the once-defunct helpdesk show in London was reborn and took the theme of 'all roads lead to the helpdesk'. This was an industry-wide recognition of the view of the helpdesk as the point of access for all IT services within the corporation. The service culture, once the premise of the helpdesk alone, had spread across the whole of IT.

Many companies had seen it coming. I noticed back in 1996 that the computer press was carrying ever fewer want ads for the position of 'helpdesk manager'. In effect, the job was being downgraded to a supervisory position. In its place, the new rank of 'IT services manager' appeared. The service culture, invented by the helpdesk, was now being institutionally inculcated into other processes and functions, such as procurement, applications maintenance, problem management, infrastructure management and so on.

The other major force contributing to this change, at least in the UK but with international presence, was the Information Technology Service Managers' Forum (ITSMF). That esteemed body meets regularly to deal with the strategic issues surrounding the concept of service in IT. But it is so much more than just another sectoring of a market to sell conferences. This is because it takes as its backdrop the body of literature known as the 'Information Technology Infrastructure Library'.

ITIL considers various functions in IT and documents them separately in dedicated volumes. But although the volumes are distinct, the ideas therein are co-dependent – so that a methodology adopted by one service group, say the helpdesk, can feed into and dovetail with a methodology elsewhere, say in problem management. What ITIL describes is not just a set of functions, but an end-to-end IT management process. There's nothing else like it on the globe and its importance is increasing steadily as ITIL-compliance is sought by a rising number of corporations.

But for all the usefulness of ITIL, it is in my view not a total answer. Nor could it be. It was originally invented for a limited market, namely IT in public bodies in British national and regional government. It is being adopted more and more by commercial enterprises and some of them feel, as I do, that ITIL is a mechanism, not a mindset. ITIL tells the IT department what to do – but it cannot, nor should it, tell the manager how to do it.

So we have:

- the spread of service mentality across IT
- the integration of IT services under one management structure
- the professionalization of that process.

1.2 Purpose and scope

The chances are that as a reader of this book, you are already an experienced and competent manager, either of the whole of IT services or a significant function within it. You already have years of experience. You've developed your vision, you have your goals, you know your responsibilities and you're politically astute. You don't need to be patronized by a 'how to' book. So that is not my intention with this volume.

Instead, I offer this book as something you would have done if you had the time – namely to document the whole of the process and its functions in one place. Use it to contrast with your own structure and services – see if you got the same results I did.

The scope of this book is limited to *services* provided by IT – namely the IT operations and provisions that keep the company going – as opposed to *development*, which plans and implements the company's future IT. This distinction between 'present' and 'future' computing is crucial. For me, it is the defining factor when deciding whether an IT function is a service or not.

1.3 Special disclaimer

Throughout this work I have used case studies to illustrate points or arguments I am trying to make. It just may be, especially if the reader is a client of my consultancy practice, that he feels he recognizes his own company in my words.

I therefore feel I must point out here that no single company is represented in any of these case studies. They are amalgamations of practices I have witnessed in several companies. So if I criticize or congratulate a certain practice or methodology, and the reader recognizes this as something that happens in his organization, the reader can be assured that he is not alone – several other organizations are guilty of, or can be praised for, the same thing.

1.4 Electronic version

Some of the tables in this volume are extensive and could be used as the basis for a service level agreement or a service catalogue. They can be supplied in electronic form, for importing into a word processor, thus saving your fingers. The electronic version includes a right to use those tables in your company's internal documentation. Contact services@noelbruton.com for details.

2

2.1 The service culture

IT services as a technology group

On the face of it, the IT department is a section of the corporation serving the information and communication needs of the business. Its primary focus is technology, its people are largely engineers. This is one way of looking at IT. But it is one-sided and divisive. It is the view from outside IT. Technology? Engineers? These are simplistic terms, mere categorizations. The problem comes when the IT department comes to see itself in these terms, in other words adopting a view of itself as created by those who never really understood IT in the first place.

This misconception is of course often assisted by IT's internal structure and culture. May I offer an all too typical scenario.

Our technological legacy means that management attention and remuneration tend to go to those who have the most technical experience. Too often this can cause senior technicians to get promoted in order to stop them from leaving, because the system says they can only be paid more if they are given management rank. So we find ourselves promoting people beyond their level of competence; so they continue to be technicians and make a hash of their management responsibilities.

In the middle of all this, we are under pressure to improve the service ethos in IT. But that's immensely difficult because our line managers are predominantly ex-technologists. However, we find there's a part of IT that apparently already has a service culture – namely the helpdesk because they talk to the users all the time – so we send that group on customer service courses to make them even better at the 'customer service' side of things.

So we have now made a faithful nod in the direction of 'customer service'. We have all the calls go through the helpdesk, where service culture has been concentrated. We've also pulled off the political coup of simultaneously exonerating all other parts of IT from having a service responsibility. And meanwhile, we can now brag that we have a service culture because the helpdesk call-takers have been on a customer service course.

IT services as a business

There is another way and it starts from a reconsideration of exactly what the IT department is. We're often accused of not being sufficiently 'business-aware'. The business itself can claim this accolade, because it has external, paying customers or clients, whereas we, apparently, do not.

Too often, the accusation is well founded. While we continue to see ourselves as a discreet department within a business, I would argue, the foundations of that accusation will remain firm. Another way of seeing the IT group, however, is as a business in itself rather than as a functional department.

IT has everything any business would have:

- a market (the userbase)
- untapped opportunities within that market (use of 'vertical' applications with imported user support, new business needs, new versions of technologies etc.)
- a set of products and services
- a production line (the various end-to-end services and processes that produce them)
- resources (staff, skills, technology) to produce those services
- identifiable cost of production.

In fact, about the only factor missing from that list is an identifiable profit or margin above our production cost. Or even if the accounts system in the corporation does not allow for individual departments to profit off others, then perhaps what is missing is a range of formulas for cost-justification.

If we could complete that list and view the IT department from that standpoint, then customer service would become as much a part of our modus operandi as it is for the business proper. Instead of seeing 'the business' as a parent, let us see them as our marketplace.

The consequence of competition

Once we start to look at it that way, we start to see other commercial factors creeping into our philosophy. Chief among these is the concept of competition. It may appear, because our user base is effectively a captive market, that we are free from the ravages of competition, but this is not so.

Competition arises when there are several suppliers or potential suppliers of the same thing. Perhaps the users have to get their computer equipment from us, because it must be connected to the corporate network, which we own and administrate. That's a monopoly, not competition. Perhaps the users must always call the helpdesk for user support, because we've stipulated for the purposes of controlling support costs that all enquiries must be formally logged. So our helpdesk too is a monopoly. But that's not the point – this type of monopoly is a mirage.

First, they certainly must get their kit from us, but that doesn't stop them reading the computer magazines and finding that in the real world, computers cost a third of what we charge for twice the processing power and features. Second, the rule may state 'log all enquiries with the helpdesk' but that doesn't stop the users from first asking each other.

Case study:
The cost of using the helpdesk

The IT services department happens to be located in one of the factories, because there was space there after the corporate administrative from all the factories was centralized. The factories are all over the country. Centralization of non-specialized work made sense, to reduce the overhead costs of administrative staff. Of course, all these administrators were the ones who produced the corporate management information, so the centralization became part of a larger project to house all the executives in one place. The executives needed good rail and highway links to the capital, good local hotels for visiting clients and so on. So the new executive block was built in the nearest major city, which happened to be some fifteen miles from the IT services department.

Two things raised the IT services manager's suspicions. The first was the nature of enquiries coming from the executive block. They indicated a level of IT competence much lower than anywhere else in the corporation. That was no surprise – the executives were notorious for never attending IT training courses and their secretaries were known for booking on the courses but cancelling at the last minute, usually blaming some unforeseen, high-level corporate emergency.

The second factor was the quantity of calls coming from head office. Given the number of users there, many more enquiries would have been expected. Given the level of competence, it should have been higher still. Where were these calls going? The answer was astonishing.

It is quite commonplace in large corporations for groups of users distant from the IT services group to establish an unofficial local IT support person (often without telling IT of this person's existence, which plays the devil with calculating support costs, but that's another story). In the case of the executive block, this role had by default fallen to the assistant marketing director. Not the assistant-to, but the actual assistant director, a man whose salary was three times that of a desktop support technician, yet that was the job he found himself doing half of his working day.

And then there was the attitude of some, indeed too many of the users in that building. They hated the fact that they had to queue to make an enquiry to the helpdesk – even though the average call pickup time was less than thirty-eight seconds. So rather than risk the queue, users with technical enquiries would spend much longer periods of time touring the building looking for another user who might know the answer to their question.

The waste was tremendous. Users interrupting other users, causing lost productivity. Highly paid staff surrogating lowly paid work. All this fuelling an unnecessary poor image of the IT services department.

Things only changed when the new IT director took hold of the situation. In various presentations, regardless of the risk to his polit ical popularity, he forced the head office users at the highest level to acknowledge their behaviour and its corporate impact. It took a while and a political solution had to be found. It meant a premium service for head office users and an establishment of a permanent IT presence in the executive building (even though the two technicians who staffed it were often unoccupied). A new training regime was established – one-to-one training for everybody over a certain rank, so they would not have to face the embarrassment of showing their IT-illiteracy in a classroom of lower-ranking employees. And the appearance of discreet but insistent posters all over the building bearing the legend 'Save money – call the helpdesk first.'

When a market comes to perceive that there are numerous potential suppliers of similar products, the product then becomes a commodity. The only way to differentiate between commodities is price. One could maintain that price is not an issue in the provision of internal IT services. There in the catalogue, is what we charge for a computer and its connection to the corporate network Mr User – your options are to pay that price or go back to pen and paper. And the helpdesk doesn't charge for its services, nor does applications maintenance charge for bug fixes and forms redesign, so how could price be an issue?

When it's not a matter of money, other factors come into play. Part of the cost of an IT service comes from its availability. How much effort is required on the user's part to avail himself of the service? He will avoid that effort as much as he would any avoidable cost. So to the user at least, the competition is real. Which is the cheapest way, not just financially, but also in terms of my time, to get this service? One option is IT services – another is to go outside, ask a friend, fetch in a contractor, whatever. Because at least some of what IT services provides could be construed as a commodity provision.

There are two ways to deal with competition. One is to remove it from the marketplace by a takeover. I've seen this done – in a company that used several vertical applications in addition to its standard, horizontal office software. The specialized software and associated support were provided by external parties, often trading directly with specific groups of users. In some cases, the only thing IT services knew about these was that they existed and servers had to be provided to house them. But the service manager had other ideas. He knew that his department was not the only group providing some form of IT support to the users, and that the standards of those alternative support offerings varied enormously. So he determined to set an overall standard for IT product and service provision to the corporation's users, regardless of source. He then made that insistence on these external companies and took full responsibility for their performance. In effect, he acquired those external provisions because in terms of service quality they must report not to the users who engaged them, but to the IT services department.

The other way to tackle competition is to defeat it by adding value to our own provision. If the user sees his request as being satisfied solely by the provision of a hard product or solution to his enquiry, then that licenses him to seek alternative providers of that product or solution. But our response should be to take the focus away from the hard end-product – to make the user value it not for what it is, but for what it means.

Take the example of the desktop computer – purchased from IT at a price that seems higher than that advertised by the local computer store. He's seeing it the wrong way. We do not provide computers, even though that's what it may look like on the surface. We provide a connection to the corporate network. That connection, which is our product, consists of the ability to exchange emails with other parts of the corporation, access to central data, alternative ways of storing and printing those data, a secure data environment, use of corporate applications for input and output, a guaranteed availability of all this at certain times and oh, by the way, a computer to get at all this.

Take the other example of the solution to the technical enquiry. We know the user can ask another user. But does that other user guarantee to be able to answer the question? Or to be available all day and every day, within minutes, to accept the enquiry? Or to manage the escalation of that enquiry if a solution is not immediately to hand? Because we do. We don't just solve technical problems. We provide a complete and guaranteed service by which technical problems are solved.

These examples are to some extent subtle questions of perspective of course, but it is a particularly important perspective. IT services delivers its offerings to a captive market. Nevertheless, competition exists in that market. I believe that the acknowledgement of this existence of competition is a crucial philosophical leap in seeing our own function as a business in its own right. With that leap having been taken, then IT services must necessarily be as 'business aware' as the corporation that hosts it – simply because it too is a business. Therefore, all the functions of IT, including those placed furthest from the users, can be said to be at least as 'business aware' as those employees of the corporation at large who are similarly removed from the commercial front line.

This also puts the idea of 'service' into a deeper context. The service ethos never could be purchased from a training company anyway – only the skills. And just because we place low-ranking employees on customer service training courses does not necessarily mean that service mentality will percolate through the department. This is unlikely, because skills are not mentality. A football fan may understand how a midfield strategy works but that does not therefore mean he could coach a football team to success. A musician may recognize a ninth in a Bacharach tune, and even be able to play the chord, but that does not necessarily mean any musician could have written 'Walk On By'. The mentality comes first – the skills can be honed later.

We do this by instinct anyway – for example, the helpdesk and procurement staff are gregarious people who like talking to users in any case. The engineers, however (at least in this example) are not really that 'good in front of the customer' – if they were they would perhaps have chosen a more customer-facing career. So it is apposite to concentrate the service training where it would be put to best use, which is in the more service-minded helpdesk.

But without a deeper service ethos in IT services as a whole, putting a few skills into isolated pockets of the department will have a comparatively tiny effect. Service is a culture, which impacts a structure and methodology, not a few isolated behaviours by a small minority of politically less influential and low ranking staff. The service mentality has to start at the top – no, better to say it has to be woven into the very value system of the IT services department. The top is only one place where a service ethos can reside. And let's be pragmatic; senior management proclamations can often be routinely ignored in the quantity and complexity of hourly work by the people who actually have to do the job. (Incidentally I feel this is why so many corporate mission statements are often received by deaf ears or with a smirk at their meaningless hyperbole.)

Furthermore, this isolated inculcation of 'service skills' is risky, especially when done to people who by their natures empathize with their clients. Customer service is not just a bolt-on to the product or service on offer. It is actually part of the offer itself. As such, just like the product, it has a cost of production and a margin of value. If too much 'service' is offered against a request, that carries with it the twin risks of increasing the cost of provision and raising customer expectations the next time a similar request is made. Either of these risks can ultimately have a budgetary implication.

So the way 'service' is delivered, the parameters surrounding it and associated limitations of authority of the service operative, all of these have to be as well-defined as the product itself. In other words, the 'customer service' element must be a defined and inextricable part of the process of delivery itself. So just like the product, just like the process, it has to be designed, not just left to the staff in the vain hope that their 'niceness' will produce high levels of customer satisfaction.

I see this in my work as a consultant all the time. One of my favourite questions in interviews with users is 'What's good about the service?' If I get the answer, as all too often I do, 'Well they're really nice people' or similar such as 'They'll bend over backwards for you', I start looking at the design of the service process – because comments like that, especially in the absence of anything more substantial, set alarm bells ringing for me. They often suggest that the service ethos exists only in the smiles of the front-line staff and not in the production process.

2.2 Who is responsible?

So we end up with the following steps:

- Acknowledge the fact that for whatever IT services provides, competitors exist.
- This competition gives the user what he perceives either as a potential choice of suppliers or as a yardstick against which to judge the offerings of the IT services department.
- Use that reality as a basis for seeing IT services not merely as a department, but as a self-contained business in its own right.
- Design IT services as a production line to deliver products into a competitive market.
- Thereby, cause a market ethos to pervade throughout IT services, paralleling that in the corporation at large.
- Encourage that market ethos to create service awareness at all steps of the production process.
- Add service skills as appropriate only after the service awareness takes root.

So in a way, everybody in IT services is responsible. They all have to adopt that market thinking. But they cannot do that without some basis. They were hired for their engineering skills, not their commercial awareness, so we cannot expect them to become service-conscious overnight.

So somebody has to profess the truth about the competitive environment in which IT services finds itself. This means there has to be a vision somewhere, one so bright and obvious it cannot be ignored. And that requires leadership and invention and – dare I say it – passion.

Passion is an emotion, and in the received wisdom, there is no place for emotion at work. We're all supposed to leave our emotions at home, because otherwise they tend to interfere with the dispassionate objectivity we must adopt in our business relationships. We're all supposed to be cold and clear of egotistical distraction. To subdue ourselves to emotion is to be unprofessional, or so the thinking goes.

We all know examples of people who by professing their passion have caused themselves to be tagged as having clouded judgement. The problem with emotion is that it is just about as honest as honest gets. Imagine if everybody were absolutely honest? The advertising and public relations industries would collapse. Negotiation would be nigh on impossible.

We fear emotion. We fear even more those who express it, for they may be nerds or nutcases. But most, we fear the fact that they can be honest and we dare not. But without honesty there can be no sincerity and without sincerity, credibility is difficult to attain. Try it for yourself. Put up a few 'motivational' posters or some hyperbolically worded 'mission statement' and see what reaction you get. Smirks, sniggers and cynicism I'll warrant, especially here in the UK. These posters and mission statements are all very well, but they must have a context. If they profess emotion or a value system – e.g. 'the customer is king' – then they must stem from an emotional basis – in other words that everybody truly believes that the customer is king and not, as might be the case by default, that the customer is a pain in the —.

So the responsibility must lie with somebody who is in a position to conceive of and express a passion. That must be somebody pretty high up, confident enough in the security of his position to make declarations others may fear to make. Somebody who can back up those declarations with both the political clout to deal with peer detractors and the authority to implement policies and designs to turn vision into reality. In other words, the most senior person in the IT services department. The one who must be the most dispassionate and clearest of thought is also the one who must, for the sake of meaningful leadership, also be the one who is most passionate about the vision he or she has ordained.

2.3 A structural basis

Figure 2.1 below gives an overview of a basis for a service design and delivery strategy. This schematic is designed to emphasize that if we see IT services as a business, the first thing it would need is a business plan, based upon a detailed consideration of the market. These are the steps we might go through in the creation, delivery and assessment of our IT services 'factory'.

2.4 The IT delivery process

Market understanding

The 'market understanding' could come from our experience of the needs of our users, but there is also a place for some negotiation with the business and its computer users, to arrive at an objective and agreed assessment of the 'business needs'. This step alone may be complex – often, the users may not be willing to offer the same level of commitment to an IT services design

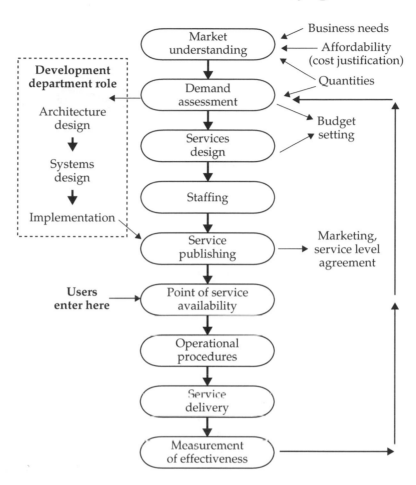

Figure 2.1
Overview of the IT
delivery process

strategy, especially if they are broadly satisfied with the service as it is. Nevertheless, the ideal is to assess our market before we start designing or staffing services, and we must be at least amenable to discussion and consultation with our users. So we must encourage them to play an active role.

Affordability

As part of this initial step of understanding the market, we should also calculate what the market is willing to pay, perhaps even in terms of what the company can afford. If we do not decide this at the outset, there may be difficulties later on, especially if cutting costs becomes an issue. There must be a financial value attached to every type of demand for every type of service. That way, as we shall see later, any decrease in the financial status of the IT services department will equate to a service or a service level. The position we need to be in is not that the business decides to spend less on IT services, but the

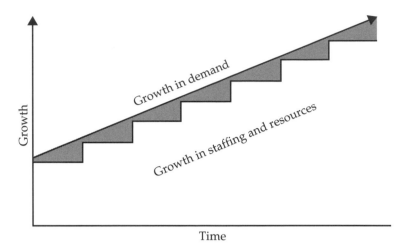

Growth in demand

Growth in staffing and resources

Growth

Time

Figure 2.2
Reactive recruiting

business decides which services it can do without or what consequential reductions in service levels it is willing to bear.

So the financial side must be sorted out right at this early stage. The problem is that IT services departments already exist, so they are dealing with an existing legacy, which will include an existing policy of recruitment. All too often, this recruitment is reactive, giving rise to the situation shown at Figure 2.2.

This gives a model which uses as a basis the fact that the demand from the users tends to rise steadily. Because the users outnumber the IT services staff, this rise can be depicted in an analogue form: whereas in relative terms, the headcount in the IT services group rises quantally, i.e. in steps of one head at a time. The tendency here is to recruit new staff after demand has risen by a certain amount, because that is the point at which a staff increase can be justified. But if we increase headcount after the demand has already risen, we will always be in a state of lagging behind demand. As a result, the service we can deliver will always be less than adequate, with the shortfalls in our ability to meet demand depicted by the shaded areas.

The alternative to reactive recruiting is of course proactive recruiting – namely hiring staff in anticipation of needing their skills and the production capacity they would bring. These days, of course, that is extremely hard to justify. The thought of hiring people and deliberately keeping them under-utilized in the anticipation of demand rising to eventually consume the potential productivity is a definite taboo. It sounds like a waste of money. Paying somebody to do nothing? The very idea! But the alternative is that shown in Figure 2.2 where throughout the existence of IT services, the department is *never* actually able to meet demand.

So in the end it's a matter of what the corporation is willing to finance – a service never able to precisely meet business needs or carrying the cost of idle resource with a guarantee of being able to meet those needs.

A favourite analogy of mine for this is the fire station. At some point of the day, there will be a fire crew sitting around drinking coffee, waiting for an emergency to happen. Even though our taxes are paying for this apparent idleness, we don't begrudge it – because we know that when we do call on their craft, they will save us much more than their temporary idleness could ever cost. If a computer user needs a service, for every moment he has to wait for that service is a moment during which he will be making less money for the corporation than he would had he been working normally. Factor into that the possibility that many users could be affected by a service shortfall, and the costs soon mount up.

The point of decision lies in the very purpose of IT services' existence. What that department ultimately serves is the productivity of the corporation. If it cannot absolutely fulfil that duty, what ultimately suffers is corporate productivity. If IT services isn't there or has reduced capacity – if it takes too long to deliver a machine, fix a bug, reschedule a batch job, resolve an enquiry, repair a fault etc. – then during that time, user productivity is reduced. It would be less reduced if service levels were higher, and while increased productivity in IT can raise service levels, so can increased headcount.

Assuming that the IT services people are all working as diligently and efficiently as they can, the only remaining option for increasing service levels, and thus increasing the amount of the user's working day for which he is making money for the company, is to have more than enough people in the IT services department. So don't let the business abdicate that decision, and make sure they understand it. What they are deciding is not simply whether to spend less on IT services or not, it is in fact whether to reduce corporate productivity or not. This perspective must be encouraged. The way to point it out is to give the business a real decision to make. Which would they rather have? One or two idle resources in the IT department? Or idle users all over the business because their computer requests remain outstanding due to IT being short-staffed?

Demand assessment

This is a tricky one. How much demand will there actually be? We need to assess this for each of the services the group will eventually produce. The two main ways of doing it are by using data from benchmarks (there are a number of companies providing these, best known being the Gartner Group). But even these tend to be limited to simple things like ratios of service staff to user or machine populations, and all that tells you is what happens in terms of headcount, or what companies happen to be doing now rather than what is possible. In my own experience of benchmarking helpdesks, for example, the figures show that the average performance of helpdesks, especially second-line support staff, is adrift of what is possible by factors of up to four. In other words, the best helpdesks are not just a little bit more efficient than the average, but up to four times as efficient. Given a difference as stark as that, the value of benchmarks becomes questionable.

Furthermore, that only deals with the easily gathered statistics, such as number of helpdesk calls, number of training interventions, mean time between failures (MTBF) and mean time to repair (MTTR). There is no such benchmark that I am aware of for number of email administrators, how many network infrastructure technicians and so on. Nevertheless, there has to be some set of numbers against which we can parse the likely demand from the users. We'll look at this in more detail when we examine the individual services in Chapter 3.

Services design

Continuing with the theme of the IT services department as a factory, then each of the services it offers is a production line in itself. One line is making moves and changes, another is making solutions to enquiries, another delivers new computers and software upgrades and so on. A mistake we can often make is to see our department in terms of a group of people, whose aggregate output is that of all the services.

If however we see the services as separate and distinct, this can give us a different perspective. How efficient is each of the production lines? How many people does it need, etc? In some of the roles, this separateness is clear – for example the procurement staff do only procurement, so their input, activity and output are ring-fenced. The problem comes when we have a department whose staff are involved in work to produce several services, or where the 'service' as such is the output of effort of more than one workgroup. Take the second line, who fix assigned problems, but also install computers, carry out moves and also conduct numerous projects. These cannot be so easily separated.

One way to do this is to take a snapshot of your staff's commitment of time to the production of various services. The precursor to this is that the services must have been defined first, perhaps coming down to a list similar to that in Chapter 3. Then give each of the staff a table to complete (see example at Figure 3.1). On the vertical axis is the list of services. The horizontal axis depicts the working day broken down into fifteen-minute chunks. Then for a week or so, have your people put ticks in the cells, thus showing how much time they spent delivering each service at what time of the day. Gather the sheets in and calculate the total number of fifteen-minute chunks per service and then divide the totals by the number of such chunks in a working day. The result will tell you the amount of logical (as opposed to actual) headcount you have committed to each service. Comparing that with the output will give you an index of how much manpower you are currently consuming to produce your current output – and that can be a basis for calculating headcount against growth in demand for each service. I call this a 'resource usage table'. It's also a good indicator of what might happen to one service if you moved resources from it to shore up performance in another service.

But keeping the services separate is not just an aid to assessing resource commitment internally. It is also a key factor in bringing to the user's attention just how broad (and appropriate to the business) is your range of services. Your clients need to appreciate that you are more than just a group of people they call on for help – that you are a factory with a range of distinct products that they consume.

Staffing

As mentioned above, the resource usage table is of immense use in predicting staffing levels, but it only pertains to where those service activities already exist. A key point here is where in the process design strategy the staffing levels should be considered. My preference, where possible, is to design the service portfolio first and only then decide what staff (and thereto headcount, skills, abilities and attitudes) are needed to deliver that service. What we are to produce is more important than how we produce it. It could be argued that we can engage staff with certain skills and then decide how to put them to use, but this is to put the technology before the business needs. The business comes first – therefore the services must precede the staffing.

Service publishing

First we assessed the market, how much business there was out there for us and what the market could afford to pay. Then we built our factory and recruited its workforce. It's almost time to set the production lines running, but first we have to tell our potential customers what's on offer.

This brings us to the stage of publishing our services – in the analogy of IT services as a business, this is the marketing, the advertising and possibly even putting the reps on the road to do some selling. The obvious reason for this is to bring the customers in so we can justify the scale and cost of the production lines and start to deliver their promised benefits into the business. But there is another, more important reason, particularly so if we are delivering to a captive market such as the userbase employed by the organization that ultimately also employs us. And that is to set and keep on setting our customers' expectations.

One of the main ways for us to publish our services is by setting up a service level agreement (SLA) between IT services and the business. This is essentially a management document. It describes the services along with a regime for managing how well these are delivered. It states our commitment to range, quantity and quality of services as service providers. But in that it is an agreement, it should also state the customers' responsibilities, not least in terms of how the service provision shall be financed. There is always a risk that a service provider will be exploited.

Case study:
Innocent exploitation

'This business got where it is today by being quick on its feet', the CEO proclaimed. Around the table, highly placed heads nodded sagely. 'So we don't need the overhead of centralized administration.' The CFO smiled – that'll save a few quid, he thought. 'And nor do we need to spend a fortune on IT – we don't have complicated processing needs and the business units are autonomous. We should let them choose what computing they need.'

'So should each business unit have its own IT section?' the CIO enquired.

'That would just increase duplication and push costs up', said the HOD of HR.

'So let me get this straight', the CIO continued, 'We do without central admin, but we must have central IT, but IT must serve the different needs of different businesses without standardization?'

'That's the company culture,' added the marketing director. 'Can-do attitude.'

'Quite right.' The CEO confirmed. 'Just as I said before. Serve the business needs in a changing market. That's how we stay ahead.'

And so it came to pass that the 'can-do' ethos was built into company culture. The effect was to give licence to every request on IT from anywhere in the company, regardless of how unreasonable that request may be. Any user could buy any technology they felt would serve their individual, esoteric or even eccentric business needs and expect the IT department to make it work. Seventeen different types of mobile telephones soon appeared, along with eleven different brands of personal digital assistant, eight desktop operating systems, four financial packages, three email clients and five office software packages. Then came the interconnectivity requests, spanning from the exciting and cutting-edge, through the reasonable to the downright weird.

'Now listen here, IT. I want to connect my new USB digital camera to my Windows 95 computer and I want it done right now. And if you say it's technologically impossible once more, I'll hold you up as an example of how IT does not conform to the company's 'can-do' value system. I don't see the need to pay for a new computer when I've got one here that's done me perfectly well for the last seven years.'

It is in the nature of human beings to abdicate responsibility where possible. In the work environment, this is exacerbated by the fact that everybody is busy – if they can pass part of their burden onto another department, it is tempting to take that opportunity.

A department that provides people with a service is a perfect target for dumping responsibilities should the customer be so inclined or so overworked as to have no choice. In the hypothetical case above, the corporate culture actively supports the practice of blaming IT when the user has an unreasonable request. For this reason, any service level agreement (SLA) we draw up with the business must be two-sided. It must outline the responsibilities not just of the service provider, but also of the service consumer.

What happened above was that the users were given the option to judge the effectiveness of IT services not just on any formal recognition of performance against the service level targets, but also on whether the service met the users' expectations. In other words, a scientific form of measurement was allowed to take a lower priority than an emotional one. It's to be expected – users are under pressure just as we are. But that must not be allowed to overshadow that this is essentially a business relationship, in the mass production environment that is IT services. If we have to deal with too many exceptions as are caused by unreasonable demands, or senior staff jumping the queue by virtue of their rank rather than their need, then we cannot effectively plan our service delivery – and if that happens, everybody suffers. The expectations the users are allowed to have should therefore be cemented at the outset, at as high a level as possible in the organization and change should thereafter also be agreed at that level. Flexibility in service delivery is all very well – but it must either be minimized, or tightly controlled, and in all cases where flexibility is demanded, it must be paid for. I know of numerous clients where senior staff have their own premium subset of IT services to exploit – and this becomes a separate, premium service in its own right, planned for and financed just as stringently as any other service.

Of course the SLA may not be able to set the expectations of all users. It is an esoteric document, intended primarily as a form of government. The user on the Clapham omnibus may simply never get to read it or hear about its provisions, regardless of how widely we may publish and advertise it. This suggests a need for something more accessible in addition to the SLA. This can be as simple as an extract from the schedule of the SLA, where the service expectations are summarized. Sometimes known as a 'service level statement' (SLS), it should be distributed as widely as possible. One site I know of used to have the main stipulations of the SLA printed onto mouse mats and delivered to each new arriving company employee in the human resources induction pack.

Even the SLS may not be enough. Users come and go, the pressures they are under may change, new deadlines may appear. The SLA should have the means of changing itself built into its very structure, to allow for shifts in business needs. Beyond this, there may be a need, from time to time, for reminding the user populace about the service provisions (once they have read the SLS, there's a reduced chance that reading it again will be a future priority for them). So it may be an idea to back up the SLS with a proactive communications channel to provide those reminders. Examples of this may include:

- regular IT services newsletter, structured in such a way that it always contains new and unmissable other information so that customers have to read it
- reiteration of service expectations on job tickets etc. or customer satisfaction surveys
- standard service level message given out by helpdesk staff on all incoming requests.

Beyond the publication of services via the SLA and marketing media, there may be scope for a more direct relationship, via an IT services 'customer manager'. If IT services were actually a manufacturing company, this role would parallel that of an account manager or field sales representative. The function is one of representing the products of IT to its clients – to make sure the clients are getting the most they can out of the provision and that we are providing them with the most appropriate service we can. This person can also be a formal channel for complaints or enquiry escalations, or act additionally as a co-ordinator within IT services for requests requiring action by more than one section of the department.

Putting this role in place often tends to be a luxury for larger user populations, it must be said, especially given that it may consume dedicated headcount. However, it need not necessarily be so. Several organizations fulfil this purpose by giving managers within IT services the duty of representing the group to various user groups or parts of the business.

If there is scope to create the role, it can become a new career opportunity. Because it is not a technical role, but essentially a service one, and because one of the necessary skills is the ability to manage relationships with customers, this function can be seen as a rare career path option for first-line helpdesk staff who don't want to take the technical route. It's a way of keeping and growing those important customer relationship skills.

The customer manager can fulfil an additional role as the 'supplier-side manager', this being the one who represents IT services in meetings to review performance against service level targets.

Point of service availability

The factory is built, the products have been designed and advertised, the operational methodologies are in place and the reps are on the road. Now at last it's time to open the sales ledger and start taking orders for our products. This is the gateway to the services as we present it to the users. Most commonly it is the helpdesk, or with separate entry points for procurement, development or change requests.

Operational procedures/service delivery

Once the requests of various types have been collected by the point of service availability, they go onto the various production lines for completion. Here are the internal, operational procedures, largely invisible to the users, governing things like request logging, ownership change, job recording, escalation, resolution and closure of which more throughout this book.

Measurement

Measurement will be stipulated by the targets in the SLA, so that we can prove to our customers that they are getting what we promised and what they are paying for. However, there will be internal measurement to assess the effectiveness of our internal processes, our productivity and how well our skillsets match the demands of the job in hand. The measurement is there not just to tell us how well or how badly we did in the last reporting period, but to give us data which we can later feed back into our anticipation of changes in demand levels and of our ability to cope with those.

2.5 The difference between a service and a process

'I blow through here. The music goes round and round, oh, and it comes out here.' These lyrics, written by Riley, Farley and Hodgson about playing the trombone and famously recorded by the Tommy Dorsey Orchestra, describe a process. It starts with a causal event, to which a value is added within a purpose-built mechanism to produce an end result. If we just look objectively at the sequence of events then the process is clear, a procession of isolated but integrated cause and effect relationships.

But that is not the service. To see that, in effect we have to ignore the process and just listen to the end effect as it rolls sweetly out of the horn of the trombone. The service is the music, magically created by something that is patently not music, the controlled forcing of compressed air along a brass pipe. To observe the process, plug your ears and watch what Dorsey does. To receive the service, close your eyes and listen to what Dorsey is giving you.

On the other hand, maybe the music itself is not the only service. I'm a guitarist and I like to watch other guitarists play, to see what I can learn from them – which is why I never watch 'Top of the Pops' because the BBC cameramen seem to think that the right hand does the work, so they focus on the up and down strumming of the right hand. To me, that's not the service I want. My need is for them to focus on the left hand, where the notes and chords are shaped (Paul McCartney and other south paws excepted). So the left-handed emphasis of the camera operators at the Cambridge Folk Festival on TV the other night did indeed constitute a service for me. In other words, by watching the process, I actually received a service other than the one the guitarist intended to produce, namely the music issuing from the speaker attached to his amplifier.

Two conclusions emerge:

- the service is invoked at the process entry point and received at the delivery point – while the process can be (and usually should be) invisible to the user
- the service is what the consumer perceives it to be, and it may not necessarily be the service the provider thinks he is producing.

It can be said, for example, that within IT services, the helpdesk is a process. A sequence of events begins with a user request. Once the request is made, it is sucked in by the ITS machine, going through several procedures, modifications, additions of value, escalations, recording, changes of ownership and so on. This sequence is the process. And then out of the other end pops a resolution of the original request. The *service* of the helpdesk is the provision of the gateway through which the request may be entered and the resolution may be received. All that stuff in between – that's 'process'. But the user sees a service, so for him, the helpdesk is a service.

There is a debate, especially in ITIL circles, as to whether the helpdesk is a process or a service. To my mind it's both, the separation being defined only by who is observing the helpdesk. The provider may see it as a manufacturing process, but the user sees it as a service. So then in my view, the debate comes down to one of priorities. If the ultimate purpose of our existence is to provide services to a clientele, then their view should be the overriding one when we make our assessment of our nature. To the philosophical question 'Is what we do a service or a process?', the most appropriate answer is 'If the customer sees and uses it as a service, then it's a service.'

> **The service is:**
> - *not what we do*
> - *not what we provide*
> - *what the customer consumes*

2.6 Principles of service identification and design

If the definition of a service is that the user sees it as such, then this is the logical place to begin to design our service portfolio. The starting point should be the question of what uses the user community will make of our skills and resources. So we decide on our services from the outside in – from what the customers need to use rather than just what we propose to offer them. It's a 'garden path' approach: if the gardener lays the path in the wrong place, people will still walk across the grass. The wiser gardener sees where people need to walk first and that's where he lays the path, thus fulfilling the ends of optimizing the service for path users while simultaneously protecting the lawn.

If the services are not offered in a manner in which the users find them most convenient and effective, the users will invent their own access points. We see this all the time in IT. The user finds the queue for the call centre an irritating waste of time, so finds a way to bypass the call centre and talk direct to an operative. We could complain that the enquirer is just being selfish and difficult – the enquirer could counter that the service is not sufficiently accessible. The truth is probably somewhere between the two, with the user not fully understanding the implications of his bypassing behaviour, which are as follows.

To each service, there is a process, which is essentially a sequence of integrated events, each event contributing to the production of a resolution to the service request. These events have a cost, in terms of resource consumed. Where the number of simultaneous events exceeds the number of resources to cope in that moment, a queue is created. Where the number of production requests consistently exceeds the number of resources to deal with demand, the queue becomes a backlog. This means that the process has to be meticulously planned at each stage of production to ensure that any queues, which may build up from time to time, do not turn into a backlog. There must be a constant monitoring of the match of demand to resource at all points in the process. If by some fluke or deliberate act, a demand is allowed to enter the process at a lower point than the proper entry point, this becomes an unplanned demand at the actual entry point. That part of the process therefore has a higher demand than was anticipated – and having to deal with that demand thus may force a queue to form at any part of the process earlier than that illegal entry point. Thus, any user going direct to a second-line operative rather than reporting his request at the first-line entry is more than just a mild aberration – it is a direct threat to the service level we can deliver against all other requests in production at the time.

So putting the garden path in the right place is indeed our duty – but we will probably find that even after we have so carefully and beneficially laid the path, we may still have to line it with a fence. That 'fence' is a matter of ensuring the users' expectations of the service (to the point of telling them what to expect) and ensuring that they understand that if they walk on the grass, they may also thereby spoil the path for everybody else.

2.7 Going into detail – types of services

So that gives us a set of principles for structuring the services. Then we get into the detail of designing individual services. Some of these appear to be obvious – the user needs a place to submit requests for technical assistance, therefore we need a helpdesk. But even that raises difficulties, chiefly stemming from the type of enquiry the helpdesk should be able to field. I want to examine the type of helpdesk we put in place, because that alone can tell us a lot about how services come into being.

My contention here is that the service design process is not necessarily a rational or objective one. From IT's point of view, we are often guilty of offering services because we can, not necessarily because we should. But the issue of 'should' is also clouded – because who gives us that compulsion? For if the compulsion comes from the users, often that may not be rational either. Follow my argument.

It is perhaps unfortunate that the term 'helpdesk' has become so widely accepted across the industry, for it implies something that most traditional desktop support desks are at pains to do – namely to 'help' the user. The job of the helpdesk is not usually to assist the user in his use of the computer as a work tool. It is to accept and manage the resolution of reported failures of the machinery to function as the users expect. This is not assistance – it is problem resolution. Nor does the helpdesk even 'help' the caller to solve the problem, but retains the capacity and responsibility for resolution within its own auspices. I report a problem to the helpdesk, and they come and fix it.

The term frequently leads to false expectations within the user community. It is in most cases not reasonable to call the traditional helpdesk with a request for immediate assistance in the use of an application of the computer on which it resides. The helpdesk could not reasonably be expected to have such expertise, as unlike the users, they do not use the business or desktop applications hour in, hour out, in the same way the users do. Few so called 'computer support analysts' could reasonably be expected to understand a spreadsheet application as well as an accountant who works with numerical tabulations all day. No computer technician could understand the fine details of a word processor as well as a trained typist. So the use of even the common-or-garden, horizontal desktop applications would fall outside the expertise of the typical support operative. When the scope of this is broadened to include task-specific tools such as computer-aided design (CAD), process control and so on, the gap widens still further, because to use such tools requires specific knowledge and understanding of terminology and techniques specific to a certain profession, which may itself have required specialist training. A computer support technician cannot assist a draughtsman with a CAD system because to do so, he would first also have to be a draughtsman to even understand the context of the user's question, let alone the question itself.

When we get to the level of the business applications, the problem is similarly acute. These applications are absolutely purpose-designed, to the point of reflecting the financial or business processes of that very corporation. To understand the tools here, the computer technician would have also to understand the business processes. He could not really do this – his job of fixing computer problems keeps him too busy to learn the finer points of fiscal process. In any case there is no recruitment market for 'applications usage support people'. In the case of the vertical applications, such support people might be drawn from the development team. For vertical applications, they may be recruited from the users.

So why am I banging on about what the helpdesk can and cannot support? Because in the middle of that question lies a much bigger one of how we go about providing services of any description. The solution can only be that we should provide the services the users expect us to provide. They expect support in the use of applications – oh, yes they do – my research suggests that the days are long gone when the two top questions coming from the users were 'I've lost my password' and 'my printer won't print'. The top enquiry coming from users is now most likely to be 'How do I ...?'

We have been subject over recent years to a massive change in the way computers are used. In early 1996, when I first put my Internet email address on my business cards, some people I met working for large corporations were surprised to see such a thing – the facility for Internet email just did not exist in a lot of large companies. Back then I used to carry telephone extension cables and adaptors (and occasionally a screwdriver!) in my luggage so I could rig my hotel bedroom telephone to collect my email. A short two years later, everybody had Internet email addresses and modem jack points started appearing in hotel bedrooms and motorway service stations. So the idea that executives now had the duty of collecting their email when they were on the road had become ubiquitous in less than two years. This meant they were also composing their own email messages, finally sweeping away the culture that highly placed people tended to have somebody slightly lower in the corporation to read and write their emails for them. Five years ago, one might have seen a computer in the office of a senior executive, although it may seldom have been switched on – but no longer.

And senior executives never go on training courses – let's face it, some of them would not attend a classroom session where people of lesser rank in the corporation might be seen to be more expert than they – it would undermine their authority and hierarchical mystique. So we have a new, senior rank in the corporation that has come at a late stage to realize that they too must use the computer they have avoided having to understand for so long. These are new users, powerful people who can have a service expectation rather higher than that of the lower and middle operational ranks. Since desktop computing first started seriously, back in the mid 1980s, it has always been the preserve of lower ranks, because essentially, computers have been about data input and output – a clerical, not an executive function. But not any more – computers are now also about communications, in a much bigger way than the old company-internal-only email systems sitting on the mainframe.

But if executives are being forced to communicate from their computers, then they will also be creating material to send and receive. Not so very long ago, if I was a corporate manager and I need to make a presentation, I would scribble a few notes and pass them to my secretary. She might make a start with the presentation, perhaps incorporate some data downloaded from the mainframe and drawn up in a spreadsheet, and pass this on to the public relations department for finalization within the corporate house style. Not any more. Now the corporate house style for presentations, letters and so on resides in public templates on a server to which everybody in the corporation has access. A fully configured suite of office applications is on every computer in the company. There is no longer any need to pass the material around the clerical functions – everything you need is on your desk. Besides, the clerical functions have all been downsized, so there's nobody there to pass it to anyway. Nowadays, executives are doing it for themselves – some of them are struggling of course, which attracts low level 'How do I...?' calls from the seniors to the helpdesk.

But the issue goes much deeper than that. Use any decent office software package and it is likely to be rich, if not bloated, with features. There are several ways to achieve similar results. In one respect, this adds to functionality – in another, it simply leads to confusion. To resolve that confusion, computer users need support and the helpdesk is one of the first places to look. And provided that the helpdesk is one page further in the software manual than the users are, perhaps they can stay ahead and remain in a position to turn confusion into progress.

Then we have the idea of 'time-to-market'. This refers to the period of time that passes in industry from having an idea for a product, coming up with a prototype, developing that into a finished version, deciding on how it will be marketed and distributed and finally placing it on shelves in stores. That period has shortened dramatically in recent years. An example is the CD-ROM drive. I first saw these at the Hannover Fair in the early 1980s. It was all of several years afterwards when they started to appear on desktop computers with any real regularity. Nowadays, that period from innovation to wide availability has shortened from years to months, and in some cases to weeks. But it's not just in the computer industry, it's everywhere, affecting every company and every type of product or service. To stay competitive, companies have had to dramatically shorten their time-to-market. This means that the employees of the forward-looking company are always having their knowledge, skills and competence stretched, because the company is constantly innovating and pushing those innovations into the market with increasing speed to cut development costs and increase returns. The administrative systems (including the computers) have to keep up with this. Therefore the users are constantly faced with some new way of working, some new business process, which requires user support.

Then we have globalization. It becomes ever easier in most countries to start a company and build a business, and once that business exists, it may well become a potential target for acquisition by a larger company in a more established overseas market.

Acquisition is a relatively easy way of grabbing market share or establishing a presence in a region. Market share and presence are important for survival – they have become as important as the product portfolio itself in the competition between market players. For the IT department, this means the arrival of new corporate divisions, with the accompanying high-level need to integrate the various businesses for the purposes of uniform management reporting and reduced duplication. So IT finds itself with one computing system suddenly having to incorporate another company with a different system altogether, with all the accompanying rollouts, installations, user retraining and enquiries from users who missed the training (even though they may have attended the course!).

So what have we got?

- new users with new expectations
- changing computer environment
- more challenging applications
- new uses for the computers
- a different type of user, more senior with more power
- rising service expectations
- users rapidly reaching the limits of their computing competence.

To me, these are irrefutable arguments for new types of IT services. These have to be more flexible, more usage-oriented, providing assistance rather than mere problem-solving, more business aware, more pro-active and anticipating business change. We simply cannot continue to do it with the limited 'buy your computers here, report your problems there' approach any more.

The minimum we have to do beyond our limited past is to add computer usage assistance and customer relations. That usage assistance has to go beyond hiring a trainer to run a few courses – it has to be 'just-in-time', in exactly the same way as the company as a whole is generating new products and entering new markets just-in-time.

The customer-relations side of things has to improve also. In the past, the relationship between IT services and the customer base has been largely passive and limited to providing somewhere for the customers to call to acquire and report faults with computer equipment. Perhaps there has also been a regular meeting to review IT services performance against agreed service level targets. The development side of IT has handled some of the relations – it might dispatch a project manager to respond to a user department's stated need for a new application to represent some new business process.

In the future, IT services will have to go much further than that. To truly reflect the changing nature of business, IT services is going to have to become much more directly involved in how its customers are using its services. I know it's a cliché to say that business is changing. But really, it is, so fast and on such a scale that it's mind-boggling. Down here in IT we tend to miss out on just how fast business is changing. We think we are keeping up and being ever so terribly innovative just by bringing in new technologies – but that's a myth. I hate to be the bearer of bad news, but broadly speaking, the new machinery we peddle is just that – new machinery. That's not innovation, that's just reacting to the latest market manipulation from those lovely people in Seattle. In the midst of it all, we stay much the same – developers are paid more than support staff, we put our least technically skilled people in front of our customers, we subsidise low productivity among second-line technicians, our computer login screens still confront lay users with weird messages that only network technicians can understand, we still wait to be asked to do something rather than touting for business. The typical IT services department adheres to outdated philosophies and structures and still looks the way it did ten years ago. It continues to react to its market rather than control it. It ignores competition and deals with changing demand after, rather than before the fact. Meanwhile, out there in the business world, much of that thinking has long gone.

We need to be much more directly involved in the process of bringing IT itself and the accompanying integrated services to the market consisting of our users. We need to know what they are up to, from the outset. We need to be as much a part of the business as the users are, so that our service design methodology works in tandem with the changing needs of the business. We have a new obligation to be there at the point at which the new business need is identified, so we can design our resulting services in parallel with that and not (as I believe we are now) in a state of resentful surprise after the business change has already taken place. We need people Out There. We all can relate the story of how the applications department sneaks up to the servers in the middle of the night and installs a new application without telling anybody except the users it is aimed at, only to leave the IT services to hear about it the following day when a user calls in with an enquiry about the use of that application. If the business changes, so must we, procedurally as well as structurally – and simultaneously, not a little later with a plaintive and often refused request for more staff.

In designing our IT services, I believe we need an approach much more like the one taken by the very business that hosts us. We need to look at the service in terms of what is needed, not simply in terms of how we can shoehorn it in to what we've already got. If after we have taken that strategic look at the situation we decide that a shoehorn is indeed a more appropriate tool than a drawing board, then all well and good. But too many shoehorns will later lead to corns, and then it's too late. Planning must always come first.

You may be able to see the effects of shoehorns around you now. Users love quick fixes – that's why we do it – it makes them think we are flexible, getting them working quickly instead of subjecting them to unnecessary bureaucracy. So sometimes we bend the standards a little, skip the documentation or maybe omit to strictly adhere to the change process. But the tendency to go for the 'quick fix' and grab the users' gratitude while it's on offer can – no, eventually *will* – lead to long term problems. The following paragraph is an amalgamation of IT services planning situations at a number of companies. Does it also describe yours?

Here and there around the company, there are a few machines populated with software that perhaps does not have a complete listing on the assets management database. But we ignore it because the user bought the software anyway and has a direct relationship with the supplier for support, so he doesn't need to bother us. There are a few users who are logging in with somebody else's ID, but it's OK because they've got by for a while doing it that way. A few of the desktops are connected to different ports on the network switches than they used to be, but it works, so nobody's really that bothered. A couple of the departments retained their old printers when we upgraded them, so the drivers are getting out of date and there won't be any drivers when we update their operating systems, but we'll cross that bridge when we come to it. A few of the Portakabins needed network extensions but they're only short term, so we just cobbled the new links together for the time being. When the new acquisition took place, we had to change the procurement process a little to accommodate that, but the operations staff learned the new way quickly and we didn't have time to update the procedures manual. A few of the newer network infrastructure staff haven't been on the procedures training course yet, but that's all right, because they've learned what they need to know from their colleagues. Some of the users still haven't been taught how the new corporate templates work, but they know enough to get by, and the helpdesk deals with any problems they may have so it doesn't cause any issues anywhere else in IT.

This is a pile of cans in a supermarket. The one on the bottom left-hand corner is starting to buckle, but nobody has noticed, because their heads are too full of all the undocumented exceptions elsewhere in the pile. And when that ignored can finally goes, the whole lot will follow and it will take ages in time and manpower we don't have, to sort out the resulting catastrophe.

But it's never happened yet. We'll get by.

3.1 The specifics of individual service design

The main feature of this chapter is the list of individual services we provide. It is based on the principle that the service is not what we do, but what the customer consumes. For the purposes of this exercise, I am assuming that we have already been through the process of identifying the market for IT service and that the following is a list of service needs we have arrived at.

I mentioned in a footnote in the Preface my contention that 'customers' is not a synonym for 'users', even though it may fashionably have come to be used as such in recent times. Although most of the services outlined below are aimed at users, some are designed for other groups, such as financiers (financial reports), managers (management reports) and user line management (user performance monitoring). It is thus perhaps more accurate in this chapter to use the more generic term 'customers' rather than the specific 'users'.

There are three main reasons for identifying the delivered services to this level of detail.

- **Justification**
  These are our products – these are what our customers pay us for. So the customers have to see what they are getting for their money. This level of detail makes for a more accurate representation of the use to which our customers put us. Therefore, our catalogue should also be as detailed as this. My experience is that too many customers view IT services as the bit of IT with the helpdesk in it, and fall back on the limited understanding that IT services provides nothing more than 'somewhere I can phone to ask for something'. This can lead to all sorts of other misunderstandings, like the classic complaint that the service should be better because IT

has so many people. One way to deal with that potential complaint is to highlight the fact that the customer gets a great deal more than just a telephone answering service.

- **Resourcing**

  Every single service we produce requires staffing. Those staff will need particular skills. Every service needs a set of processes, which will have to be defined and kept up to date and the staff trained in their operation. We need a detailed list of services so that we can keep abreast of the operational and manpower demands the production of each service will have. If we don't have a defined service, how do we know whether we are committing enough resource to it?

- **Reporting**

  How well are we doing at providing service A? And if we're doing particularly well there, is that to the detriment of service B where we seem to be doing not so well? If our IT services department were a bakery, we would want to know that our croissants were nice and succulent, not too dry, not too burned. But we would need to know the same about our farmhouse white and oven bottoms. Just because our pork pies are great does not give us licence to neglect the fact that our baguettes are coming out all blackened and bendy. We have to keep an eye on the performance and quality of all our products – not just the most obvious or heavily used ones – and the first step in having that breadth of management information is to define all our products. You never know, there may be too much salt in the breakfast rolls, and unless we knew the difference between a breakfast roll and a brown wholemeal tin we might never spot it. And that means that the bread shops may start going elsewhere for their supplies of certain lines. At the risk of stating the obvious, if we are managers of all our services it is our duty to know about all of them.

For reasons of financing, planning and management, we have to distinguish all our products – because in essence, no one product is any more or any less important than any other. We simply cannot afford to fall into the common trap, as many do, of seeing our output through a haze of confused activity, which just happens to produce results.

In Section 3.2 below is a hypothetical list of IT services, with an outline of what each service is and its main outputs in terms of user benefits. The 'description' merely states what the service 'is' to ensure its individual identity and highlight to the customer the fact that it truly is a separate service.

The 'main deliverables' lists what the client obtains from his subscription to the service. I urge the reader to see the 'deliverables' that way and **specifically not as a list of IT services activities** associated with the service. Our activities come later in Chapter 4 when we look at the process. For now, this is about not what we *do*, it's about what the client *gets*. There is a difference, and that difference is a core theme in this book (which is why I keep repeating it!). The services must be seen from the client's point of view *first*.

A pivotal reason for a list of services this complex is to point out to the client that absolutely everything he receives from us is part of a structured service and not merely an accidental consequence of some activity we happen to perform. The client receives none of these services by accident. Similarly, he does not have a right of default to receive any of them just because he is our client – and this will be further cemented in Chapter 8, when we look at how we charge for, or perhaps more accurately, recoup the costs of these services.

As an example of this, let us consider the twin services of 'helpdesk' and 'problem solving'. In many IT services departments, these two separate services are amalgamated into one. They have no separate identity. The temptation to make this merger is a strong one because of the apparent need for the so-called 'end-to-end process' – put a demand in one end, a finished product comes out the other. The end-to-end process is very professional and very desirable – but it's irrelevant here and it can confuse the issue of designing separate services. It also may confuse the user as to the nature of the services he is getting. The process is not the service. We cannot sell the user a process because it happens entirely within ITS and invisibly. We may bundle services together, a point I cover later, but that does not preclude our need at least at the outset, to identify separate services. The problem with bundled services is that it may cloud the user's expectation, allowing him to make a simplistic assumption like 'I call the helpdesk, with anything, and they send somebody over'.

Even that first presumption, 'I call the helpdesk, with anything' is false, for several reasons, the main ones being:

- **It doesn't have to be a helpdesk**
  If we offer the client a problem solving service, we may insist that to report a problem, he approaches the helpdesk. But we don't have to do it that way. We could for instance insist that he goes to his own manager and reports the problem there,

and then the manager had to fill out a form in triplicate, send one copy to the finance department to solicit payment for our eventual response to his request, keep one copy for himself and attach the other to the leg of a pigeon, which happened to know there was birdseed and a dry bed waiting for it in a cage in the server room, and so once released, would take off for said destination with its cargo of a trouble ticket.

It is presumptuous of the client to expect that just because he has been granted one service, means he gets another by default. You only get it if you pay for it my friend, because it's a different service.

- **It doesn't have to include problem solving**
  Take the similar presumption that just because a request is reported, means that IT will send a chap round or even assume the responsibility for solving the problem. That is not necessarily the case. One of our options, in terms of service provision, is not to offer a problem-solving service at all. Of course that is unthinkable for internal user support – surely we must solve the problem after the user reports it, mustn't we? Not necessarily. Think of all the mail-order computer companies who ship a piece of kit to your home address and offer a technical support number you can call and maybe a hardware maintenance service – but no problem solving. If your problem with your mail-order computer is software, you might find out that you're on your own with that one. If the machine is not obviously broken and thus not in need of a hardware repair, they won't necessarily despatch a technician to your side, because for the mail-order companies, providing an on-the-road technician is a separate service.

  So it should be with us. Problem resolution is not a given. It's a separate service. That's why we have the optional service of 'remote resolution', which is a lot cheaper to provide, because some of our users, even though they may like the idea, may simply be unable to afford the high cost of a mobile technician (see 'The high cost of second-line support', p. 37)

Take another example, that of change requests and applications maintenance. Just because the user wants a new field on a form in one of the business systems, does not necessarily mean his request will be passed from change request receipt into the applications maintenance service and his request acted upon. The services may be procedurally linked, but that link is internal to IT services which does not necessarily imply that from the customer's point of view they are the same service. Similarly, IT itself may instigate a change to the applications as a way of improving the service to the business without that change being the result of a user request. We accept requests for changes to applications. We change applications. Linked, but different.

The same goes for 'data conversion and transfer'. Your user has an external client who stores a database in Lotus Notes, but your corporate standard happens to be Microsoft Access. The user could probably do the conversion himself – there are tools around to help – but he wants somebody else to do it. That's a service.

Perhaps when he upgrades his desktop computer, he wants all the data moved onto his new machine. He could do it himself, by copying everything up to the server or cutting a CD-ROM – but he'd rather you did it. Often, we offer this as a part of the procurement service, because installation is one of our internal processes associated with that service and data transfer is bundled with the installation. But it doesn't have to be that way. Just because we happen to link our internal processes together does not necessarily mean that these processes are not separate services.

Of course for marketing reasons, we may indeed lump some of these services together and call them one service. For example, if every department is forced by corporate insistence to use the same central computing environment, then every group of users will thereby be forced to take the 'computer operations' service. So bundling services together and marketing them as bundles may be our prerogative – but for the purposes of emphasizing the fact that these services require different resources and skillsets, for the fact that they constitute separate deliverables, the list below keeps the various services strictly apart from one another.

Case study:
The high cost of second-line support

Let us assume I am running a helpdesk with three first-line people, whose salaries are around £16 666.67 per year. That means my total first-line salary costs are £50 000 a year. Those first liners take 25 000 calls a year, so the salary cost alone of their handling an enquiry is £2.00. They resolve about 50 per cent of these enquiries over the telephone. So we have some resolutions that cost only two quid. Great, nice and cheap.

The other 50 per cent, the ones that require some careful diagnosis or a deskside visit by a technician, are 'assigned' to the second line. Those people each work about 220 days a year and resolve (typically, according to industry surveys) about eight problems per person per day.

But they are also paid more than the first line – on average, the salary for each of them is about £25 000 per year. So each second-line technician solves 8 × 220 or 1760 problems a year. And at a salary of twenty-five grand, that means that each resolution they produce costs £14.20. But then each of those enquiries had to go through the helpdesk, thus incurring the £2.00 cost there also.

So a first-line resolution costs £2.00 and a second-line resolution £16.20.

There are a number of implications here. First, if the user had to pay the actual cost of problem resolution, he would opt for the first-line fix, because it's massively cheaper – and the fact that he would make that choice means that *logically, second-line problem resolution must be a separate service.*

But another implication goes right to the heart of how we structure and finance IT services.

For as long as there has been user support, we have persisted in this topsy-turvy nonsense of paying our second-line technicians more than our first line, when it is plainly obvious, in pure business terms, that the first line brings in a hugely greater return on investment.

We even give license to this. We think it's normal and acceptable that our better technicians should be freed from telephone duty. Hands up all those who have ever heard a second-line technician utter words to the effect that they don't go on the phones any more. A commercial consideration of that abdication must lead us to the conclusion that somebody with that attitude is too expensive to hire. If we put our best technicians on the telephones, they will have a higher first-time-fix rate because they are more technically competent – and that means we will fix more problems at a cost of two quid and fewer at a cost of sixteen quid.

If I were the king of IT services, I would issue a royal decree that second-line staff who don't go on the phones get paid less than first-line staff, because they generate a poorer return on investment. And I would make subsidizing low productivity in the second line a punishable offence. In my regal wisdom, I would accept that some problems are trickier to solve and thus require greater expertise, which costs more. But I would not thereby accept that just because there were some people with greater expertise, I had to put them in a department further away from the customer, because that wouldn't make business sense.

3.2 The service list

In arriving at this service list, I am assuming that we have already defined that these are the services needed by our market. That definition was done as part of the 'demand assessment' we looked at in Chapter 2 (p. 15).

Service	Description	Main deliverables
1. Account management	Strategic representation at management level between user group and IT services	• Named contact • Regular service review meetings • Complaints response • First point of request for new services
2. Anti virus	Protect users from attacks by malicious software	• Configurable firewall • Regularly updated, automatic virus monitoring and eradication tools on all processors • Removing executable files from incoming mail prior to end delivery • Provide isolated computer for inoculating incoming storage media
3. Applications maintenance	Upgrades and repairs to existing in-house business software to ensure continuing match to changing business needs	• Deliverables as per 'User applications development'
4. Archival	Offline data storage and retrieval	• Timed, automatic data backup • Minimization of system downtime during backups • Secure, fireproof storage • Restoration of data by request
5. Business continuity	Disaster recovery	• Anticipation of potential major loss of IT infrastructure • Planned alternative data processing and communications systems • Agreed prioritization of systems
6. Change requests	Receipt, recording and processing of changes to any IT system or process	• Agreed prioritization of change • Agreed timescales • Statement of change ownership

(continued)

Service	Description	Main deliverables
		• Management of change through approvals process • Implementation
7. Computer operations	Management and provision of central processing	• Accessibility of applications and associated data • Overnight and batch job administration
8. Consultancy	Assistance with choosing information technology	• Business needs analysis • Market research for appropriate solutions • Technical advice
9. Data conversion and transfer	Transfer of data between formats and processors	• Provision of a range of data format conversion tools for users • Assistance with conversion • Special conversions by arrangement • Data moves between computers as part of upgrades
10. Environmental	Assistance with preparing the physical features of the desk environment for computing and communications tools	• Provision of surge-protected mains power source • Network connection point • Telephone connection point
11. External support standards management	Provision and management of performance standards for external IT support suppliers	• Documented standards for support performance • Service level recommendations • IT services involvement in contracts negotiations • Performance monitoring and reporting • Liaison with external supplier
12. Financial reports	Information on financial implications of IT services activity	• Access to hardware assets database with reporting tools • Access to software licensing database with reporting tools • Regular reports on current hardware and software assets

(continued)

Service	Description	Main deliverables
		• Periodic reports on IT equipment expenditure against budget • Periodic reports on IT expenditure on personnel against budget
13. Hardware maintenance	Replacement and repair of faulty hardware	• Maintenance of local stock for rapid replacement • Management of maintenance service supplier • Guaranteed service levels • Preventive maintenance of non-solid state equipment, to include printers, fax machines and network-connected photocopiers
14. Helpdesk	Reporting point for user enquiries	• Single point of contact for all IT services enquiries • Gateway to other services, with assignment as appropriate and agreed • Job number for every enquiry • Guaranteed immediate resolution of certain types of enquiries
15. Infrastructure	Provision of corporate data communications, storage and processing machinery	• Guaranteed availability and continuity of connection • Guaranteed processor-to-processor response time • Standard for desktop computing environment to include operating system, office applications, • Internet browser, email client and usage
16. Installations	Making new hardware and software available for use at the usual point of use	• Delivery, unpacking and installation of new desktop equipment to appropriate location • Installation of non-IT services supplied equipment by special arrangement • Disposal of old equipment

(continued)

41

Service	Description	Main deliverables
		• Disposal of packaging • Brief acquaintance of user with use of new equipment
17. Loans	Provision of temporary equipment	• Library of corporate standard equipment • Delivery and installation • Collection on usage termination
18. Management reports	Periodic documented management information	• Reports on usage made of IT services • IT performance against agreed service levels • IT performance against available manpower
19. Moves	Changing the location of equipment	• Disconnection, porterage and reconnection of equipment • Specialist temporary installations in meeting rooms and external sites by arrangement
20. Network connection	Account on corporate computer network	• Secure user ID • Server-based data storage space with backup • Logical connection to monochrome and colour printers near desk • Logical connection to fax output • Internet browser • Corporate internal email address and client • Internet email address • Logical connection to necessary business applications • Logical connection to necessary office applications and software tools • Peer-to-peer data sharing within workgroup • Access to account from any corporate computer • Access to corporate document templates library
21. Problem solving	Resolving computer problems reported to ITS by users	• Assignment from point of problem receipt to diagnostician

(continued)

42

Service	Description	Main deliverables
		• Problem diagnosis and resolution • User instruction on use of resolution • Deskside visit as deemed necessary by IT services (see 'Remote resolution')
22. Procurement	Acquisition of IT equipment	• Standards for appropriate equipment • Liaison with suppliers • Delivery to corporate location (for delivery to desk, see 'Installation')
23. Projects	Ad hoc projects	• Project identification and specification • Assignment of appropriate resources to project • Project management • Regular progress reporting as agreed • Implementation of finished product • Handover
24. Remote resolution	Resolution of problems by remote control	• Remote control software client resident on user's computer • Secure access by agreement with user • Real-time resolution in presence of user
25. Telephone connection	Account on corporate telephone private automatic branch exchange (PABX)	• Extension number • Membership of necessary hunt groups • Internal telephone directory • Access to corporate speed-dial directory • Voicemail account • Automatic divert-on-busy to client specifications
26. Training	Provision of computer usage training	• Regular training courses on use of standard company IT hardware and software • Liaison with external IT training suppliers as required
27. Usage support horizontal applications	Assistance with use of standard applications as	• At-desk assistance • Brief training on elements of applications

(continued)

43

Service	Description	Main deliverables
	provided by network connection service	(for training on whole systems, see 'Training')
28. Usage support vertical applications	Assistance with use of business and specialist applications	By special arrangement to include: • At-desk assistance • Brief training on elements of applications (for training on whole systems, see 'Training')
29. User applications development	Provision of resource for writing new, ad hoc systems for specific user needs for desktop, laptop and palmtop processors	• Assist with system specification • Software creation • Management of contract developers • Development progress updates • Agreed delivery dates • Gateway into change management process for adding created software to 'supported products' catalogue, thus bringing these into full helpdesk support
30. User performance monitoring	Feedback to line managers on employee use of helpdesk	• Nature of feedback by arrangement • Training needs analysis and recommendations
31. Videoconferencing	Provision of videoconferencing facilities	• Conference suite booking service • Guarantee of compatibility with main videoconferencing protocols • Video, voice and stills transmission and receipt • Directory of addresses of other commonly used videoconference terminals

3.3 Applying service levels

We now arrive at the question of how much of each service each group of users will actually need. This is the issue of 'service level' – not just the provision of the service per se, but the variety of involvement, ownership, speed, detail, quality or responsiveness with which the service is provided. Your users may need a fast service, but perhaps can only afford a slow one. These are the differences in service levels.

Commonly, IT services providers offer a 'blanket' service. Everybody gets the same – it says so in the service level agreement, so it must be true. Well, OK, not perhaps everybody. There's the human factor, of course. See that big bloke over there? He can be a bit obstreperous at times, so we treat him with kid gloves and deal with him more quickly than most of the users. Oh, and of course there's the directors. If any of them ring up, we leap about frantically, dropping everything else because they are so powerful and important. And then there's the human resources department – the people in there are so nice, they always make you a cup of coffee, and it's so relaxed, it's a delight to change a toner in that office.

We are bound to make exceptions, if not by agreed stipulation, then at least by instinct. Even if we have 'blanket' service levels as a formally agreed structure, our innate understanding of the business (and perhaps our own agenda or motivation – we're only human) will cause us to differentiate service levels between certain user groups. We know by experience that some departments are commercially more important than others and we will adjust accordingly our workload priorities even though the formal service offerings do not allow for such adjustment.

We are back to the 'garden path' argument I raised in Chapter 2. An SLA that stipulates a common service level, which is then ignored for the sake of reality and pragmatism, is a garden path that was laid before we had observed where people needed to walk. It may be that the reason people follow these instinctive and emotional ways of setting service level priorities is because they work and are acceptable by provider and consumer alike. Watch for these instinctive service levels – there may be a truth in their necessity, and we should not dismiss them all as aberrations even though some of them may be just that.

3.4 Wasted service levels

Blanket service levels are popular in some IT services departments because they are easy to understand from the points of view of both the provider and the customer. They have all the benefits of mass production. They are relatively easy to produce, easy to train the service staff how to produce them, cheaper to produce than exception-based services. They simply both service administration and the service level agreement itself. But they rarely reflect the reality of the real customer environment, which is why we tend to diverge from them at the point of delivery.

The impact on the company of a 'blanket' service level is shown at Figure 3.1 below. The upper of the two charts in this figure shows the actual position in terms of service needs. The service level is on the vertical axis. The horizontal axis is divided into various user groups and the height of the columns represents differences in real service level needs. In this hypothetical case, the two departments who need and can justify high IT service levels are the factory (because that's where a significant

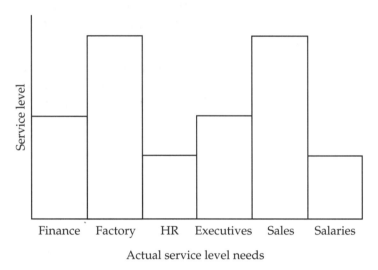

Actual service level needs

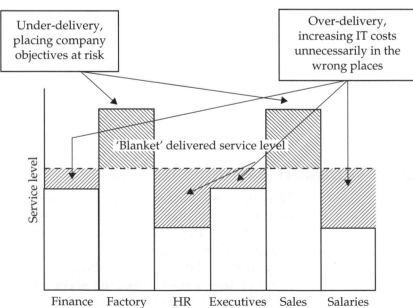

Figure 3.1
Risks of blanket
service levels

proportion of the corporate costs are incurred, and if the factory stops working we have nothing to sell) and the sales department (because if the selling is impeded, the company makes less money than usual). The finance department and the executives need a medium level of service because of their handling of the company's money and representation of the company respectively. The administrative departments need the lower of these three service levels, because they are less important than the other functions.

In the lower graph, we have superimposed a 'blanket' service level, indicated by the horizontal dotted line. This depicts how the whole company gets the same service level from ITS. The shaded areas show the effect of this. Below the dotted line, we have four departments receiving a higher service level than they actually need – incurring a cost in terms of ITS resources in the process. But the blanket service level means that these less commercially critical departments get an artificially high level of service at the expense of the departments that actually need a significantly higher level of service.

In this example, the 'blanket' service level is actually detrimental to the company's fortunes.

3.5 Differentiated service levels

It is not safe to assume that all users will need all services, and all to the same level, all the time. Some possible reasons:

- **Service portfolio requirements will differ between clients**
  Not everybody will buy everything we sell. For instance, the catering department simply will never use the videoconferencing service, but changes to their kitchen management procedures cause them to need the projects service to update their local systems. The facilities department uses a lot of casual labour and external contractors who have to use the company's computer systems only for a short while, so they will need applications usage support but will almost never make use of training.

- **Service portfolio requirements will differ over time**
  Some clients may be satisfied with a certain set of services at fixed service levels for most of the time, but suddenly and temporarily need a change to their service portfolio and/or the service levels offered within that. An example is the Finance Department. Normally quite happy with a standard service level, all that changes in the last week of every fiscal quarter,

even more so at the end of the financial year. At those times the users in that department may run programs and routines that are not run at other times of the year. Their processing needs rise, and the department's systems may be running reports all night as opposed to routine use during office hours only. At these times the computer operations service becomes a particularly high priority, whereas for the rest of the year, the user may ignore that service or receive it by default. An 'out-of-hours' user support service may also be required, just for that short period.

- **Urgency rises and falls with circumstances**
  I know of another example, in this case a legal practice. Normally, the IT service is fairly routine. But in their preparation of legal cases, their comes a point called 'completion', immediately before the case goes to court, where all hands are expected to come to the pump. Activity rises exponentially and temporarily as the 'completion' takes priority over all other matters. ITS must play its part, providing computer installations at short notice and on-hand technicians into the small hours. In this case, the ITS department has created a 'completions support' service. Staffed by people of appropriate skills, who otherwise would be fulfilling other duties, this is in effect like a hospital 'crash team'.

  Just as in the case of the finance department's special requirements at period ends, the 'completions support' services are fairly standard in design, but have significantly elevated service levels.

- **Those who claim to need high service levels may actually be wrong**
  As I mentioned earlier we may, by instinct or by our understanding of the business, offer higher service levels to some groups of users than others. But that may raise the question as to whether we do it out of actual business need or perhaps some other reason, such as fear or respect for political status. The CEO has his secretary make a routine enquiry to ITS on his behalf. This is not a 'system down' announcement – it is a routine enquiry. Does it actually deserve a service level we would normally reserve only for 'system down' just because the caller is (by proxy) the CEO? By what measure do we set the service levels – by the importance of the need or the importance of the requestor?

  Even when our service levels have been formally set, there is still a temptation during day-to-day delivery to react more promptly to he-who-shouts-loudest. And even if the artificially elevated service the shouter is calling for may not be justified in reality, it is still difficult to resist. This is because shouters have a tendency to go over our heads and pester senior and powerful people to get our priorities temporarily changed in the shouter's favour. And because senior and powerful people have more important things to worry about than somebody throwing his toys out of the cot, they may also be tempted to take the quick and easy way out and support the shouter just to rid themselves of the bother he is briefly creating.

There is a way of dealing with these false claims for service level. It lies in the way we design and authorize our service levels at the outset, because dealing with them at the time of request is extremely difficult to withstand.

- **Those who hardly ever use us may actually need us desperately**

  Several years ago, I was engaged by a company operating in a new market. In the UK, that particular market was relatively immature – while in the USA, it was well-established and its IT needs catered for by several external bureau services. The client in question had found it necessary to solve many of its computing system problems from within its own resources, so its IT services team was constantly innovating in terms of services and support methodologies. Then almost overnight, the market exploded. Several more players appeared. The established American IT service suppliers noticed the change in the UK and offered their already mature provisions. Within a matter of a few short months, this company had moved from taking its IT services from a single internal supplier to no less than six external suppliers of various IT services in addition to the incumbent group. Service levels between these various providers differed considerably, if not exasperatingly. Because of the proliferation of suppliers and supporters of mission-critical systems service levels across the company were beginning to differ. Consistency in service levels became nothing more than a pipedream, and the variety began to affect the reliability with which various interdependent departments related to one another in the corporate workflow as a whole. It was getting more and more confusing and definitely not conducive to business continuity. In the face of this, the chief information officer (CIO) decreed that Something Must Be Done. He imposed the responsibility for all IT service standards on the IT services team, regardless of the initial source of the service. The various departments who had engaged these external companies had no point of reference by which to judge the level of service they were being offered at the time, and so had accepted whatever had come with the IT offering itself, and this had led to the variation in service levels. The CIO's new strategy would unify service levels around a template he had drawn up in the IT interests of the company as a whole. The users engaging these services had concluded that as they were buying the service from outside, they did not need the internal IT services department – but as a result of that narrow conclusion, they had unwittingly contributed to a larger problem affecting the whole company. Users may not realize they need us, even though they do. Consequently they may make less use of us than they should and may underestimate the service level they actually need us to provide. Just because a user department does not use IT services does not necessarily mean that they do not need us or they could not benefit from our involvement.

3.6 Why we must formalize service levels

The user shouting louder to get a higher level of service and the executive pulling rank for the same or perhaps political reasons are examples of abuse of the service. Unless the increased service level these users actually gain is justified – which can only be the case if it benefits the business as a whole – then such requests should not be entertained. It's nothing better than cheating or jumping the queue. Our resources are finite, and ideally planned to give as high as possible a service level in the most cost-effective way we can. If somebody jumps the queue, no matter who it is, then somebody else must suffer. Commonly, ITS does not have spare resource, otherwise unemployed, just waiting for somebody to demand a service level outwith the provisions of the contract they have with us, so to deal with a sudden elevation in service levels, we have to rob the resource from some other part of ITS that is already fully employed delivering a service elsewhere, or we have to reduce a service level to somebody else.

The queue jumpers cannot have it both ways. I maintained earlier that it is difficult to withstand pressure to artificially increase an isolated service level at the moment that pressure is placed upon us. Difficult, that is, but not impossible. It takes a strong IT services manager to do this, but the actual results of these demands can be pointed out to the perpetrators. If the demand has caused an aberration to service levels to other clients, you could calculate exactly what was the size of that aberration, document it and advise the perpetrator of the actual corporate effect of temporarily increasing service for him. You might point out that this was not the initially contracted service level and that as a result he was in breach of contract. You might also observe that you as IT services manager cannot be held responsible for producing consistent service levels if others deliberately jeopardize your consistency by pulling rank.

If you are the IT services manager, then either you are in control of the service level or you are not. If you are to be held accountable for the service level, then it falls to you and you alone to control that service level. If a higher power suddenly asserts a right to change your priorities temporarily, then in that moment you are not in control of the service level. And if you are not in control, then you cannot be held accountable.

Of course you will allow this to happen occasionally – this will demonstrate your flexibility, and you'll let it go because you don't want to cause a scene or ruin a working relationship over a small matter such as an isolated incursion into your influence in your own department. And even if it starts to happen more often – and it will, because once you've increased the service level once, that's the level your client will expect by default next time – but even then, you are not likely to go banging on the CEO's office door sporting statistics to show him just how much damage he has done by his abuse of the service.

You may choose the alternative tactic of approaching the offender with your calculation of what service level he routinely demands, what level of resource this is likely to consume and how much it will cost to provide such a high priority user with such a high service level on a routine basis. See 'A VIP service' below.

Case study:
A VIP service

A certain organization was set up by an international governmental trading block and it constituted one of many representations they made to other nations not within the block. So it was very high profile, very political, very sensitive to external views of itself. Those individuals who represent the institution do so on an international level, under the watchful eye of even government ministers. The performance of the institution and of those who represent it is under considerable scrutiny. Because of their high profile, those representatives are placed in a particular category within the organization, that of Very Important People. The recognition of their status and importance goes right through the organization, even to IT services – where the service level agreement allows for one level of service to most users, but a very much higher one to these VIPs, even to the luxury of having a certain amount of idle resource to wait on the demands from the VIPs.

3.7 Client categorization

The ideal solution is to cover all the bases as early in the service level setting process at as early a stage and as high an authority as possible. My preferred method is to categorize groups of users in terms of the business criticality of their function. A definition of 'business criticality' will of course be needed. Possibilities may include 'make most money for the company', 'save most money for the company', 'contribute most to the corporate mission', or 'be of most use to the corporate executives'. The nature of the definitions may also differ between private and public sector organizations, civilian and military or police bodies, merchants and charities and so on.

But once those definitions are in place, they can next become the basis of both proactive prioritization and concrete service levels. By 'proactive prioritization' I intend to suggest that we assign to each user group a unique priority number, which in effect is a rank in the ladder of all the corporation's user groups. So every group has a different priority level, which matches their importance to the business. The only way a user group can increase its priority level is by increasing its business contribution as stipulated by the agreed 'business criticality' definition. Of course, both the definition and the priorities should be agreed at board level.

This pro-active prioritization means that a client's service requests are prioritized even before the requests are made. However, they are only prioritized in terms of the relative importance of the client – the request itself, when it comes, may have to be further prioritized against its urgency as compared with the urgency of all other outstanding work.

Clients may now be categorized in terms of their respective pro-active priorities. Higher service levels go to high-priority clients, lowest service levels to the lowest priority clients. And because the categories have been based on business contribution, we in

IT services know that we are dealing with the most important clients first and fastest.

The beauty of this is that because it is agreed with the board of directors on the basis of real business contribution, no user can berate IT services for an inadequate service provision. Because given that IT services always meets its agreed service levels, and because those levels and client categories have been agreed with the board, the user's complaint is not with IT, but with the board itself. The user does not have to prove to IT that he needs a higher service level – he has to prove to the board that his department makes a higher contribution to the business or his service level stays where it is. Complaints then only have meaning and legitimacy where IT services fails to meet its service level targets.

This can add a whole new meaning to the concept of 'user satisfaction' with the service. Satisfaction is an emotion – but the process I have described here is arithmetical. There is room for debate as to whether satisfaction has any import at all where the level of service is strictly dictated by business criticality.

3.8 Service level examples

So far, this chapter has introduced the idea of service levels in a naked form, i.e. as they will be published to or used by the clients. Further ideas on the day-to-day delivery of the services as part of the client relationship is offered in Chapter 7. But even at this stage, prior to applying services and service levels directly to clients, we are already in a position to design the basis of the service levels.

In the service list above, we've come up with four main types of services:

Service type	Meaning	Services (examples)
Response and resolution	User makes request for the service	Applications maintenance, change requests, consultancy, data conversion and transfer, hardware maintenance, helpdesk, loans, moves, procurement, projects, remote resolution, training, usage support horizontal applications, usage support vertical applications, user applications development, user performance monitoring, videoconferencing

(*continued*)

53

Service type	Meaning	Services (examples)
Production	ITS provides the service as part of routine production IT	Anti-virus, applications maintenance, archival, business continuity, computer operations, environmental, infrastructure, training, videoconferencing
Consequential	Services typically invoked by use of other IT services	Environmental, installations, network connection, problem-solving, telephone connection
Administrative	Services producing information	Account management, external support standards management, financial reports, management reports

Note that some of the services appear in more than one category – 'training' and 'videoconferencing' are examples of this. We would provide a training service in any case, but the service may also be directly requested. We provide a fully equipped videoconferencing suite as a matter of course, which makes it a 'production' service – but we also offer a booking register for the videoconferencing suite, and receiving bookings is a 'response' service.

The 'consequential' services would typically be brought into use as a result of another service being used. For example, a user request against the 'procurement' service to prepare a workstation for a new employee may cause us to automatically also offer the 'environmental' service to prepare the electrical connections for the arriving user's new desk, offer a 'network connection' and a 'telephone connection' and an 'installation' of the new computer.

We can now come up with generic service levels for each of the main service types. These generic service levels can be used as the basis for a negotiation with our clients. Because we are doing this in advance of any specific negotiation, these can only be for standard services, and not for ad hoc requirements (such as the 'completion' service in the legal practice discussed above). However, we can present service levels for both regular users and VIPs as suggested in Figure 3.2.

To add another layer for interest only, I have allowed for the possibility that some of the services may be outsourced – provided by an external supplier – and how the implications of that may be catered for in the service level statement.

Service level	Standard service level				Premium (VIP) service level	
	ITS to satisfy		External party to satisfy		ITS to satisfy	External party to satisfy
Service type	User productivity impeded	User productivity not impeded	User productivity impeded	User productivity not impeded	All cases	All cases
Response and resolution	Response within thirty minutes Resolution within two hours	Response within two hours Resolution within one working day	Response within thirty minutes Resolution within one working day	Response within two hours Resolution within one week	Immediate response – resolution within one hour	Immediate response – resolution within two working days
Production	By special arrangement	9 a.m.–5 p.m. Mon–Fri	By special arrangement	9 a.m.–5 p.m. Mon–Fri	24/7 availability	Mon–Fri availability
Consequential	As per resolution guarantee					
Administrative	All cases – monthly data feeds				Monthly data feeds and additional information on demand	

Figure 3.2 An example skeleton service level statement

4

The processes

In order to move a unit of production from a starting state to a desired finishing state, a number of things have to happen, involving and affecting that unit of production. This application of a string of effects to the unit as it transits the production line is known as a **process**. As each event takes place, value is added to the unit. This 'added value' is created by the consumption of resources. If we were making bread, we would add the flour and water, knead it, add the yeast and knead it some more. We'd put it somewhere warm to rise, then bake it in a hot oven. Throughout, we would have been consuming hard ingredients, fuel, space and the energy and skills of the baker. All of these have to be paid for, but in laying out those costs we have constantly added value, until at the end we have a loaf of bread, which is worth more to the end user than the ingredients alone would have been.

So it is with IT services – for although we may not have such an emphasis on raw ingredients, nevertheless we still consume the time and expensively gathered skills of our staff. By taking, for example, a situation from problem to solution or a hardware installation from absence to presence, we are adding value as our process progresses.

This issue of adding value is important – if we were in manufacturing we would watch it very carefully. We would not want to add more value than necessary, for we might not be able to recoup that outlay at the point of sale, thus reducing our profits. We may tend to ignore the issue in IT services, for the apparent absence of competition in our market may de-emphasize the cost issue – if nobody else is providing our users with equipment or solutions, we don't have to compete with anybody so there are apparently no profits at risk. However, all our processes consume resources – and if the process is inefficient, then it is in effect robbing us of resources we could use to make another service more effective. We should take care to add only the value we need to add for the final outcome to serve the user according to his needs. Anything more than that is both a waste of resources and a potential risk to the efficacy of other services.

At a higher level of detail than the processes come the **procedures**. These describe how we should conduct the activities within the process. Take for example the process for installing a new computer, which may go something like:

1. user places order
2. ITS verifies necessity of equipment and budgetary authority for the order
3. ITS passes order on to vendor
4. vendor delivers equipment
5. ITS technician installs equipment.

As a process, this works. It tells us what has to happen, in what order and where the responsibilities lie. But it is only the *what* – it says nothing about *how*, which is why we need to go to the higher detail of procedures.

So for 'user places order', the procedure may state 'user downloads equipment request form from the Intranet and fills it in. Then he takes it to his line manager for signing. Then he passes the completed form to the ITS administrator, who responds with an estimated delivery date.'

Case study:
Necessary bureaucracy

The obvious problem with procedures is the necessary bureaucracy that accompanies them. I witnessed an exchange between a particularly distressed user whose new computer was apparently late in arriving and a flustered IT office clerk.

User: 'But I put my order form in weeks ago!'
Clerk: 'Well I didn't see it.'
User: 'No, you were at lunch, so I gave it to one of the technicians.'
Clerk: 'Which one did you give it to?'
User: 'It was Dave.'
Clerk: 'Dave! Did you see that form?'
Dave: 'Don't think so.'
User: 'I put it in your in-tray.'
Dave: 'I haven't got an in-tray.'
User: 'Yes you have, there on the corner of your desk.'

Dave: 'That's my work-in-progress tray.'

User: 'Well don't you look at it?'

Dave: 'I don't have to – I know what's in it because I'm the only one who puts things in it.'

User: 'What is it with this place? Don't you people talk to each other?'

Clerk: 'There are procedures here.'

User: 'Yes, and look what good they do. There was nobody here to accept my order. What kind of a procedure is that? And in any case, all these procedures just slow things down.'

At this point, the helpdesk manager, who had been listening in, decided to join in. Manager: 'Let's see if we've got this right. You didn't follow an advertised procedure and that's our fault. You didn't follow the procedure because it was too slow, thereby making delivery of your computer even slower and that too is our fault. The procedure says "give the form to the clerk" and you chose to leave the form lying around in this office and that's our fault also.'

It was clear that this user had scant grasp of the need for procedure. The company in question installs some sixty computers a month. Nobody could hold that kind of detail in their heads, so there simply have to be procedures. To some people they may appear a hindrance, but without them, more mistakes would be made. The user's real problem was that he did not appreciate the scale of the ITS operation. The more we tend towards mass-production, the more uniform must be the way we work. Of course there should always be scope for exceptions, but exceptions are risky. So we establish a norm of operation to minimize that risk. However we may dislike bureaucracy, it will always be with us because sometimes (not always) the bureaucratic way is the best for everybody's interests.

At a higher level of detail still come the work instructions, which are the individual tasks to be carried out during the procedure. The process may say that we take a change request, put it through the approvals process to accept or decline the request and upon acceptance pass the request to a project manager who will oversee the resources and activities to be dedicated to bringing the change about. Within that process, there will be a number of procedures, such as logging the request, requiring the use of a form. The work instructions will dictate precisely how that form should be filled out. Where the processes give a functional overview, and the procedures govern the method of carrying out those functions, the work instructions are specifically about the mechanics of a detailed task.

In this chapter we shall be focusing mainly on the processes, with a few nods to procedure to give those processes some flesh. The work instructions will vary so much from company to company that they are outside the scope of this book.

Broadly speaking, we shall be looking at processes according to the services defined in Chapter 3.

4.1 Designing processes

There will be dozens of processes in any IT services department. Most of them will govern the production of a service or the output from it. Others will be administrative – such as that for recruiting a new member of staff or advertising the department's services. In later chapters, we shall look in more detail at those administrative functions. For the sake of clarity, I intend to confine the remainder of this chapter to only those processes that produce a service output.

Extended service process identification method

Our purpose here is to define processes, which by being followed will create, run and manage our services. The services produce desirable results, so underlying them is a manufacturing process. But before the service can begin to start working, it too has to be created or manufactured, so there is also a process at that level. Just as any other product, the service must be designed, tested, documented, published and marketed. Then it starts to run on a regular basis. While it is running, as we would with any machine we own, we may start to think of ways of improving it, and acting upon those observations may take us back to the design stage for the service.

So one could say that a service could be in one of four states, resulting in an overall 'service management' process.

Service state	Description
Design	Creating the service from scratch
Provision	Moving the service from design to delivery
Managing continuity	Operational state, with the service being routinely provided to its intended market
Change	Re-engineering, improving, growing or de-emphasizing the service, leading back to 'design' state

And within each of these states, there are further processes pertinent to the conduct of that state.

We are now at the point of 'process identification'. Considering these states individually, the following questions could be raised for each one of them.

Question	Description
What has to happen?	What outcome are we looking for? What is the necessary sequence of events to reach that outcome?
Who does it?	Who will be in charge of attaining that outcome and who will actually do the work? Is this more than one person or body of people?
How do the doers communicate?	What information needs to flow between people working on producing the events?
What measurements should we take?	How do we monitor our activities to know that everything is happening as it should?
How do we measure it?	What tools should we use for that monitoring?
What should we report on, how and to whom?	Which authorities need to be apprised of our progress, what elements do they need to know about and in what format do they want that information?
What action should the recipient take as a result of the report?	What do we need and expect from those authorities as a result of that information?
What do we tell the customer, why and how?	If we are at a stage in the service design where the customer is involved, what is the nature of that involvement?
How do we hand over to the next state?	How do we know when this stage is complete? What is the interface to the next stage, so that stage can start work immediately?

If we combine those two tables together, we end up with a single form of reference for the state of any service, with all of the detail affecting that state. The table might look something like Figure 4.1 opposite.

Thus there will be one of these 'process identification' matrices for each service. The matrix starts off as a guideline for the service design project team to use for their brainstorming and research to compose the contents of each cell. Once the matrix is complete, however, it becomes a reference point for all processes, affecting all services.

One of these matrices for each service, and there are thirty-one services listed in Chapter 3. Each service can be in one of four states and there are nine issues with each state. So to design the processes in our IT services factory, we have to ask ourselves at

Service name: 22. *Procurement*	Design state	Provision state	Managing continuity state	Change state
1. What has to happen?				
2. Who does it?				
3. How do the doers communicate?				
4. What measurements should we take?				
5. How do we measure it?		*Details in each of the cells here*		
6. What should we report on, how and to whom?				
7. What action should the recipient take as a result of the report?				
8. What do we tell the customer, why and how?				
9. How do we hand over to the next state?				

Figure 4.1
The amalgamated process identification matrix

least one thousand, one hundred and sixteen questions. Put that way it seems daunting. You may feel you don't have the man-power to go through an exercise like that. But then how many questions could we expect to have to answer if we were building a factory that made thirty-one different product lines?

The fact is that even if there are no formal processes, at least some of those eleven hundred-odd questions probably get asked and answered every day as the ITS staff go about their daily business, having to decide what to do next as regards whatever job they are currently working on. Look at it another way – suppose the absence of formal process means that some of those questions are asked and asked again every time a new job comes in? That people have to repeat their thinking, because nobody has examined and formally documented the process? How much more does the duplication of that thinking cost, com-pared with only having to do it once and training everybody in the results? And what does it cost when a lack of due process causes a lack of consistency in the work output, so the quality of the output becomes variable? Consider also the slackness of the grip the services management can have on the department if there is no process there to be monitored.

When I'm building one of these for a client, my preferred method is to put in each cell a hyperlink to a document containing the details from that cell. The resulting database of documents can be quite extensive, but assuredly complete. And because 'change' is built into this design methodology, no service need ever stagnate if the methodology is followed as a matter of routine.

Up to now, we've been looking at service and process design as though we were working on a greenfield site. In such a situation, there would be nothing else to take into account. Empty piece of paper, carte blanche, do as you like, create as you will. I remember several years ago listening to a lecture by a representative of the product design team at a major computer manufacturer. 'The reason God could create the world in only seven days', he contended, 'was that he didn't have an installed base with which his new products had to be compatible'. (If you've been in this industry for over ten years, you can probably guess which manufacturer that was.)

Abridged service process identification method

Where the site is not that greenfield, there is an abridged process identification table I have used before now. It assumes that the services are already grouped and teams of people are already responsible for them. One significant grouping is user support, which deals with all first- and second-line support calls, moves and installations and hardware maintenance. This department is pretty much self-contained. Another is infrastructure, which deals with any technology from the computer to the network wall point, and all central horizontal applications – so the file, print and email servers sit here, as do the firewall and virus screening. All non-technical functions are performed by administration, typically including all the procurement, training bookings and management reporting.

As a matter of principle, I see this as back to front – it should be services first, then necessary processes to deliver those services, from which we identify what skillsets we'll need, which tells us what sort of staff to hire. But I have to acknowledge that not everybody is in a position to fire the existing headcount and shut the IT services department down for a few months, while we rebuild the service and process matrices and hire people more suited to the new strategy. We have to start with what we've got, not least to ensure service continuity while we re-examine our methods.

So assuming that we have the departments listed above, we may end up with a table like Figure 4.2. It still asks questions to define the processes, but there are fewer questions. No concept of change to the services is taken into account and some of the questions have been amalgamated for simplification.

Processes	User support	Infrastructure	Administration
What has to happen?	• Take and log enquiry or standard change request, fix immediately if possible – else pass to second liners, who resolve enquiry or conduct installation and update log. Pass all non-standard change requests to administration • Pass all complaints to manager • Pass all training requests to human resources	• Monitor capacity of all servers and network trunks • Various ad hoc projects to improve network capacity • Keep anti-virus up to date • Nightly data backups removed to secure location	• Check non-standard change requests against pre-agreed budgets and pass to manager for approval • Liaise with suppliers on all purchase requests • Check pricing of equipment • Produce monthly reports for service level meeting • Update assets database
How monitored?	• Call logging system • Telephone system	• Server and network trunk downtime • Viruses trapped at entry • Backup logs • Server capacity warnings	• Financial expenditure reports • Supplier contracts • Service level meeting minutes • Regular systems audit
Critical success factors?	• Backlog less than 10% of incoming workload • Queue on telephone less than three minutes • Service level agreement targets	• Systems availability targets in service level agreement • Complete absence of virus incursion	• Equipment delivery targets in service level agreement • Buying equipment at competitive price • Reports ready in time for monthly meeting • Assets database accurately reflects installed base
Points of failure?	• Staff availability • Skills match nature of enquiries • Users exceed agreed call quantities	• Firewall • Excessive storage of emails and files • Users keeping business data on local drives	• Supplier stock levels • Availability of service performance data for reports • Second line not returning installation reports

Figure 4.2 An example of a completed abridged service process matrix

4.2 Process/procedure design – management or staff responsibility?

One of the main problems with an overview like this is that it does not go into detail. Many more of the processes are left to be enacted at 'procedure' or 'work instruction' level. This is the detailed level at which individual, lower ranking members of staff work out their own way of managing the stuff coming across their desks. This means that much more of the work done by each of the departments is transparent to the ITS managers.

On the one hand maybe that's a good thing – it lets the staff take control of their own jobs, which is good for motivation and ownership. It leaves the managers free of involvement in the hour-by-hour work, so that they can take an overview of operations and be less likely to have their thinking bogged down by detail.

On the other hand, this level of simplification makes no provision for exceptions. If something unusual comes in, an incomplete set of processes like this may not be able to cater for it, and it will get shoved upstairs – so the manager may find himself daily having to make decisions on fairly low level work in any case. The other threat of leaving the staff to work out how to do it for themselves comes from where one draws the line between management and staff responsibilities.

Draw it too close and you may find managers designing small-scale processes they will never themselves have to carry out, and their lack of experience at that level of detail may cause them to design processes that are incomplete. In such an event, the staff will just end up doing the work their own way anyway. Draw it too far, with less management involvement, and the staff's natural focus on the minutiae of their own day-to-day work may cause the process to be incomplete the other way, in that it may not take sufficient account of the dependencies of other departments and processes on the work they do apparently alone.

There is a question of balance here. Workers will always try to exert some influence over how they actually do their jobs, in the same way as the accoutrements and ornaments with which they surround their desk space will reflect their personality. They'll always do their own job in their own way in some respect – so we let them, of course we do. But they must do it against a backdrop defined by a manager or a committee that has a higher view of the context in which that function exists. In the case study below, the manager drew the line too far away.

Case study:
Leaving process to staff initiative

Julie the ITS administrator was the sole clerical authority over the equipment procurement process. All the user requests came through her desk, she managed the relationship with the suppliers, she received the arriving goods, she booked the installation engineer, she arranged for the user to be available on delivery day, she kept the inventory database up to date, she processed the vendors' invoices and got the payment requisition forms signed off. Everybody thought Julie was a godsend. She always knew the status of every order. Julie was a bright and motivated self-starter, doing a complicated job with diligence and good humour. Nobody else was involved in her job and she was so good at it that she was left to do it her own way.

In the absence of formal tools, Julie had devised a personal spreadsheet to help her manage the complexity. It ran on her own, password-protected machine, and was full of her personal acronyms that she used for the idiosyncrasies inherent in her function. When Julie decided two weeks on the Mediterranean would be good for her, nobody begrudged her that.

A few days after Julie left, a lorry arrived with forty crates of computers and peripherals. In Julie's absence, somebody had to sign for them, so one of the installation engineers took it upon himself. Because of a general lack of space in the department, he stacked the boxes in the hallway, where coffee-carrying staff routinely collided with them.

'We need to get rid of this lot,' the helpdesk supervisor complained. 'Why don't we just install them?'

'We don't know where they're going,' replied the installation engineer. 'Julie knows, but she's on vacation until the end of next week.'

That afternoon, one of the company project managers happened to visit IT, and he too collided with one of the boxes. He immediately paid a visit to the IT services manager.

'I've a customer project starting next week,' he said, 'and we've been waiting for you to install six machines for it. Tell me, are our machines among that lot in the hallway?'

Knowing the efficacy of his procurement process, the IT services manager smiled confidently and said 'I'll soon find that out'. He picked up the phone and dialled Julie's extension. He got her voicemail.

As managers often do, this one got round the embarrassment of his loss of control by making this user an exception. He had the installation engineers rifle through the boxes to find something like the equipment the user had ordered and install it immediately. He knew he was taking a risk that this would impinge another order, but that would be another bridge later (in the event, he got away with it).

The manager also organized a process review workshop to take place on the day of Julie's return.

A notable risk with leaving the operational ranks to define too much of the process is that the resulting thinking may be too insular. The tendency will be to consider the internal processes of each functional group rather than how those processes may impact or be dependent on processes underway in other groups.

An example of this can be seen in Figure 4.2. The user support department is taking not only support calls, but requests for 'standard' changes – these are changes already anticipated, for instance a call-off of a purchase of a computer against an already-agreed budget. These change requests are passed to the administration department for processing. So we have an isolated process in user support, upon which another in administration must depend. The interface between these two departments is therefore crucial for the whole process to be 'end-to-end' – but with two separate departments each focusing their internal processes, the question arises as to who is designing the interface between them. There's a story 'Damn the second line … ' below that illustrates this. It really happened – no point in mentioning in where, because I've seen it or something very like it so often at so many sites.

Case study: 'Damn the second line...'

…the helpdesk manager complained. 'My staff log the call, carefully fill out the trouble ticket and assign it to second line. And for all the good that does, we may as well have written the call details on a brick and thrown it into the North Sea, because the second-line technicians never get back to the user unless they're repeatedly kicked. And then we get it in the neck from the user. And they never fill the solution field in. Best you'll ever get is 'fixed' from somebody who won't take the time to do his job properly.'

'Yes, that does seem like a problem,' concurred the process consultant, before wending his inquisitive way towards the second line's frantic and slightly messy office.

The second-line manager was just as reciprocally insistent.

'Damn the helpdesk,' he proposed, instructing his computer to print off a summary of the calls recently assigned to his team before thrusting it toward the consultant's retreating nose. 'Here. Just look at some of the rubbish they send us. It's like as soon as they believe any enquiry to be even slightly technical, they shut their brains down and press the 'assign' button. As a result I get hundreds of unnecessary and badly written assignments. My staff have to come in early and work late every day. We have to chase the user to ask him questions the helpdesk has already asked. It's annoying and embarrassing.'

'Yes, that does seem like a problem,' the process consultant agreed, secretly conceding to himself that it was perhaps time he started earning his fees. 'What do you think is causing it?'

'It's straightforward,' came the emphasized response. 'If the helpdesk only asked a few simple questions, they would be able to diagnose many more of these enquiries and fix them on the spot.'

'What questions are these?' enquired the consultant.

'Oh, various,' offered the second-line manager.

'Have you ever given the helpdesk a list of these questions?'

'Now when would I have time to do that?'

So the helpdesk manager had a dependency on the second line, which in return had dependencies on the helpdesk. These issues had never been formally discussed between these two. The process consultant briefly wondered whether his most appropriate and professional response would be to write a report on the absence of a working interface between these interdependent functions or to drag the two so-called managers into the car park and violently bang their heads together, ranting 'Talk to one another, for pity's sake!'

4.3 Interfaces

The interfaces between the processes are as important as the processes themselves. Somebody has to oversee that, since we can't always guarantee that the separate operations will sort it out between themselves. They're all overworked, they all have patches to protect, they all have to supply increasing job satisfaction to their staff, we're all looking for a way to reduce stress. The interfaces are a form of infrastructure, and where there is an infrastructure, there is a probable need for a government, providing a tactical overview of the whole process to ensure not just that the individual components of the process pay their roles, but that those roles dovetail together. I like to use analogies, and one of my favourites is the game of soccer[1]. It is a boon to have a good crosser on the wing, and advantageous to have a forward who is good with his head in the six-yard box, but if there is nobody working out the tactics of positional play, the

---

[1] I was born near Manchester United's stadium – soccer is in the air round there, never mind the gene pool.

centre forward may not be in the right place when the cross comes over, and a promising move simply sends the ball into touch or hands possession to the opposing side. It's not just a matter of the components doing their bit to the best of their ability – the interfaces between the components matter just as much.

Figure 4.3 illustrates an overall user support process. The interfaces, such as they are, appear as mere changes of responsibility as a unit of work moves between parts of the process. The flow-chart cannot describe the way the interfaces will work.

As we in the computer industry know, wherever there is an interface, there is also a protocol – a set of rules regarding the nature, form and structure of information passing along the interface. It is not enough to describe an interface in a workflow process simply as 'this group over here passes the work to that group over there'. There has to be a procedure by which the expectations and needs of both groups are dealt with so that when the work is actually passed, ownership and responsibility go with it, there is no cause for dispute and 'what happens next, at whose hand, by what means and who needs to know about it' is understood by both parties.

Fortunately, somebody has already designed that procedure for us – and since there's no point in reinventing what already exists, may I suggest that we design our workflow gateways around the principles used by the RS232 serial interface.

The analogy could be said to have its limitations – I'm only using the signals of an asynchronous interface and the separate sections of your IT services department may communicate synchronously!

Common (GND)

Both the sending and receiving departments are linked together in a permanently live circuit with no leaks. Any exchange of information in either direction also has a trace presence here. If the 'common' wire were not in place or its connection were intermittent, one or other of the ends of the circuit would assume its counterpart to be in no position to communicate, and so wouldn't even try. Without some 'common ground', communication cannot take place.

In IT services, this common ground is the established mutual recognition that both departments sharing the interface are part of the same mechanism. It is the understanding that each department is part of a larger process; that they each have their own, specialist role to play in that process, that they are co-dependent, that neither department is 'more important' in the process than any other and that neither is the slave or master of the other. This cog does not turn that one – they both turn together. OK, now I'm mixing my metaphors, but I feel it necessary to emphasize the point.

I have used the analogy of a 'common ground' connection to highlight the idea that the relationship is a permanent one. There is always the possibility of a signal passing along this interface, so these departments are in a constant state of readiness. They are aware of their dependence on one another, and in continuous expectation of a need to be suddenly expressed by a connected department.

This co-dependence and mutuality cannot be stressed enough. Even now, although we have lived through the service-oriented 1990s and put 'the customer is king' posters in the public areas of our offices, in my view the legacy of the IT industry as a technocracy still maintains in some quarters.

This history gives some of our number a licence to regard the work of some IT departments (notably the first line helpdesk or administrators) as 'less important' than that done say by the development or network support departments. I will concede that any section of IT will have specific goals and purposes, which they will naturally regard as their top priority, and thus demands arriving from other departments will necessarily take a lower priority. But too often this has come to be psychologically linked with the alleged technical superiority of some departments over others.

The unjustified prejudice that thereby arrives by the mix of these two ideas is that helpdesk/clerical/administrative work is less important simply because it requires less advanced technical skills. The result of the prejudice is that support requests (for example) are given a lower priority and in the worst cases, ignored altogether. The most suffering victim of this chauvinism is the company as a whole – for the productivity of the corporation's employees is consequently delayed just because somebody in the technically elevated parts of IT decides that being asked to do a certain job by a technically more lowly colleague is beneath their inflated dignity.

The fact that some parts of the process require more detailed technical knowledge than others neither diminishes nor de-emphasizes the importance and value of the other parts of the process. If you have IT staff who still think their paper qualifications authorize them to dismiss their team-mates out of technocratic disrespect, perhaps it might be an idea to take the offenders to one side and have a few words with them. Some of those words might be 'anachronism', 'teamwork' and 'professionalism'. For the worst offenders, useful words might include 'socks', 'up', 'else' and 'door'.

Data terminal ready/data set ready (DTR/DSR)

The moment you switch your terminal on – in our analogy as soon as the receiving department comes into work in the morning – it shows its willingness to receive assigned work by establishing a permanent signal of readiness in principle on the DTR and DSR lines. The transmitting department can see these signals and know that they can begin to submit work across the interface. It might be the staff logging into the telephone system or work-flow database. It might be the installation engineer checking the schedule of network connections to be made today. It might be the applications maintenance team opening the failure reports from last night's batch run. It could be the day-shift supervisor formally accepting the handover of the incident log from his night-shift equivalent. It is that part of the process by which a department formally states to other departments that it is ready to do what it will be asked to do.

Transmit (TXD)

So here comes the transfer of work, but it cannot be any old stream of data or the receiving end won't understand it. Both sides of the interface have been completely programmed in such a way that the data coming across have to be sent in a certain order, in a certain size and shape of packet, with the right accompanying information. A simple 'please do this' won't suffice.

It is not that the receiving terminal has insisted on the information coming in a particular format – it is that both parties in the process have agreed on the protocol. It means there can never be any gaps, disputes, misunderstanding or presumptions. Admittedly, this overcomplicates the simplest enquiries – but it also simplifies the more complex ones. It gives uniformity to all instances of ownership change, which makes the change smoother, more predictable and easier to manage, while making the real exceptions stand out so they can be dealt with in a special way.

The transfer should contain evidence that the transmitting process step has already added value to the work in the way it should. It should enable rather than hinder the smooth conduct of the next link in the chain.

Receive/acknowledge (RXD/ACK)

The protocol should make it clear that ownership has indeed changed hands. With computer communications, this is the 'Acknowledge' signal. In ITS, it is not always possible to acknowledge every change of ownership. The technical side, with its often purpose-built tools, may indeed have an acknowledgement function, but the administrative functions may not.

I remember when we first started using fax machines. People didn't really believe in them. It was common practice, after the fax had been sent, to telephone the intended recipient to confirm that the fax had been received. It is this need for acknowledgement of ownership transfer that we ought to consider when designing our IT processes. When I pass a job to the next step, how do I know it has been fully understood, that somebody has taken ownership and that the action I expect will actually take place? I need to know that the job is owned by a human being.

It is for this reason that one of my preferred features in workflow software is the 'claim' function, where the party receiving the work must acknowledge in the system that he has taken ownership. This gives clear closure to the delivering party, leaving them free to get on with their next job without wondering whether the previous one will get the attention they'd hoped it would.

Receive/non-acknowledge (RX/NAK)

If there is an 'acknowledge' function within the process, it follows there must be a 'non-acknowledge'. We cannot assume this will happen by default. A wrongly formatted or otherwise incomplete reassignment is as likely to find its way to the bottom of the receiving party's in-tray ('Don't understand that one – looks tricky, so I'll think about it later') as it is to be immediately returned for repair and reassignment. In my view, a failed attempt at ownership change must immediately be returned to sender to stop it from falling into a black hole. This 'non-acknowledge' function needs to be as formal a part of the process as is the actual transmission.

4.4 Processes in practice

If the services are what we provide, then the processes are how we go about manufacturing the services. The list below is of some of the processes and procedures that enable an IT services department to do what it does. It is by no means exhaustive, but it covers most of the processes common to most integrated IT services departments. Some of the absences can be accounted for by their being part of something else – for example, if your ITS develops applications for desktop use, you may note that 'software development' is missing. However, any such development would have to go through the change process, probably as a non-standard change, and thus would be allocated a developer – the fact that the developer reports to the IT services manager is beside the point, for the process of getting the development approved and started is already dealt with.

I contended earlier that processes are at a different level of perspective than procedures, and the following treatment of IT service activities illustrates this further. The activities by which we deliver a service to the user community have a distinct 'end-to-end' feel about them and this is what makes these processes. The administrative activities are rather more intermediate, being contributions to a greater end rather than complete processes in themselves – so more precisely, these are procedures rather than processes.

Fundamentally, there are only two things IT services does – it either supports or changes computer usage. An enquiry is a demand for support. An installation is merely a change from absence to presence of an item of equipment. Both of these fit the description of a process as something that takes a unit of production from a starting state to an end state. So there are really only two main processes – take an enquiry from request to resolution – or take a change from instigation to implementation.

These are complicated by the fact that so many different and often technically advanced skills are needed to make these happen, and so we may group the responsibilities for different types of support or change in different departments. But this is only for the purpose of structural or managerial convenience. The network support department is different to the helpdesk by virtue of its skill set and the fact that it supports and changes machinery rather than computer usage, but it may still use the same basic processes, at least for solving problems or changing systems.

In a way, network support is the anomaly here. Its functions are the maintenance and continuity of the network services, such as data storage, backup, system and email accounts, capacity management and so on. But these are not processes because of their very ongoing nature. There is no end state to what network support does – there is only continuity. As such, network support is probably more correctly defined as a set of procedures rather than a process.

Figure 4.3 offers an example of a user support enquiry handling process. It accounts for changes of ownership as the enquiry

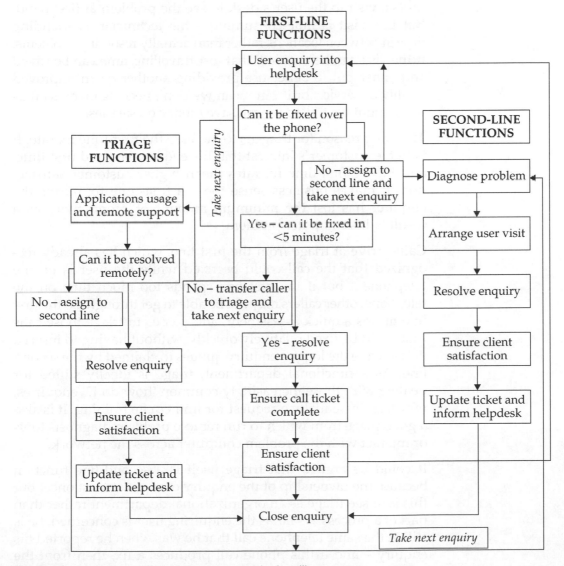

Figure 4.3 An example of a user support enquiry handling process

moves to resolution. In this case, the enquiry may variously be owned by three separate user support departments; the first-line helpdesk, the 'triage' desk and the second line. First- and second-line support departments are commonplace – the optional triage much less so.

There are two main purposes for triage. One is visit avoidance – second-line technicians invariably resolve fewer enquiries per day than their first-line colleagues. One reason for this could be that the enquiries themselves are more complex, which is why they have been sent to what is often a technically more experienced department. Another reason is that the call actually warrants a visit to the user's desk to see the problem at first hand. But this visit is time-consuming – the technician is spending time in between locations rather than actually resolving problems. If the visit can be avoided, that lost travelling time can be saved and either put to better use providing another or an improved quality of service, or it can mean we don't need as many staff as we thought we did, so we can save money on salaries.

The other reason for triage is to increase the first-time fix rate. It is in the customer's interest that his enquiry be fixed first time, and higher first-time fix rates mean higher customer satisfaction. It makes business sense too – a first-time fix means the enquirer has lost the minimum amount of productivity as a result of his computer problem.

Calls arrive at triage from the first line, which has already recognized that the call could be fixed while the user is on the telephone – but if the first line spends too much time on the telephone, other callers may not be able to get through. So the first line makes a quick assessment, and passes to triage those calls that could be fixed relatively quickly, without having to insert a delay while the logged enquiry queues to claimed by the second line. As a functional department, triage is ideally suited for dealing with those increasingly common 'how do I?' enquiries, which are essentially a request for immediate training. It is also a good place from which to run remote problem diagnosis tools or interact with the problem computer across the network.

It could be argued that triage itself is a second-line function because the ownership of the enquiry changes at least once. But this is to see triage as an organizational department rather than part of a process. As far as the enquiring user is concerned, he is still in the same telephone call that he was when he reported his enquiry – and if this phone call produces a fix, then from the user's point of view it is a first time fix.

For me, a second-line function is one where the enquiry is logged in a database in order to be claimed by or assigned to another individual. The original conversation the enquirer was having with the support department has been terminated. Now we wait for the second line to respond. I call this the call going 'cold' as opposed to the 'hot' transfer between the first line and triage. As such, I see triage as a first-line function.

The second line as described in Figure 4.3 is essentially a traditional desktop support function, but it does not have to be so. I know of companies, usually the larger ones, that may have dozens of second-line departments, perhaps supporting enquiries about various specialist areas or systems. Regardless of this the second-line really needs to be represented in the support process only once. The actual differences between these various types of second line are only at the more detailed level of internal procedures or that department's staff work instructions or the specific nature of the item they are supporting. So long as the inputs and outputs of those departments take a support enquiry from a start to an end state, then regardless of their differences, the process can and should be made to represent all types of support enquiry at the highest level. The trick is not to get bogged down in detail – leave that for the design of the procedures.

4.5 The change management process

All changes to systems, methods, processes, installed base etc. carry with them some element of risk. This is because a change is a disruption to the current status quo.

A change in one area may produce imbalance somewhere else, necessitating further change – for example, installing a group of computers in an office may suddenly increase network traffic to that area, thus decreasing the service to all others in that area. A change to the way a program displays information may benefit the group of users demanding the change, but another group using the same program may find the display no longer matches their ideal. Furthermore, a change to the way computing is provided may necessitate a change to operating procedures, both in the IT services department for supporting the altered systems, and among the user community for operating them. Changes to IT thus do not only impact the technological environment, but also the business one.

So the practicality of any requested change has to be assessed in at least four aspects:

- Technical feasibility – can it actually be done, what technical consequences may it raise elsewhere and do we really need the change or can the systems already support the implied business need?
- Supportability – what will be required to satisfy the request in terms of user training, support staff training/recruitment, new support procedures etc.?
- Risks versus benefits – what if it all goes pear shaped? Is it worth taking the risk given the operational benefits the users and the business will receive?
- Cost versus return – the change will cost money: will it pay for itself?

These questions are normally asked as part of an approvals process (see Figure 4.4). However, this can be bureaucratic, slow and consume resources. It may be cumbersome to invoke the approvals process for every change. Take for example the purchase of a new desktop computer, printer or software package. This may be such a routine event that it can be standardized. The company may anticipate and prepare for these changes, so when the request is made, it goes through on the nod.

This brings us to the topic of 'standard' and 'non-standard' changes, the difference being dictated by the level of simplicity.

Standard change

A standard change is one that is expected, and that will happen as a matter of routine in the normal run of business. An example of this might be the replacement of a desktop computer, or indeed the replacement of several as the existing installed base moves toward obsolescence.

Let's suppose that at the end of the financial year, the IT services department realizes that a third of the installed computers are now three years old, are likely to struggle with the next version of office software they will be expected to run and have been depreciated in accounting terms so that they are close to worthless. They can be replaced, and with a useful life of three years, this means that we can expect to replace a third of the desktop hardware every year. Furthermore, the company has 1000 users now and appears to be growing at about 10% per annum. So we shall have to replace 333 computers and acquire around 100 new ones next year.

Knowing this, the network support section examines the implications of a ten per cent increase in network traffic, data and applications storage and backup requirements. They look at both the technical loading and the logistics, do an impact analysis and determine that because of this demand, they will need to put two more servers in the computer room and add more network switches and patch cabling. They discover where these new users will sit, and follow standard policy for ensuring groups of users will have access to a nearby printer. This also goes into the mix.

The software licensing administrator anticipates how much more will need to be paid to the vendor of the computers' operating systems.

The IT services training section looks at the growth and determines a need for a new trainer to look after the knowledge needs of these 100 new employees and the training of the 333 people who will get new machines next year. A bid arrives for a new member of staff.

The helpdesk manager realizes that this means a likely 10 per cent increase in user enquiries, so more technicians may be necessary.

The installations team gears its staff and procedures for installing 433 computers.

Depending on how IT is financed, the users may have to stump up the money for all this. So they make their bids for next year's budget. The usual negotiations take place, some things are approved and others not etc. but at the end, the IT services department knows that over the course of the coming financial year, there will be a certain number of orders placed for new machines.

Ideally now, everybody is ready and the new financial year can commence. When the requests start to come in, these have in effect already been through a mass-production approvals process, so such requests are deemed to be 'standard changes' and thus may take a fast track to implementation.

Non-standard change

We cannot anticipate everything. During the year, there will be shifts in the business environment. The company's competitors will attempt to take us by surprise. Legislation may change. Unforeseen commercial opportunities may arise, which the board of directors may decide to take immediate advantage of. One of the users may suddenly have a brilliant idea for doing things in a more efficient or cost-effective way. We'll suddenly find a dangerous bug in the ERP system so the software maintenance section needs to change some code. For a number of reasons, we may be forced to revamp our computer systems and methods on the fly, in ways we could not have predicted. This is where the non-standard change comes in. It is for this reason

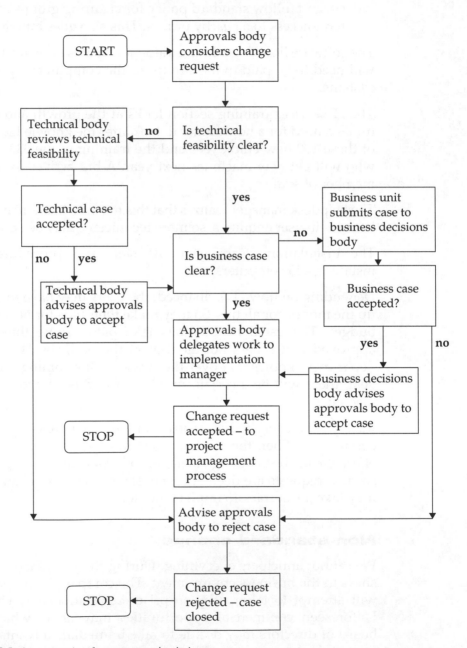

Figure 4.4 An example of a non-standard change process

that we have a formal mechanism for assessing the practicality of a change request and approving or rejecting it.

These sudden changes will be on top of the strategic ones we expect to make. Software as well as hardware can become obsolete. We may decide to develop new applications software for business purposes, and that such a development will impact everybody, so it will have to be planned, and it too will go through the non-standard change process, albeit hopefully not as a surprise occurrence.

In fact the non-standard change process can be used for any change at all affecting IT services – even for changes to its own processes and ways of working, to its recruitment and staff promotion.

4.6 Some IT services procedures

Within the main processes there will be a number of procedures or sub-processes. As a process is a function by which a unit of production moves from a starting state to an end state, a procedure is the way in which that is carried out. The line blurs when by following some of those procedures, we move the unit of production to an interim state, thus preparing it for its next step along the production process – such procedures are known as sub-processes.

Mindful of the fact that there is no reason to split this particular hair any further, the list below is of some of the procedures and sub-processes an IT services department may use. It is not meant to be exhaustive or particularly detailed for that would be outside the scope of this work – for example I have left out any procedures to handle software standards, which in some companies is an IT services function, while in many others it comes under the regime of IT development, which would take it outside this volume's remit.

The tables are meant instead as an indicator of how processes and procedures can be mapped onto services and the types of procedures that certain services might necessitate.

The tables also include a list of some of the administrative procedures that might be followed in IT services. These differ from 'user assistance' and 'systems management' in that they do not directly result in a service to the end user or the business, but are probably necessary for the smooth running of the service delivery machine.

Table 4.1 User assistance services.

Service	Procedure	Description
User support	Helpdesk/call centre	• Take and log all incoming enquiries into purpose built database • Assign enquiries to appropriate triage or second-line function
	Horizontal applications support	• Offer first-line triage for all enquiries related to general office software on desktop and mobile computers
	Business applications support	• Offer first-line triage for all enquiries related to business-specific systems and applications. Requires specialist knowledge of business operations
	Telephone support	• Offer first-line triage for all enquiries related to desktop and mobile telephones and related devices including fax machines • Manage procurement of telephone equipment via standard change procedure • Manage changes to telephone system, e.g. extension numbers, hunt group inclusions, call barring etc. • Maintain database of telephone and hunt group numbers • Update and publish corporate telephone directory
	Second line	• Retain ownership of all assigned enquiries until resolution • Ensure customer kept informed about progress
	Escalation	• Advise line manager of all outstanding enquiries where service level is about to be breached, with proposals for rectifying
	Administrative	• Maintain catalogue of specializations of all second-line support groups
User training	Training support	• Log all requests for user training • Conduct training as requested
	Vendor management	• Maintain database of approved training suppliers • Liaise with vendor to supply training
	Administrative	• Maintain and publish user catalogue of available and recommended training • Maintain database of all training courses attended by users

Table 4.2 Systems management services.

Service	Procedures	Description
Equipment provision	As per change management process	
Operations	User account management (includes email accounts)	• Enable secure access of users to network • Provide data storage area • Provide access to standard desktop applications and appropriate business systems • Liaise with human resources department to ensure leaver's accounts are deleted
	Virus protection	• Maintain up-to-date, memory-resident virus protection software on all processors • Offer on-demand inoculation service • Have rehearsed policy for unexpected virus incursion, to include network-sector shutdowns
	Firewall	• Provide systems to lock out unsolicited outside calls to network computers • Maintain database of known spam and virus/trojan sources and delete messages from these on arrival • Retain configurability of firewall for making exceptions on demand
	Backup routine	• Take regular backups of business and user home data areas • Provide for secure, offsite data storage
Availability	Network monitoring	• Routinely monitor network traffic to identify and eradicate bottlenecks
	Capacity monitoring	• Monitor usage of live data storage areas • Anticipate need to increase data storage capacity – do so only via change management process • Produce and maintain policy on data storage by users and pass this regularly to training section

(continued)

81

Table 4.2 (*continued*).

Service	Procedures	Description
Continuity	Disaster recovery	• Design and regularly rehearse actions in the event of catastrophic loss of computer and communications systems • Liaise with corporate facilities management and human resources department to ensure logistics plans are up to date
	Routine maintenance	• Maintain redundant server and network capacity to minimize real downtime during routine systems maintenance • Maintain list of contacts among user community for announcing unavoidable systems downtime

Table 4.3 IT services internal administrative procedures.

Procedure	Description
Service availability	• Maintain and routinely publish shift rota • Ensure all shifts have necessary redundant[1] skills
Work allocation	• Ensure all ITS departments, including non-reactive ones have staff dedicated to providing support at all times • Ensure all known workload is allocated to named member of staff
Enquiry closure	• Check that all resolved enquiries are fully documented • Ensure client satisfaction with work done • Ensure properly resolved enquiries are closed to minimize backlog
Assets database	• Maintain register of all updated equipment cross referenced with user register (below) • Link with change management procedure to record all new installations • Include register of training courses attended by users and support staff[2]
Software licensing	• Maintain register of all installed software and versions, cross-referenced to user accounts register in systems support services and to user register (below)
Service catalogue	• Produce, publish and update catalogue of services offered by IT services department
User register	• Maintain register of all known computer users by department and location

(*continued*)

Table 4.3 (*continued*).

Procedure	Description
	• Link with change management process to include new users • Link with user accounts procedure in systems support services
Charging	• Administration of charges for use of IT services (dependent on charging policy, see Chapter 9)
Quality survey	• Conduct regular survey of customer satisfaction with individual enquiries and with IT services as a whole • Produce regular report for IT services management
Service level management	• Monitor and report on IT services department performance against stipulations of service level agreement
Problem management	• Analyse resolved enquiries to look for patterns that suggest deeper problems in IT systems and applications • Report findings to applications maintenance department
Supported products catalogue	• Maintain catalogue of products and systems IT services is prepared to support • Act as change manager for all requests from user community to include products in the catalogue, by putting such requests through the non-standard change process • Formulate training plans for helpdesk and second-line staff who will have to support newly added products
Skills management	• Maintain register of known skills in user support department • Ensure all skills are covered by sufficient alternative staff members to cover for staff absences[3]
Project administration	• Keep log of all projects conducted by IT services staff as allocated by standard and non-standard change processes • Monitor project progress against agreed milestones and deadlines • Produce regular report on status of project work for IT services management and IT steering committee

[1] 'Skills redundancy' is my terminology for having cover for all levels of knowledge, so that our staffing is not limited to a 'single point of failure' – in other words that we are not dependent on a single individual in any shift for a given technical skill – for if that individual must be absent for any reason, this could leave us so exposed as to have to postpone provision of a service. I cover this in more depth in Chapter 6.

[2] Knowledge is an asset.

[3] Covered in more depth in Chapter 6.

4.7 Procedures in the non-standard change process

Figure 4.5 is a composite of change process procedures I've witnessed or designed at a number of client sites. It highlights who is responsible for doing what at what stage of the process. It will undoubtedly be different at your own company, so is not meant to be a recommendation. The reader is asked to see it only as an example of how we might move from the 'process' to 'procedure' level in something as complex as non-standard change.

This chart introduces a number of conceptual departments and governing bodies in and around the IT services department, such as the IT steering committee. These will be covered in more depth in Chapter 5.

Non-standard change types	Raised by:	Authorized by:	Assigned by:	Scheduled by:	Reporting:
Infrastructure	*Either*: IT services department recognizes need	Change manager invokes change approvals board	Change approvals board delegates to network support manager	Network support manager	Change manager produces uniform progress report with highlights from project support office (projects registry) and project or operational managers – and then submits this to all IT services managers and to the IT steering committee
Applications maintenance	*Or*: User recognizes need and gains approval from own head of department to submit change request	Change manager invokes business systems analysis team	Business systems analysis team	'Tranche' (scheduled block of program releases from applications maintenance team)	
Business applications development (minor)					
Business applications development (major)		Change manager invokes business systems analysis team (short scope for business case) then to IT steering committee	IT steering committee appoints chairman of project board	Project board (minimum membership – project sponsor and project manager) – exists only for duration of project	

Figure 4.5 An example of non-standard change procedures

5

IT services organization

What form should IT services take? What should be its structure and how might its hierarchy operate? I am a great believer in the principle of 'as above, so below'. The macro-scale forces and influences affecting us give us a hint as to how we may reflect those circumstances. The principle suggests that the best way to deal with our circumstances is to mirror their structure in our own organization. If the company is localized and hierarchical, then it behoves upon us to have a similar layout and culture in our IT services organization. On the other hand, if it is globalized and anarchic, then to serve it to the best of our ability, we adopt such a structure ourselves. As providers to a market, we organize and conduct ourselves like that market so our provisions match our customers' needs and they in turn can understand what we do because it looks like what they do.

5.1 Relating to the business

This is how businesses prefer to have their IT behave. It is a common accusation levelled at IT that it is not 'business aware' – or as I heard a user put it, rather more stridently at a recent client project – 'wall-to-wall technicians and not a manager among the whole lot of them'.

The problem these days is that businesses are trying to become ever faster on their feet, ever more responsive to market vagaries and more entrepreneurial. Simultaneously, IT becomes increasingly complex, its technicians ever more knowledgeable and the gap between the technical practitioner and the even competent user continues to widen.

It is the view of this author that we'll never really be able to escape the 'not commercially minded' tag with which our host companies seem so keen to label us. While they're off entrepreneuring, somebody has to be minding the store. We produce and manage systems. These have to offer a reliable and predictable output. They are machines, so they will probably do that anyway. So we have to have a systematic mindset and culture so that we can design, install and run the systems. Let the entrepreneurs fly off in their various market-chasing directions and accuse us of low business-awareness. If we didn't produce that consistent output from the systems, then neither they nor we would have a business to be aware of in any case. We'll never think like them. And on the whole, it's probably better that way.

5.2 A dichotomy of structure

The problem faced by many ITS groups is the natural dichotomy of structure. A common design in many companies is to have different profit centres producing different products for different markets. So each of these divisions may have their own identity and operational methods, with consequently different IT needs. On the other hand, we in IT have a natural tendency to standardize our IT infrastructure where possible. This ensures compatibility and increases the scope for communication between and integration of systems. And standardized systems give rise to, if not indeed necessitate, standardized support services. The result can be a cultural divide between a highly flexible host company and what is perceived as an incompatibly rigid IT.

We cannot escape this flexibility in the corporate world. The concept of the large company that started small and grew big but still retained its unity of operation is now an outmoded one. We are much more likely to see a corporation of exceptions than one of universal cultural compliance. There are forces acting against rigidity.

Many companies these days have reached their present size by acquisition of other companies. They do this to capture markets once held by former competitors by subsuming those competitors into a corporate structure. They may do it to enter niche markets at a stroke by taking over a company with an established presence. They may do it because smaller companies may often be able to see and react to approaching bandwagons with a fleetness of foot long sacrificed by larger companies for the sake of easier governance.

But these acquisitions bring with them an existing and alien structure, culture and mode of operation. No matter how the holding company may try, it may not be easy to get the new arrival to behave entirely in accordance with the methods already adopted by the larger parent company. The reasons for this will extend all the way from a real desire to harness unchanged the skills and motivation of the acquired company's personnel, through contractual obligations to honour their share options, right down to individual members of staff who see no reason to change how they run their desks just because there's a new logo on the letterhead. The acquired company may well retain its old ways of operating, and that will include how it uses and supports its IT.

The holding company itself may shun investment towards getting any one division to comply entirely with head office culture. This is not just to allow the division maximum scope to turn its self-expression into business success, but also mindful of the possibility that one day, that division may be sold off. As such, it may be less attractive to a potential buyer if it looked too much like the company it came from.

In IT services, we have to cope with this diversity. If anything, IT appears to be clinging on to corporatism while corporations themselves are becoming more culturally fragmented. If 'as above' is starting to look more diverse, then here in the 'so below' of IT services, we are going to have to mirror that so our now various markets of users can best understand and use our services.

In any case, there may be more myth than must-do in the idea of integrated IT systems – so we do not necessarily have to see IT services as needing to be uniform just because the systems ought to be. What the corporation needs is not necessarily uniform systems but uniform reporting. The purpose of IT is to record information and then report upon it for the purposes of business decision-making. If all these different systems within the corporation can produce compatible reports in such a way that the executive corridor can easily understand and act upon what it is reading, it does not really matter to the senior managers that this information comes from disparate technological platforms.

As for systems needing to be uniform so that they can talk to one another – this can be achieved almost as well by protocols between those systems rather than the similarity of their internal workings. Of course there is the cost element – different systems tend to be more expensive to provide, maintain and support than if everybody were using the same one. But if the corporation has already decided to allow difference for business reasons, then it has by implication decided to bear the cost of that difference. Nor may it be absolutely compulsory that our internal practices are alike across all geographical iterations of IT services. So long as the output looks the same to anybody who may measure it, then how that output is produced should be immaterial. And in the 'anybody who may measure it' category, we should include not just the users and the corporation employing them, but the IT services managers themselves, even though they may be in a head office thousands of miles away and monitoring several IT services operations in a range of countries or regions.

The flexibility of the corporation takes a higher business priority than the resultant inflation in IT costs. It's expensive to be flexible and varied. If there is such a thing as a scale, with standardization at one end and flexibility at the other, we'll probably go for standardization. It keeps the costs down and businesses tend to like that outcome. But – and it's a big but – if the corporation decides that flexibility is its maxim, and they want us to be flexible too, they will have to pay for it. If they are willing to do that, then we in IT services may be left with no reason to stick to a uniform structure and process, and every reason to be just as diverse and flexible as the company that gives us our budget.

So it is possible, at least in theory, for us to de-emphasize standardization and become as flexible as the company. The way for us to do it is first to identify how much more expensive will be the act of matching our structure and methodology to that of the business and get corporate endorsement for that. Next, even though we may have to run IT in different ways depending on what market-orientation or geographical part of the business we serve, we must insist for central management purposes that all parts of IT conform to a certain reporting structure. This is so that when we take decisions based on those reports, we are comparing like with like. Third, we must put ourselves about in the business locales. Even though we talk a different language among ourselves, we must establish a regular rapport with our customers at all levels. This is not just for the professional purpose of understanding and relating to their business needs – it's because people are less likely to think or say bad things about people with whom they get on well.

5.3 Towards a basic IT structure

Any IT department contains a number of different functions. Historically, there have often been three basic ones. These are a development department of programmers, an operations department of operators looking after batch jobs and backups on the central computers and support, staffed by helpdesk and problem-solving technicians. When local area networks of computers based on Intel-type processors and Microsoft operating systems took off in the 1980s, so began the demise of the central operations department as the mainframes and minicomputers gave way to file and print servers, and the arrival of client-server applications and 'lights out' computing in the 1990s accelerated this.

Client-server computing

Instead of all the intelligence being held at the central computer with 'dumb' terminals providing user access, the intelligence is now shared between the central server computer and the user's desktop machine. So instead of a terminal talking to a program, now there's a program at both ends of the communications line. This means the desktop machine does the forms processing, most of the calculations and the whole of the user interface. The network link is only used for database queries and updates and so less data needs to travel across the link. The processing workload is thus shared, making for faster computing and increasing the scope for more powerful, shared applications.

'Lights out' computer rooms

Because computers are so fast nowadays, there is less of a need to save big jobs for overnight runs when the computers are in less demand, and applications have become much more interactive and real-time, so much more of the computing work can be done during the working day. So there is much less need for the overnight batch computing runs that were so much a part of data processing a decade or more ago. So we don't so much need a computer room full of operators monitoring job control scripts as they run these batch jobs. So in theory, we don't need the lights switched on in the computer room.

As a result, nowadays the job of looking after the central servers tends to fall to a team of network support technicians who have their desks in a regular office rather than a computer room[1]. And because the servers tend to use the same processor and software manufacturer, the network team is more likely to be associated with the desktop support technicians than being a department in its own right.

---

[1] In fact, sometimes they even have a *window*, for pity's sake! They don't know they're born, young computer people these days, do they?

So a new division of labour has emerged by default in many companies, where IT is split into development and services.

Another basic format for the IT department comes from the infrastructure–superstructure idea. Rather than the above method, this is philosophically rather than technologically based – there is a principle upon which the organization's structure is to be founded. At least in the UK, where I'm writing this, this idea gained momentum in the 1980s at a time of privatization in the rail industry. So many people have used the railway as an analogy for IT, it's perhaps useful to relate it here.

At its start, the railway industry in Great Britain consisted of a number of private companies around the landmass who bought land, laid track, built trains and stations and each ran their own patch as a separate company. There would be one company who would build and own everything needed to carry you north out of London King's Cross to Yorkshire, and a separate one to take you west out of London Paddington to Bristol. In the middle of the twentieth century, the government bought all these up to create British Rail. And so it remained until the government decided to sell off the rail industry in the 1980s, to make the railways more efficient by putting the system into private hands (or to increase the treasury coffers without raising taxes by disposing of public assets, depending on your politics). The split they arrived at was between the rail network along with its stations, which became Railtrack, and the train operating companies who would then buy the use of the rails and stations from Railtrack.

So there was a distinct split between the *infrastructure* of the rail industry, which was managed by one type of company – and the *services* that ran on that infrastructure, managed by other, theoretically competing entities. This model was tried by a number of companies for running their IT. Infrastructure (computers, servers, network, cabling etc.) would come under one department and services (support, training, access to applications, etc.) would be the responsibility of another.

Such a model offers opportunities for outsourcing certain parts of IT, just as it did in the rail industry. The problem with such a model is that when you have a number of players, there is a risk to communications between all these operating factions. Different working practices among the players may get in one another's way, and when something goes wrong, it can be difficult to identify where the responsibility lies so as to fix the problem. The natural co-dependence of infrastructure and superstructure may turn out not to run as smoothly as it should. And in the example of the UK rail network, that's what appears to be happening recently, as different operating companies' trains collide with one another, running on tracks that some think are not being maintained as well as they ought to be. I've noticed that in recent years, fewer managers in IT are postulating the infrastructure–superstructure model.

I much prefer the idea of an organizing principle rather than an historical default for deciding upon a structure. A principle can be born of a vision, hammered out into a strategy and followed as an absolute truth. Historical default – like for example the one that has for so long said 'technicians and non-technicians should be in separate departments' – just leads to glass ceilings as it does so commonly in IT. We've looked at the principle of infrastructure/superstructure and at that of organization around similar technical skills and I've argued why neither would be my ideal for most companies. As a basis for a fundamental structure to the IT organizations, one of my favourite principles is that of 'present and future computing'.

5.4 IT structure – the present–future split

Back when I first started working in computing, oh, decades ago now, the structure of the data processing (DP) department in most companies was quite simple. There was a development manager, a helpdesk manager, a support manager and a networks manager, each with their own group of specialists and reporting to the DP manager. Purchasing and procurement of IT still came under the finance department to technical specifications laid down by DP.

Then in the 1990s, all that changed. Commonly now, the information technology group is split into a development section and a separate, amalgamated IT services (ITS) section. Figure 2.1 (p. 13) shows the parallel role carried out by the development department while the ITS group is designing its own strategy. Once the assessment of demand for IT and associated services has been made, the development side takes its own track. This includes designing the overall architecture of the computing technology, then breaking that down into what individual systems will be needed within that architecture. The final stage is implementation.

This is always taking place. As new technologies arrive, the developers are looking to see how the company could benefit from these, and how they would fit into the overall architecture. The users need increased power and functionality, and request the development group to assess these needs, then create or acquire the technologies to satisfy them.

So while 'development' is essentially about the envisioning and implementing future of the computer systems, ITS is about maintaining the present, keeping the systems going and the users producing. So within ITS, we find the helpdesk, desktop support, procurement, network infrastructure and perhaps even a group looking after telephones. Reprographics may come in there too, as the fax and printing systems they used to manage become connected to the network.

The change makes sense. This structural separation of 'future' and 'present' computing is a business-minded orientation, rather than the old, largely technocratic hierarchy. But even this may still reflect some of the old technological barriers. Anything 'mainframy' goes into the development department while anything Microsoft-ish or vaguely Intel-esque is ITS's responsibility.

This historical patch-protection can throw up some weird anomalies. For example, in larger companies, 'development' may be subdivided into one team that specifies and writes applications and another to maintain the systems thus devised. But the 'program maintenance' element is decidedly *present* rather than *future* computing – and if we're sticking to a business-based rather than technology-oriented organization, applications maintenance should logically come under IT services. For that matter, so should computer operations, the bit that makes sure the backups are done among other auspicious tasks.

More anomalous still is the often-overlooked 'applications support' team. Functionally, they are just like the good old helpdesk. They take requests for assistance from users and resolve them, often over the telephone. Its role is unquestionably production support – i.e. present, not future computing. Yet although the helpdesk is part of IT services, applications support remains firmly wedged in among the developers.

The reason is one of the orientation of the applications being supported. Microsoft Office and its ilk are undoubtedly horizontal – these applications can be used anywhere and everywhere in the corporation's business, in all departments and at all ranks. Word-processing, email and desktop number crunching are ubiquitous and in a way ancillary to the ultimate business in which the corporation is engaged. If you're a shoe manufacturer, you can use any email program and it won't make that much difference to the final quality of your English brogues. Hence the term 'horizontal'.

What will make a difference are the vertical systems. Those applications so specific, or so purpose-built that no other cobbler could use them. They are woven in such a way as to define and reflect only your own business processes. These vertical applications may be based on a horizontal foundation – such as SAP or Oracle – but the workflow and financial processes they have been customized to reflect, are those of your corporation and no other.

This means that any group of technicians supporting the vertical applications has to understand not just the technological platform upon which these applications run, but also the business activities the technologies represent. That's a particularly specialized knowledge base, with which the traditional helpdesk could not compete. While the helpdesk may take calls on horizontal applications, it can seldom pretend to be able to support their use. Few helpdesk analysts would have a reason to build complex spreadsheets like those in hourly use in the finance department, so they could never be as expert in Microsoft Excel as any user could.

Microsoft Access demonstrates this point especially keenly (is it all IT managers who hate Access, or just the ones I've met?). Unable to persuade the overstretched IT department to come up with a huge number of small-scale, low-userbase yet mission-critical applications, the users have taken to cluttering the servers with dozens of unsupported unpoliced Access databases. Standards and version numbering are ignored, and the first IT gets to hear about them is when the user who wrote the system leaves the company and the application develops a fault that nobody in the helpdesk can repair. The application was written on a needs-must basis and now the absence of formal support for horizontal applications usage threatens to leave a user department exposed.

This horizontal–vertical split is the spanner in the works of business-oriented IT structure. Often, the reason is simply that the technical skills of supporting the different types of systems have historically resided on one side of the divide or the other, and nobody's got round to moving them yet. I could also be cynical and say that if in organizing IT, the principles of present–future computing were adhered to rigorously, then IT services as a department would dwarf the development group, and in some companies, that might create an unhealthy imbalance in the power bases of IT managers, let alone the effective demotion of the development manager as the structural shift was implemented.

Nevertheless, there are strong commercial arguments for putting all support of production IT in the same place. It's not just about applications support, it's about any department responsible for keeping the computers going today, as opposed to preparing something the computers will be doing six months from now.

The first is the reduction of duplication, but that itself implies other reasons. Vertical support over there, horizontal support over here, both short-staffed, neither understanding the other's skillsets, often using different call-logging systems. Bring them together to share knowledge and resources and broaden the availability of all manner of user support – while reducing costs by eliminating any duplication. Increase obvious career paths so that horizontal people can learn about vertical systems and thus give themselves the option of climbing either tower of technocracy.

I realize this view suggests that hitherto mainframe people may suddenly end up working for a hitherto desktop department. In the initial stages, they may feel a little isolated. Nobody in this department knows the first thing about Oracle. No bad thing. You can teach them. Here in ITS, you vertical people are rare and valuable, while over there in development, user support was just something you did between projects.

But another argument, one I believe to be crucial, concerns the development of the service ethos. Developers work for months in isolation from the customer – and that's as it should be. Development should indeed have a rarefied, even academic quality to it, to foster creativity as well as productivity. But in ITS, the atmosphere is rightly one of urgency, of do it today or the company stops. This atmosphere is gradually (in my view too gradually) causing the rise of real specialization in service management – which is very different from the techniques and principles needed for the management of pure technology. By and large, IT still needs more service-minded thinking and cementing a present–future structure could help foster that.

5.5 The ITSC – the core of IT management

Information technology is no longer just an administrative tool. The fact that it can integrate the business from product design through manufacture to stock control and invoicing, means that it pervades all sectors of the organization and meshes them together. With automation come consistency, cost reduction and increased efficiency. So IT has allowed us to take on more customers and products than we could ever have managed with manpower alone – indeed in many companies these days (take the Internet book retailer Amazon.com for example), automation has become the only thing that would make the business viable. We can't do without IT.

All this means that while on the one hand, the commercial side of the corporation will entreat their IT people to better understand the business, those commercialists must equally understand the importance of IT. The two can come together in a core management structure to define the IT strategy and commission the technicians to deliver the technologies to satisfy that strategy.

One of the most common ways such a structure emerges is in the **Information Technology Steering Committee** (ITSC). For all matters relating to IT, this is the most senior body. It consists mostly of representatives of the business. It convenes regularly, to deal with the requests for non-standard changes (see Chapter 4), but for these, it chiefly behaves as the provider of a stamp of authority and corporate approval. Its main purpose, however, is to act as a council for deciding at a strategic level on how to progress the corporation's IT. The big questions will be asked here, with the analytical detail delegated to various experts around the company. The members of the ITSC tend to be senior managers or their direct delegates.

For anything major to happen with IT, it must go through this committee. If they decide against it, it won't happen. This is where IT and the business really come together, where the true purpose of IT is realized. If we were to compare the role of the ITSC with its counterpart in a national government, it would be the legislature. The IT department and to a certain extent the user departments would form the executive, carrying out the wishes and decrees of the ITSC. It is not a part of the IT department – it is an external and superior governing body to which the IT department must defer.

This is illustrated in Figure 5.1 below where I offer a hypothetical structure for an IT department.

Managing the IT Services Process

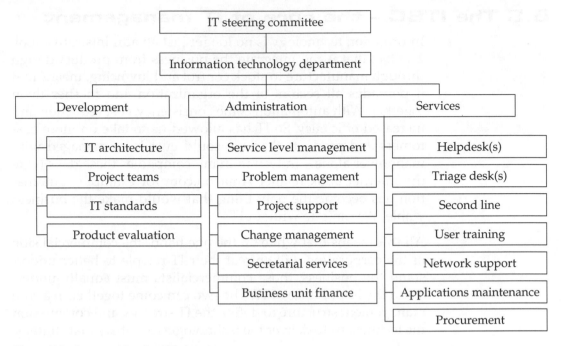

Figure 5.1 An example of an IT department structure

5.6 Functions in the IT department

I have suggested a three-way split to IT. It may not necessarily be perfect for your organization, even if this is the way you are already set up. The shape of your IT organization will be influenced by the services strategy you identify (Chapter 2), the services you choose to offer (Chapter 3) and the processes you follow to produce those services (Chapter 4).

In the structure above, the two technical sections stand alone, with development looking after future computing and services dealing with the present. Another way of seeing this is to compare it with a manufacturing company. There, research and development would invariably be separated from actual production. Similarly, the 'head office' functions of measurement and overall management would be at least structurally divorced from R&D and the factory.

And so it is with my suggestion of making 'administration' a distinct section. The purpose of this group is to serve not the technology or IT's customers, but IT management itself. Its main job is to gather information and feed that into the process of performance assessment and decision-making.

These next few paragraphs outline the duties and responsibilities in the IT department, following the layout in Figure 5.1.

5.7 IT development

This department *produces* all the *major* computer hardware and software systems in use at the company. I use the word 'produces' in the same sense that one might use it in the movie industry – for the development department's role may be as much in the actual physical work of doing what they do, as in the commissioning of vendors or other parts of the company and IT department to do it on their behalf.

Furthermore, the emphasis is on 'major', for they may not be the only group producing computer systems. Desktop computer environments usually have considerable programming functionality in themselves, of which users may take advantage, producing small, tactical programs and routines for limited or specialized use. Again, some user groups may have such a specialized need that there is no need for a generalist IT department to be involved, and thus deal direct with software and systems vendors to meet these limited needs.

So the responsibilities of the development department blur markedly at the edges. However, where it matters, namely in the systems that will run the company as a whole rather than isolated operational departments, development plays a crucial role.

However, it is not a services function, thus placing too detailed a consideration of it out on the fringes of this book's scope. It produces an output, then hands that finished article (be it a computer networking strategy, corporate database structure or major application) over to support – and it is here where IT services takes over, to distribute the delivered systems and keep them available to the userbase on a day-by-day basis.

I see IT development as having four main functions.

I use the term **'IT architecture'** to denote a policy authority with a technical remit. The following analogy is taken from city planning. The political authorities overseeing a city realized that they had a certain traffic problem. Somebody had to decide on the best way to deal with that, whether it should be to increase the capability of public transport or improve the roads. If the solution were to be the roads, then should these be improved within the city or by bypassing it, so traffic wishing to cross to the other side of the city could do so by going round it rather than through it. The ease and cost of long-term maintenance and effects of increased growth would have to be taken into account. Chosen technologies would need a long life before obsolescence, so the solution would have to be future-proofed. These high-level decisions would need a mixture of strategic vision and technical knowledge. They are the sort to be taken by an architect.

So it would be the IT architect who would decide that the solution for a given company would be a centralized ERP system rather than a suite of discrete programs, or for a combination of the two, how these might interface with one another. The architects might decide on the physical network structure, and whether wireless or cabled networks would best suit the organization's needs.

The purpose of **IT standards** would be to ensure the uniformity, interoperability and quality of the installed systems.

Those involved in **product evaluation** would do just that – based on the outline strategies promoted by the architects, this function would consider the pros and cons of various products and technologies in the IT marketplace in terms of the match to corporate needs and prescribed standards.

The **project teams** are the visible face of development, the groups of programmers actually setting up the hardware and writing the code that will become the company's production systems.

Too often in my experience, IT development and IT services operate as two distinct and unrelated entities. This can be seen even in something as mundane as the career path for the IT employee – a transfer from technical support to development is known to happen, but it is not a well-worn path. Most commonly one is either a developer or a support person, even from education (the most common route into development is straight from college). It is as though the two functions demand entirely different cultures and mindsets.

However, IT services has much to offer development, for in the end, IT is not simply about the technologies as they are provided but how they are used – and IT services must deal with the usage of the computers, because it talks to the users several times an hour, rather than just at the design stage. It communicates routinely with those low-ranking people, whose day-to-day jobs are directly and minutely influenced by how the computer systems are designed. In short, where development may know what the company as a whole needs, IT services is better placed to know what its employees need. This means that potentially at least, IT services may have much to offer about the practicality of the systems – and in my view, this should be a major input at all stages of the development process, from architecture, through standards to implementation.

Implementation of developed systems is a particular bugbear of mine. The wall that too often exists between development and services is the one over which some developers too commonly throw an installed system without warning those on the other side of its imminent arrival. This leaves the support departments exposed when users must face the new software's teething troubles. These same troubles might have been avoided if IT services were involved in the design process at an earlier stage, to insist that the architects and programmers would take into account the eventual usability and supportability of the systems. A program or technology that does not cover the bases of usability well enough will eventually impede the productivity of the user. It is not just that IT services will fill the gap by dealing with the users' enquiries, it is that while those enquiries are taking place, a user is not fulfilling the purpose of his employment and thus the company is losing or wasting money.

IT services needs to understand and get involved with the development process.

5.8 IT administration

I have proposed earlier in this book that any IT department can be seen as though it were a company in its own right. If the development section is the one that designs the products this 'IT company' provides, and the services section is the customer-facing function that manages the distribution and post-installation support of these products, then the administration section is in effect the IT company's head office. This is where the whole production machine, from concept to delivery, from technology to customer, is controlled. It is an extension of IT management. It enforces management decree and monitors production, productivity and quality to ensure that management objectives are being met.

As would any management office, it will have the purely clerical functions of **secretarial** services and **business unit finance**, staffed by secretaries and accountants respectively. The secretaries book the travel, handle the complaints, look after the managers' diaries, minute the meetings, handle the correspondence and organize the Christmas party. The accountants pay the bills, watch the budget, balance the books and send out the cross-charging[2] invoices.

Some companies choose to 'insource'[3] these services – i.e. have them performed by a centralized, corporate function on behalf of all company departments. In other words, as clerical operations, these two may not necessarily fall under the direct remit of the IT directorate, and thus it is beyond my scope to study them in detail in this book. I mention them only for completeness of the structural model at Figure 5.1.

The **service level management** function within IT administration will exist by virtue of the fact that in addition to IT managers measuring their department's output, so too are their customers, even if not formally. The usual way that IT and its customers conduct their relationship is under the auspices of a 'service level agreement' (of which more in Chapter 8). This document describes the services to be produced and sets target levels of quantity and quality. The attainment of these targets must be measured, for it is in relationship to that productivity for the users that the IT department is financed. This means that money must change hands between IT as the service provider and the users as service consumers, and there will have to be some mechanism by which the users can verify that they are getting what they are paying for. The staff who carry out service level management are therefore in a way representing the interests of the users.

Putting them here in a separate section from IT services itself is the closest the IT department can come to impartiality of that measurement. It may not always be so, however. In some larger organizations, notably those who are audited by external parties, a separate corporate department may carry out service level management. This is often the way when such organizations are, for example, proclaiming ISO[4] compliance or in public

---

[2] 'Cross charging' is a financial policy used in a number of companies who have separated each of the business units into cost- and profit-centres. It places actual budgetary responsibility directly where the money is being spent, at the company department incurring the costs. I cover it and its implications for IT services in more detail in Chapter 8.

[3] As opposed to 'outsource' which would be to have them provided by an external supplier.

[4] The International Standards Organization offers published standards for the completeness of management and operational processes. A company can sometimes benefit from choosing to follow these standards in order to gain publishable accreditation by the ISO or its appointed agents. This makes the company subject to regular audits to ensure they continue to deserve the accreditation.

service where there may be a government-appointed body of auditors.

There is an argument of course for having service level management done by the user community – after all, it is their money at risk. My own experience is that it is usually difficult to get the users to do this, because they have other business priorities imposed on them by the company directors and so long as IT is good enough, it tends to be taken for granted.

Problem management looks for recurring patterns in the repeated failure of IT products and services. Its main purpose is to minimize repeat failures by searching for the root cause of these problems. I prefer to put it under administration because it is essentially an IT internal only necessity. Granted that solving repeat problems serves the users, it also serves IT, because it reduces duplication. In other words, it means that IT does not have to waste effort continually solving the same problem.

Although the eradication of repeat problems is a support activity, which suggests that problem management should be part of IT services, its findings tend to indicate a design failure, which suggests that the core issue lies in development. So it could theoretically live in either. But given that repeat problems will by default have to be resolved by IT services, and that to do so will require development to improve the quality of their output, problem management can become a case for contention between these two technical sections.

As I have argued above, development has as its core priority the production of future computing – to revisit installed software to resolve intermittent and reoccurring bugs is time-consuming and costly and diverts development from that purpose. Furthermore, often these bugs disappear as part of the natural round of product upgrades. This all conspires to suppress the priority that development will give to repeat problems, while simultaneously increasing their priority in the view of IT services. The potential contention lies in those differing levels of priority. Where there is contention, there may be a need for an independent arbitrating authority. My argument for putting problem management in neither development nor services, but in a separate section reporting directly to IT management, is that it is only there where that contention can be overridden by directly invoking senior management authority.

Problem management therefore implies a need for technical expertise, and this makes it the only function within the administration section where this is the case (the others being exclusively administrative). This will give some smaller IT departments a staffing issue. Technicians are expensive enough, and their efforts should ideally be focused on producing and supporting technical systems. I see this, however, merely as a question of perspective on the problems. By shifting the focus of problem management slightly away from identifying the root cause of the problem and more towards identifying patterns of failure, we reduce the required technical depth. The function can then become truly an administrative one, simply spotting patterns, estimating impact and prioritizing problems. It then reports these to management with a recommendation for which problems should be dealt with in what order, and whether the solution should be produced by the development section or by the applications maintenance group within IT services.

I have proposed earlier that routine bug fixes and problem changes in actuality should fall under the remit of IT services, and specifically to applications maintenance. This is to be consistent with the idea of 'present and future computing' (see above). Bug fixes are decidedly 'present', because the systems have already been handed over to production from development. So most of the routine patterns that problem management encounters will be fixed within IT services in any case.

Problem management may not, however, merely be looking for technical failure. It can also act as an overseer of the IT production line to see where they may be points of failure within IT processes, or gaps in the performance of either systems or people. As a central section, it is ideally placed to do so. It is not part of the handover between development and services and can thus theoretically be objective about how well those two sections work with one another. Its findings will benefit IT as a whole.

All IT departments have a need for **project support**, a function that knows what projects are taking place, where and to what end. The essence of development is the conduct of projects and it will have professional project managers to do this. However, invariably there will be projects in IT services also. These may be smaller, e.g. changes to document templates, small-scale computer installations, rewriting procedures, knocking together a little desktop database for a user.

The products of these projects will bring about changes in IT – in development, these will be major, in IT services less so. Nevertheless, changes in IT have an impact and though the impact of one of these may be relatively small, the impact of the gamut of them will be large. Without some governance, that impact cannot be known and without measurement, the projects themselves will deprive the IT department of resources that could be used elsewhere.

All projects consume resources and without accurate indication of this consumption, we cannot be sure that we have sufficient resources. If I am responsible for an IT budget, I want to know where my money is being spent and what benefit that will bring. I can measure my resource consumption in terms of helpdesk calls, installation requests and headcount commitment to specifically budgeted development projects, but I need to know what else is going on. I need a central authority that knows about all that 'what else', and this is the purpose of my project support office. Once I have all those projects recorded and monitored in one place, I can prioritize and make decisions about that resource commitment.

'Project support' does not conduct the projects – it merely knows what they are, where they are, what they are doing, who is conducting them and what progress is being made on them. It can spot where there may be duplication, or where one project may have an impact on another. It does this with regard to the output of both the technical sections, on behalf of IT management and it is to that body that it reports its information.

As regards to the tools used by this function, there is to my mind a gap here. For large-scale projects, there are project management systems, which will produce Gantt charts and calculate critical paths through project timelines, taking into account the consequences upon each other of simultaneous activities. This is all very well for the more sizeable undertakings – but it is often overkill for the little projects. As a result, these tend to get ignored, and I see this as a risk, for reasons of understanding impact and resource consumption as outlined above. It only needs a simple database – and I have offered some thoughts for such a system in Chapter 11.

In Chapter 4, we looked at the **change management** process. If we were to follow that as described, it would imply a need for some administration. In Figure 4.5, the non-standard change process means that once a change request is raised, it must be submitted for further analysis and/or approval, assigned to an authority, scheduled and produced, with regular reports on its progress. The change manager is the principal channel for ensuring that all this happens in the right order and management reports are produced. In this respect, this function is to changes as project support is to projects. It monitors, oversees and highlights key events of the change management process on behalf of IT management. It is a purely administrative function.

5.9 IT services

Although the whole of this book is ostensibly about the headings in the right-hand column of Figure 5.1, it is still useful to summarize them here in the context of IT as a whole.

The **helpdesk** is a point of reception of inbound communications, which usually take the form of either a request for change, a request for technical assistance or repair, or a general enquiry. It is also known as 'first line' support. There may be several of these, each with a certain technical or geographical specialization.

The **'triage desk'** is an extension of the first line. It is not contracted direct by the users, but the helpdesk will use it to resolve problems that could be fixed over the telephone, but may be time-consuming – passing such calls to triage keeps the incoming telephone lines free to take new enquiries. Triage also serves as a way of reducing the burden on the second line, by dealing on the telephone with enquiries that the second line otherwise might have had to attend in person.

The **'second line'** usually takes the form of a group of technicians. These will be mobile by default, and typically more advanced technically than their first-line colleagues[5]. Their main support function is to resolve those technical problems the first line could not. In many companies they also perform other services such as installations, one-to-one user training, upgrades, small-scale projects and network changes.

'User training' provides training to the userbase either directly or by acting as agents for external training companies.

'Network support' is usually a team of technicians looking after the server, as opposed to desktop end of the computer network. Not normally a user-facing support team, this group tends to provide less obvious services such as guaranteed system availability, capacity management, email and user accounts and so on.

'Applications maintenance' is a team of technicians providing a triage or second-line support for a specific sector of computer usage, namely business specialist applications (as opposed to the more generalist desktop of office software). This normally

---

[5] Although there is no real reason other than tradition that these two skillsets should so commonly occur together.

requires a special understanding of the way the business works, beyond the necessary computer competence.

'Procurement' is an administrative service associated with the change process, to handle requests for equipment. May require some technical knowledge given the context of the requests.

5.10 IT services geography

There comes a time in the growth of companies where the positioning of IT services staff becomes critical. This is not an issue where the business is centred at a main site with perhaps a few remote offices with a token staff – in such cases, the employees at those sites will develop a certain self-reliance across all their operations, making them less dependent on head office facilities than their counterparts in the main building. But that resilience can become an issue if not closely regarded. Remote offices have a tendency to nurture local IT talent among their populations, creating surrogate IT experts whose computer skills do not appear in their official job descriptions.

The problem with this natural response to isolation is that the IT problems that occur at those sites do not enter IT department records – they arise and are dealt with as a matter of course rather than one of procedure. Needs must. This means that the IT department does not have a complete picture of the behaviour of its systems in all circumstances.

When this situation is recognized, one common reaction is to attempt to formalize the role of these ersatz technicians, by applying formal reporting routines, training these users in IT procedures and so on. But this too can meet with resistance, as then come the debates about whose budget should account for their employment costs and to which part of the company hierarchy they report.

> **Case study:**
> **The survival of the remote user**
>
> War stories of the survivalism of remote sites abound. A client of mine has a campus site of some twenty-odd acres, with tens of buildings. In each of the largest of these, there is an unofficial helpdesk, consisting of a user or two who, in addition to their usual jobs, have assumed a quasi-technical support role. If course these users were originally hired to do something else, and their computer support activities eat into the time they can spend doing the tasks in their job descriptions.

The worst case I saw was in the executive building, where the default first point of contact for computer difficulties was an assistant director of marketing, a man paid more than twice the annual salary of a computer support technician for spending half his time doing that job. The unnecessary cost was self-evident, but his colleagues preferred to go to somebody they knew rather than telephone some distant and comparatively irrelevant call centre in the hope that somebody would come over from IT several hours later. The same model was repeated across the vast campus, with the majority of these specialists not formally recognized and completely unknown to IT.

When the company spotted the pattern, it immediately forbade any such reoccurrence, and insisted that henceforth, only IT be used to solve IT problems. With some reluctance, the users complied. However, the company did not account for the volume of work these people were doing and did not increase investment in IT services to deal with the unavoidable increase in workload. And as IT got busier, their telephone lines became ever more engaged, so the enquiries could not get through. The users survived – new local technicians began to emerge in each of the buildings but this time the emergence was accompanied by a profound conspiracy of secrecy, lest the company find out.

For all the usefulness of accountants, sometimes their single-minded pursuit of cost control for its own sake can blind us to the obvious. At the remote site, there simply is not enough work to keep a computer technician occupied all day – and it is absolutely unthinkable these days to have somebody not fully occupied. Heaven forfend, that if they were only half-occupied, they might spend the rest of the day reading the newspaper with their feet up, on a full salary. The other employees at that site would witness an expensive IT expert with an easy life and that would be politically divisive, showing IT up to be the waste of money it is. Dear me no, that would never do. Far better to have no technician there at all. Sure, that means the users will spend much more time either fixing problems themselves and thus decreasing their productivity, or waiting hours or even days for somebody to arrive from IT, but those outcomes don't appear on the balance sheet, so that's all right then. Human resources will be able to boast that all employees are working at full stretch, so their backs at least will be covered. Who cares if a few users have computer problems? Better than wasting money, isn't it?

No.

My maxim is this – that if the computer problems faced by an unsupported site cost more in lost corporate productivity than would placing an IT services representation there, then no matter how little that representation is utilized, it still pays for itself. The users who complain that the representation appears idle will simply have to understand that if it were not idle, then it would not be available to deliver those services as quickly as it does when eventually it is called upon.

The accountants are not always right. Money is not always the issue, but when it is, the financial decision should be a complete one. In IT services, it is not so simple as to ask 'Should I spend more on IT services or not?' because the lazy accountant will offer the simplest answer – i.e., *not*. But the reason the answer is so simple is because the question is wrong. The more complete question would be 'Should I spend money on IT services, or by not doing so incur a greater cost elsewhere?' Perspective is required to see where that other cost might be and how big it is so that it can be compared with the cost of service and IT headcount provision. That cost is user productivity. By his activity, the user produces a proportion of the total revenue of the corporation (in the UK, this is called 'turnover'). If, due to impediment by a failure in computing or his ability to use it, the user ceases to produce or suffers from reduced productivity, that is so much less money being contributed to revenue, and this is the case for both public and private sector institutions. For a full assessment of whether or not to commission an IT services presence at a remote site, the accountant must ask what the cost would be if there were no such presence.

The geographical placement of IT becomes crucial when the company has numerous sites of similar size and is exacerbated still further by the distance between these sites. Different parts of the world approach this question different ways. In the USA and Australia, the problem is easiest to resolve. These are big countries with a homogenous language and culture, and perhaps the only real difficulty arises from centralization of support services. Put it in the east, and the support desk has to work late because their customers in the west will still be in the office three hours after most of the easterners are heading for the subway. Put it in the west, and the helpdesk has to open at five in the morning.

The Europeans have only in recent years come to face this problem. Once, Europe was a loose amalgam of hugely varying cultures, languages and mindsets. But we Europeans have promised not to go to war with each other any more, we've largely harmonized our economies and homogeneity is creeping in. The trade between European member states increases apace, and for the growing company, it is an obvious step to establish a business presence in the country next door. Because these are all developed economies, the chances are that whatever enterprise exists in one country, there will be a counterpart in the neighbouring lands – so a comparatively easy route to growth and market share is acquisition.

With acquisition comes the question of integration, and from that follows a reduction in duplication of effort, so as to reduce business operating costs. As IT is rarely a contributor to corporate profits and particularly expensive to run, its costs will be among the first to come under examination. Sooner or later, IT managers will come to wonder what could be centralized, where the duplication could be eradicated and how the newly integrated and uniform business systems could be met with concomitantly integrated and uniform support services.

My preferred approach to a consideration of supporting remote sites is to see these as a range of markets and look for patterns of similarity. This does not have to be a similarity of approach, but one of client need. From this I can make an analysis of service provision against consumption as in Figure 5.2 below.

This gives me a map of who does what to whom. From this I can start looking for examples of duplication. This itself is not always bad – perhaps two offices each have their own second line – but then if they did not, it would take so long to move the second line from its base to another site in the event of an issue, that this duplication is actually beneficial in terms of user productivity.

Some types of duplication may suggest a possibility for centralization of certain services. The most obvious of these is the

Figure 5.2
Service provision vs consumption at remote sites

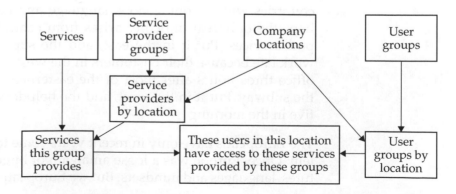

helpdesk, or indeed any other service that could be delivered by remote communications because it requires no real onsite presence. But even this is not necessarily the 'no-brainer' it may appear to be. Centralization can fail even here and not just because of language barriers:

- A pharmaceuticals company with several sites in the UK decided it could save money by removing all first-line IT services (helpdesk, moves requests, change requests, video-conference booking, telephone configuration, just-in-time training etc.) from the various sites and amalgamating them into one large helpdesk, promising better service by having more people to take the calls. **But** – within months the users were complaining that most of the helpdesk staff did not understand their enquiries. So the helpdesk was split into a number of sub-desks, each with a responsibility for the site from which that sub-desk's staff had been relocated.
- A US manufacturer of computer peripherals wanted to centralize European support enquiry operations along the American model that had worked so well there. **But** – the productivity of the various desks was so high it turned out not to be worth the expense. There would be scant headcount savings, and the language differences would lengthen call times, reducing first-line effectiveness.
- In early 2003 the UK telephone directory enquiries market was liberalized from the major telecommunications provider. Several companies would now provide a competitive service and price became the deciding issue for their customers. **But** – to cut costs, many of these outsourced their call centres to Asian providers. Customer complaints mushroomed, as the lack of local knowledge resulted in expensive wrong numbers. By late summer, one of these suppliers had already gone into receivership.

The moral is that centralization will not necessarily reduce duplication – which itself is not necessarily desirable – nor is centralization guaranteed to improve the service. It may also not reduce costs. It must be used carefully.

The problem with centralizing enquiry handling is that it can force all enquiries down the same pipe, with the same recipients waiting at the bottom. For maximum efficiency, those individuals will have to be well trained in just about any IT issue they may be asked about, coming from any geographical location in the IT regime. It may just not be possible for so much information to be held by one individual – so the first-time fix rate is low, and costs rise as more calls are reassigned for further, specialist diagnosis or farmed out to other, specialist IT services departments. Delays get inserted as enquiries change ownership and customer satisfaction becomes more of an issue as resolution times consequently lengthen.

Centralized enquiry handling works best where the types of enquiries can be well anticipated, which is why such simple, non-diagnostic services such as airline seat booking services can be centralized. In these cases, the enquirer can only ask for confirmation of an item of information to be extracted from a finite catalogue of pre-known information, such as the airline's flight timetable and price list. People who work on an airline booking desk do not need to know anything about aeroplanes. And because the only way of using an airline's aeroplane is how the airline says it will be used, there is no real need for user support. All this absence of the necessity of knowledge means that such a service can be centralized, located anywhere, even subcontracted to an external company.

However, IT enquiries are not like that – there will always be a need for some enquiry diagnosis, because the computers are being used in a certain context. The larger or more diverse the company, the more varied may be that context. Variety increases the breadth of knowledge the enquiry-handler will need, broader yet if the target is a high level satisfaction of the enquiry at first hand. In IT, centralization is not always as straightforward a decision as it may seem in the call centre, precisely because of this first-time resolution, which is desirable from a business point of view. It may be that to cover too big a company would require an impossible amount of knowledge.

One of my favourite models for geographical placement of IT services is based around a mixture of central, regional and local services. It takes the whole of IT into account, and it may not work for everybody. However, it does consider a wide range of IT development, services and administration functions and I offer it here. It is an amalgam of models I have developed for a range of clients.

Central IT functions

Summary

*Strategic and administrative function – main point of business contact – governs standards of **all** universal systems including central business* *applications and universally deployed desktop, laptop and palmtop environments – all corporate IT functions.*

Function	Comment
Information technology steering committee	An overall, board-level function to which ITS ultimately reports
Integration	A corporate planning function to ensure new acquisitions get uniform corporate IT services and ITS takes responsibility for acquired resources
Finance	IT central finance function, performing following sub functions:
Resource usage	Measuring ITS productivity and man-hours spent in service production
Transfer pricing/cross charging	Reporting on expenditure and managing ITS budget
Contracts negotiation	Financial terms of contracts, if contracts are negotiated centrally
Contracts repository	Owners of central database of all contracts with external suppliers of hardware, software and services. Allows for central negotiation of vendor relationships if available across all operating locations, or can act as a pure repository if contracts are negotiated locally
Service management	ITS central function to administrate service provision by use of following sub functions
Service level agreements	Negotiating and cementing service levels with business units
Service catalogue	Authorship and maintenance of ITS's electronic service catalogue
Service level performance reporting	Measurement of service levels actually delivered
Project support office	Overall administrative and reporting resource for all ongoing ITS projects
Project monitoring	Ensuring projects are on time and have requisite resources
Release notices	Standardized releases of all updates to group systems
Change management	Gains approval for changes, tracks progress
Problem management	Monitors repeat systems failures to seek out root causes
IT architecture & development	Overall central IT function for systems design with sub functions:
Installed systems version control	Licensing, ensuring version compatibility and supportability

(continued)

111

Function	Comment
Group network architecture design	Design of network systems
Wide area network	Management of wide area network and/or technical liaison with vendor
Group applications design	Design and standardization of all company-wide applications regardless of computing platform
Development	Cutting code for new applications
Local systems uniformity	Existing applications universally used, but not yet standardized (e.g. staff management software or taxation calculators which may differ between countries) – looking for global, uniform alternatives
Documentation	Ensuring developed systems are documented
Office systems standards	Templates, macros, etc.
Office systems applications	Selection and version control
Desktop image base	Global uniformity of user computing environment. Centralization of this can mean that single hardware supplier can be selected for all locations and given image for installation prior to hardware delivery
Change management	Authorizes changes – convened by change manager to approve change requests to group systems, includes:
Non-standard business applications changes	Project management for change implementation
Group systems change request analysis	Feasibility and impact studies
IT production	Day-to-day IT provision
Process authorship	Implementing procedures and ensuring compliance
Operational standards	Monitoring the manner in which work gets done – work instruction level
Operational tools	Describing tools needed to support IT internal operations
Configuration/assets database	Owners of central database of all known computing and telecommunications assets
Data centre	Ownership of central computing platforms
Mainframe operations	24-hour, backup and batch operations
Shared reference data	Database administration for shared data used by all business units
Applications management	Job control language scripting, batch running control

Regional IT functions

Summary

Main point of user contact. Where user computing is actually delivered.

Function	Comment
Computing and communications infrastructure	Changes to systems only as directed by IT architecture
Network infrastructure	As directed by IT architecture
Server operations	Ditto
Backup administration	Ditto
File restores	Helpdesk function via standard change procedure
Server service pack upgrade deployment	As directed by IT architecture, such that all servers are at the same level of upgrade
Workstation systems upgrade deployment	Ditto
Shift handover	Reports on overnight systems performance as requested by central production IT
Local PABX management	As per network server operations – changes to hunt groups etc. via standard change
Helpdesk	Takes calls from all users in region
First-line enquiries on all ITS topics	'Public relations' function
Business applications support	Helpdesk for business applications
Office systems support	Assistance in usage of office systems – therefore takes calls direct from users and not through 'key users'
User fax and telephony support	Ditto
Remote office support	Assists users in remote offices via remote control tools, probably through 'triage' function
Email enquiries	Provision for e-support
Triage support	Secondary helpdesk for immediate response to specialist or time-consuming support enquiries
Second-line escalation	Calling upon local IT technicians (based at local sites but reporting to region)
User database	Ensuring integrity of information on users in region
Asset database integrity	Ditto
User account administration	Provision of user network accounts via standard change
Password resets	Helpdesk function – central IT to provide tools
Out-of-hours support	Size of regional desk offers opportunities to extend hours
Non-local time zone coverage	Ditto

(continued)

Function	Comment
User training	In both desktop and business applications – may be outsourced
Local computing change advisory	For specialized, non-corporate applications only unique to that location
Non-standard infrastructure changes	Implementation of changes to infrastructure as approved and instructed by central IT
Purchasing	Verify budgets and authority of unit controller, purchase equipment
Vendor selection & contracts negotiation	For local issues only, technical content of contracts only
Standard changes	As per service catalogue
Stockholding	Physical storage, maintaining asset database
Laptop and phone loans	Ditto

Local IT functions

Summary

Not an official route for users into IT services, but user contact is assumed to be inevitable – however, these must be logged, because future viability of local IT presence cannot be guaranteed in smaller offices. Otherwise present in all offices of more than (for example) 20 users, including regional offices. Local IT is organizationally a separate function from regional IT, even though it reports to the same manager and may reside in the same office.

Function	Comment
Business applications usage support	Enquiry resolution for non-technical issues surrounding use of software application – normally provided 'user-to-user'
Desktop support	Local support for user enquiries needing deskside visit
Second-line support	As delivered from helpdesk
Accommodation moves	As delivered from helpdesk via standard change or from project manager via non-standard change procedures
Installations	Ditto

One of the attractions of this model is the fact that it describes the principles of the organization, and staff are recruited to fill the positions indicated by those principles. There may be both regional and local IT on the same site. Indeed in head office, all three tiers of the model may be represented.

Note that in this model, I have made the helpdesk a regional, rather than a central function. This is to allow for international companies, where language is an issue. So at least in IT terms, Germany, the Czech Republic, Eastern Switzerland and Austria could all be one region, as could France, Southern Belgium and Luxembourg as the member countries of these regions share a language.

Staffing

6.1 We'll always need people

IT services is a labour-intensive function. It cannot work without people. There may be automated alternatives to some of our low-level procedures but in our industry, these will never entirely replace the knowledgeable warm body. Some attempts at automation have already produced limited results. Users can consult a published encyclopaedia of technical solutions rather than call a helpdesk. A machine can verify the completeness of an arriving change request form. A procurement order can scan the requestor's budget to ensure he has funds, then pass the order directly to a vendor without human intervention. But these just nibble at the edges of the relationship between IT services as a provider and the users out there as its customers.

Users are people and will prefer to deal with people. Decisions are still taken by people. IT keeps changing, and so there will be troughs of exception between the peaks of change – and machines are not good at handling the unexpected.

Computers also make lousy politicians and diplomats and wherever there are people, those skills will be needed. Computers also fall short in the bedside-manner department – a user with a problem is not just a broken machine, but a human being with concerns about not completing her work, fear of consequently incurring the wrath of her superior and a genuine need to hand over the responsibility for the problem to a competent counterpart. In IT services, we do not just look after the machinery, but also the humans who use it, with all their anxieties, desires and expectations. And in our lifetime, no machine will truly be able to handle that. The exchanges between IT services staff and their clients are not purely cold and rational – they include necessary asides, crucial to building relationships. 'Yes, Mary, I'm printing your order off now – while we're waiting, how's the new house?' 'Tom, I think I've solved the problem with your printer – by the way, did you see the match last night?'

Damon Albarn knows that humans have another, less business-like side to them, and got MCA Music to publish his words:

> All the people, so many people
> And they all go hand in hand,
> Hand in hand through their Parklife.

6.2 Management causation of staff requirements

The staff we hire are a consequence of the work we do. We have technical services so we need technicians, we must administrate our operations so we hire administrators. For any business function that requires staff, the route to hiring is a logical track, and one that I have tried to follow in this book thus far.

We began by assessing our market. Who are our potential customers? What do they need in terms of services? How many are these customers and where are they located? What's the value of the market, i.e. how much can they afford to pay? Given that value, what is the level of service quality we should be delivering?

From that process of market identification, we moved on to designing the services we would eventually produce. That gave us a catalogue of service products, which would need to be manufactured.

That meant that we had to design a manufacturing process. We broke that down into smaller scale procedures and realized that at a smaller scale still, these would need to be augmented with detailed work instructions.

Given the size, scope and location of the market, next we considered what kind of an organizational structure would be appropriate to manage everything we had designed thus far.

Up to now, all we have considered is the size and shape of our market and the factory we will have to build under the IT services banner to tackle that market. In the scenario I have explored here, we still don't have any staff. Now it is time to populate the factory with workers. Step by step we have moved through the process of designing an IT services machine, leaving the people until last.

It never happens like that in real life. My scenario is idealistic. It assumes that you are building your IT services department on a 'greenfield' site. There are some lucky people who have experienced this splendid opportunity, but they tend to be in the construction industry from which the term is borrowed. On day one of the project, you move into field of grass and imagine that one day, there will stand the edifice you have envisioned. Those of us who have been in this powerful position will know its associated, magnificent feeling of freedom and scope and its potential for self-expression and bettering anything that's gone before. Imagine how Beethoven must have felt when he decided to write his eighth piano sonata. He hammered a single C-minor chord and thought 'Right, now what can I do with that?' To which the enormously exciting answer must have been 'Anything I damn well like!' The result was the *Pathétique*.

Sadly, working in IT is rarely an aesthetic experience such as that. You acquire your management position, or more likely it acquires you. It is surrounded by legacy, vested interests, political history, reputation and existing heads with an established if not entrenched way of doing things. You have to build with the materials and people to hand. An IT services manager who engaged me as a consultant early on in my career insisted that on a service process redesign project, I would include a service the company did not need. She did this on the basis of skills held by certain members of her staff – she did not wish to lose those people, so she wanted a service that would give them something to do, even though there would be no market for their output. Of course that is an extreme example, but it happens, to a certain extent, to all of us. No matter how clear our vision of the future we want to build, we almost always have to take somebody else's past into account and that means we must, at least in the early stages of our management, work with the staff we already have.

It gets more complex still. Unless we keep a clear focus on the strategy we designed, we too can slip into entrenchment. It shows in the 'quick-fix' way we hire to replace leavers. When a key employee departs, we could take the opportunity to redesign from the ground up. But the pressure is always upon us to deliver service continuity – we must minimize the negative impact on service levels caused by staff absence or departure. So we take the easy way out and advertise for and end up hiring a clone of the skillset of the person who is being replaced. The clone arrives, and because his skills and attitudes so mirror those of his predecessor, he hits the ground running. The dip in service levels is minimized, the users may not even notice the difference. And in fitting in so well, the arriving employee also soon slips into the same bad habits and inefficiencies as those around him. So nothing changes and we throw an opportunity away.

It is my preference – and I would encourage it to be yours – to hire the people to fit the machine of your design and not to design the machine around the people. It is an enormous management dilemma but it is not one we should shirk. Hiring the right people to do the job we want them to do is a prime expression of the fact that we, and not historical accidents, are in control of service delivery. It is one of the differences between active management and passive position, i.e. whether we are actually running the IT services department or merely happen to be hierarchically authorized to sit behind its biggest desk.

Sometimes that requires extreme courage. The received wisdom is that we will never get our greenfield site. We will always have to make the best of what we have. That may include staff who may be unwilling to do the job we have decided, through process design, is necessary. If there is one reason that seems to crop up more than any other for managers choosing not to design the service from the ground up, it is the staff already in place. Even though staff attitudes may hinder our grand design, we hang on to them because their skills would be so hard to replace, and they know the business so well. So even if they are a little inflexible, we'll continue to make the best of what we've got.

And I for one completely refute that acquiescence. The ideal is a greenfield site. If the main thing stopping that is staff inflexibility, then we have the wrong people and they have to go. Their attitudes do not just hinder your grand plan, they will hinder every other plan thereafter. They have put themselves before the priorities of the company, and that breaks the deal they made with us. So we will lose their technical knowledge when they go – so what? Technology changes so much and so quickly that we would have to retrain them in the near future anyway. So we will lose their business knowledge – so what? In a year's time, the business will look different, so new people have as much chance of coming to terms with that as old retainers would.

This is *my* department and *I* am accountable. Therefore *I* must have control over it and I am not going to abdicate that control to subordinates who refuse to run the machine the way I designed it. I know it sounds callous – but this is business. First services – then process – then and only then, people. If certain people won't work the process the correct way, then the services will go awry and that is too big a price to pay, not just for the business as a whole but for you, the IT services manager. When the services fail because the staff are unwilling, the accountability still rests with you not them. If your greenery of your field is marred by antiquated structures, then a bulldozer is a legitimate tool. Don't gamble the future of your career and the success of the business on the fact that Fred Bloggs may not like his job description. Get the right people.

6.3 The right people

For the most part, IT is still a technocracy. The more one knows about computers, the more one is paid and the higher our standing in the IT hierarchy. It has been thus ever since the Lyons Electronic Office, when the gap between the technology and the businesses and users who benefit from it was at its widest. And despite the facts that computer knowledge is now ubiquitous, that users have come to see computing as just another resource commodity to be exploited and that technology has been supplanted by services, we still hang on to that anachronistic hierarchical idea.

Our unfortunate legacy is the thing that often keeps us from exercising our true authority. While we continue to see ourselves as technocrats, we will continue to stand slightly outside the true business world and kept from influencing it too much. We will continue to be less than perfect at attracting into our industry the sort of people we need these days, namely those who understand and can use the meaning of service. Granted, computers still misbehave, and that the technology changes so often that neither the manufacturers nor we can fully grasp it before it evolves yet again. So we will always need some modicum of technocracy or we would lose our grip on the benefits of technology completely.

We must nod in the direction of our technocratic history, but not necessarily defer to it. The nature of evolution and progress is that our past does not inevitably dictate our future. Things will change anyway, as the business evolves and grows around us, as our people's motivation waxes and wanes, as new technologies shift our priorities. The future is coming whether we like it or not. We can either let that change happen around and to us or we can choose to take control of it. And we can use the process of hiring people to simultaneously raise our profile in the business and change the culture of IT to reflect a service rather than technophile ethos. While we're about it, we can start rewarding and promoting our staff on the basis of the value they deliver rather than how many computer product courses they happen to have attended.

The mistake we often make is to hire people on the basis of their technical skills. That is of course, a necessary consideration, but it does not of itself take into account that the necessity for those skills was dictated by something else. That 'something else' consists of the processes we designed, in order to make the services we had realized we must offer. The principle I propose here is that we hire staff on the basis of their match not to the technologies, but to the processes. Happily, we have a precedent for this perspective – it is in the way we hire non-technical people for non-technical jobs.

IT services is not just a computer helpdesk and associated resolvers of technical problems. There are also clerical and organizational functions, which unlike the technical ones do not bring with them any prerequisite that the candidate must be expert in given technologies. What people like this possess is not necessarily a vocational direction, nor a hobby turned profession, nor an appropriate and recognized academic qualification as we might expect of a technician – but an aptitude for the tasks and responsibilities associated with the job on offer. There is a certain imprecision about hiring non-technical people, which, I would argue, we can also use in retaining our technical staff. We are mindful of the processes these candidates will have to follow and we assure ourselves, perhaps instinctively rather than rationally so, that the candidates are of the mindset to adhere to the requirements of those processes. We know that without due process, the service delivery machine will not work smoothly, and thus the services will not be properly manufactured. We need our clerical and administrative staff to be operators of the service mechanism. We need exactly the same of our technicians, no matter how technically elevated they may consider themselves to be. So in our technicians too, we must look for an appropriate mindset. The trouble is that when it comes to technicians, more often than not, we don't.

Instead, we tend to fall victim to the common practice of hiring chiefly on the basis of technical prowess. Take a look at the job ads in any trade magazine offering positions for computer support staff – they are looking for knowledge of this product, two years' history of that product and 'expertise in the other product would be desirable but not essential'. They may also promise to take the candidate through a technical training programme as one of the perquisites. We should not be surprised then, that by following the easy track of replacing departing technical skills, we may also replace the shortcomings that often accompany them.

The image of the computer technician has almost become a cliché. That cliché is almost exclusively negative. Typically male, he finds computers interesting, so takes a job that reflects that interest. His technical skills hamper if not preclude his communications skills. He may be able to repair a computer, but his interaction with its user will be perfunctory at best. He finds users tedious, and cannot understand their lack of interest in and ability with computers. He tries to educate the user into his own interest, but in doing so makes too much use of technical jargon and so alienates himself from the user still further. He finds it difficult to express himself clearly in the written word. He avoids bureaucracy. He has a narrow perspective of his role in the business. He believes the soft skills of customer service, personal organization and motivation to be largely a waste of time. He prefers to work alone, and only nods to teamwork if this means joining with other technicians to solve a technical problem, which he does for the fascination with the problem rather than the interaction with his peers. He prefers to deal in facts, which technical activity supplies in abundance, rather than in supposition. He likes quick fixes and is unlikely to commit much time to solving a problem. He is disorganized, especially in his use of time. He is unreliable, and likely to go absent from the office without announcing his likely whereabouts – demands to solve problems for distant users give him ample opportunity to indulge this. He spends much of his time increasing his technical knowledge, in the guise of solving technical problems. He distrusts authority, believing that they do not understand how busy he is and why this is the case. His rate of activity is high, but his productivity low. He is suspicious of measurement of any kind, especially when he is the one being measured. He dislikes working on the telephone helpdesk, as the work there is not technically satisfying and is too centred on personal relationships with users rather than technology. He also sees first-line helpdesk work as easier and less taxing, thus for junior staff, beyond which stage he feels his career has already progressed. He is young, single, a follower of mass-market sport and his weekends include bar-hopping and going to cinemas showing action blockbusters. His dress is casual, tended towards the way he dressed as a student – he is a college graduate. He has a computer network at home, along with an advanced audio-video system and a sizeable music collection. Politics and the arts bore him.

Of course, not all technical support staff are like that – but you may recognize some of your own people in the tirade of the above paragraph. The clues lie in such elements as 'disorganized', 'distrusts authority', 'avoids bureaucracy' and 'dislikes working on the helpdesk'. My argument is that we should hire people whose inclination is to match the processes, not the supported technology. And these are all traits that would steer the employee away from process. We have designed a machine to manufacture a range of services – and what we need are operators of that machine, no matter where in the process they may work. This must essentially go for everybody in the machine, managers, clerks, trainers, service representatives and technicians – but especially technicians. Why especially? Because they are the real face of IT services. Unlike the clerks and first liners, they will meet the end user face to face. The interactions they conduct will be fundamental to the relationship between the IT services department and the user base – better to say the company – as a whole.

6.4 Hierarchy

There has been a tendency in recent years to 'flatten' the organization, to remove middle management and have more staff reporting to one superior. The concept was touted in its early days as a boon to flexibility, as having focused work groups who could react quickly to business change. By and large, that was hyperbole. The real reason was that middle managers were expensive, so we could save costs by getting rid of a few of them.

The idea ran through IT services like a dose of salts. When I first started in user support services, management authority was crucial, particularly in the helpdesk. There, it was considered that power was needed, to ensure staff knew where they stood – high service levels were seen as a product of strong and nearby leadership.

I suppose these days, that all sounds a bit 'theory X'[1], but it suited the nature of much IT services work. Our job tends to be

---

[1] A term coined by Douglas McGregor as the antithesis to his 'theory Y'. It contends that workers are fundamentally lazy and will avoid responsibility where possible. To motivate them out of this, they require clear instruction and monitoring of their output. The 'Y' opposite claims that workers fundamentally take pride in their work and desire to do a good job, so will be motivated by their own professionalism. The truth in most cases lies somewhere between the two.

reactive, and a measurable incoming workload requires a measurable output, so close measurement will always be necessary here. Nevertheless, throughout the 1990s, middle management jobs in IT services began to be replaced by supervisory and 'team leader' positions. The power shifted ever more upstairs and further away from the actual point of service delivery. But while we saved money and reduced confusion by decreasing the number of political influencers, we eroded both the staff career path and the scope for delegation. Nowadays, the IT services manager is a lot busier than he was, because the erosion of hierarchy has burdened him with so much more direct responsibility.

The flattened organization has its place. This is where individuality must shine. It is where a workgroup must take on a project, different to the one that preceded it and no precursor of what the group will be working on next. Creative departments in the advertising, design and public relations industries occur as instances, as do football teams. IT services is not like that. This is a production line, with a set process. It has a common workload that can be anticipated into the foreseeable future. It must be run, as a machine must be run. Staff motivation, work progress measurement and skills development are crucial. It needs managing, and there are too many people for one person to shoulder all the management required. Even if the senior manager can take responsibility for the budget, the alliances with other departments and so on, he cannot possibly watch all the people all the time. There must be leaders below him, who themselves are accountable to him for the performance of their immediate charges.

A supervisor is not necessarily a leader. The job of a supervisor is to ensure the ticks go in the right boxes – staff turn up for work, an enquiry follows the right track through the system, i's are dotted and t's are crossed. But the supervisor is doing this to a format ordained by a superior, following a design created at a senior level. In other words the supervisor is following instructions, not making them. The same goes for a team leader, despite the use of the word 'leader'. Both supervisor and team leader are also likely to be doing the same job as the staff in their group. There is no real separation except this slim, conferred elevation and a (usually) slightly higher salary. Furthermore, the salary difference is often not enough to inspire other group members to aspire to the position, so progression comes to be seen as not worth the effort and jobs stagnate – along with, all too commonly, staff morale.

The supervisor/team leader has some form of accountability, but lacking the title of manager and being hierarchically so close to her group, has little to no real influence or control. Accountability without influence never works – it just creates stress.

As I argue later, for true staff motivation to be possible, the motivator must come to understand the psyche of those who are to be motivated. Without that, it is difficult to divine what might constitute an incentive in the eyes of the employee. With too many underlings, there simply is not time to comprehend the subtleties of their individual and collective psyche.

Given all these factors, on balance I will tend to look for some way of creating a hierarchy. A career ladder may be expensive in terms of salary differentials and the threat of too many chiefs and not enough Indians comes that bit closer. But that is better than artificially limiting motivation by stymieing the aspirations of talented staff. The costs may indeed be recouped by higher productivity resulting from closer management. It may also keep your desk clearer of day-to-day internal trivia, so you get to think more clearly about bigger pictures and the issues that really matter to managers.

6.5 Career path

It is a truism that most jobs in IT services are dead-end. Not everybody wants to move forward. Most people in society are satisfied with a job they can forget at home, one that pays enough for a respectable standard of living and quality of life. Not everybody wants a career. Those who have a career in mind tend to be talented self-starters and will find a way for their career to advance, no matter what. If their current employer provides no such opportunity to advance, then the opportunity will inevitably be sought with another employer. To the driven individual, the current job position is as much of a commodity as the employee is to the employer. We use them, they use us – that's business after all. If their aspiration comes to exceed the extent to which we can satisfy it, we may be happy to let them go – else their growing frustration might become disruptive. In Figure 6.1 opposite, I suggest some career paths throughout IT.

The chart allows for the organizational structure discussed in Chapter 5, where we looked at a model for distributing IT services across large organizations and geographical spreads, hence the 'local', 'regional', 'central' and 'corporate' levels. Indeed the fact that this hypothetical organization has all these levels suggests career options at least in terms of geographical seniority.

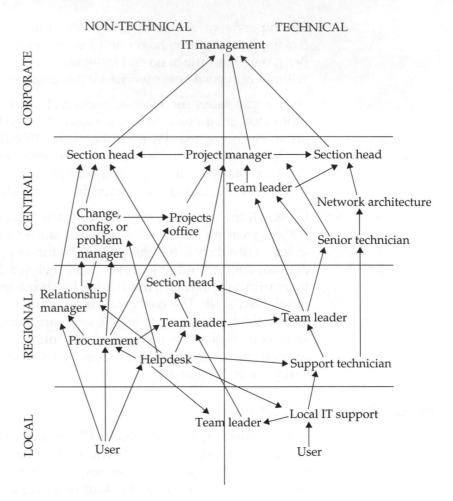

Figure 6.1
Career paths in IT services

I have divided the paths into 'non-technical' and 'technical' to suggest options for administrative and clerical as well as technicians. The administrative and clerical functions in IT services include procurement, task scheduling, statistical reporting and general duties. None of these are really IT-specific. As such, we could import a staffer from an administrative department of the userbase, and their ultimate departure could be to any other administrative position in any industry. But talent is talent and should be retained where possible and financially justifiable. But in a department where technical knowledge plays such a part, the administrator's career options may be limited.

This need not be the case. I mention the position of 'relationship manager', which in this model is a regional, non-technical post. It is a route up the ladder for administrative people or for first-line helpdesk staff, who might wish to progress their skills in dealing with customers rather than solving technical problems. If we take the analogy of the IT services department being a private company providing services to its market of computer users, then the relationship manager is the equivalent of the sales representative. This could be the official route for dealing with complaints, the one who sets client expectations, who takes part in the negotiation of service level agreements – the interface between IT services as provider and the user community or sections of it as consumer.

These career paths are only suggested – I am sure the reader can think of many more. The map merely serves as an illustration of the point that there is a benefit to be gained by publishing possible career paths. This can show the ambitious and talented, whom we may most wish to retain, that there are routes to advancement from any job and for any skillset in IT services.

6.6 Performance and motivation

Whose responsibility is it if the IT services staff fail? Ultimately, the manager must carry the can, but it is not quite as simple as that. People perform well if they are motivated – and with all that is written in management volumes and spouted from conference stages on this topic, it would be a fairly safe conclusion that the motivation of your staff is something for which you are solely answerable.

After all, if a team does not perform well, it is not the fault of the team – it is the manager who should be replaced. Anybody following a professional sport will see that repeated throughout the season. But we must not get scapegoating confused with improvement. Removing the manager may be a political act as much as it may be an altruistic one. Nor must we assume that performance and motivation amount to the same thing, because they do not.

Your team may fail to perform. That is indeed your fault. But if the team fails because it is not motivated, that is not. I'm going out on a limb here to say that the manager is not responsible for his staff's motivation. He is responsible for giving his staff the opportunity to be motivated, but that's all.

Our staff are adults, not children. Unlike children they have arrived in your employ because they made a choice to be there. The issue of choice is crucial here. Admittedly they could have been promoted sideways or reorganized in such a way as to come under your structure, and so were manipulated into the choice – but it was still theirs not yours. The reason they were moved in such a way is because the job they once did, or the group of which they were once a member, or the structure that once housed them no longer exists in the form it did. In effect, the job they used to perform has faded or been reorganized away. When they were restructured, it was something done unto them and therefore not of their own doing. We even use the phrase deliberately in the passive voice to highlight that restructuring is something done to us – 'We're being restructured.' But this still does not give them licence to abdicate the responsibility of their choice. There was another choice they could have made – they could have chosen not to follow the path they were given and thus leave the company.

But if they chose to stay, then the only remaining question is that of their professionalism. Adults choose their working environment and so must follow that with absolute professionalism. However, what can happen is that adults in the working environment can ignore that duty of professionalism and thus allow their motivation to slip. They come up with all kinds of reasons and rationalizations as to why they are not motivated. They may feel they are underpaid, or they resent the commute to work, or they think their boss is incompetent, or the job is boring, or the company is not worth working for and so on. But these are just excuses. There is no reason for low motivation at work. When people become victims of low motivation, they are choosing to be unprofessional, which is the act of a resentful child, not that of a spiritually competent adult. They are, in effect, behaving as though they were still at school, resenting the institution in which they feel they have been imprisoned. It is perhaps worthwhile to look at school life to see the difference.

We cannot expect professionalism from children. We build schools for them, herd them into the classroom system and then teach things at them. We do it to them – they are the victims of the system in which we place them – they don't have any say in the matter. So when children rebel, we should not be surprised. In fact, we need them to rebel – the very process of procreation is nature rebelling against itself. If human life were perfect, we would not need to replace the population every seventy years in order to bring in fresh ideas and show the adults that there may be better ways of doing things in the future. In a perfect world, we would have learned everything already, so we would not need to reproduce, and we would all be immortal. Children must rebel – it is their evolutionary duty. They are necessarily irresponsible. They don't owe the world anything. We even design our legal systems to allow them to be irresponsible, to be free to evade the consequences of their choices and actions. They act from their instincts and look for ways of having fun or communicating and playing with their friends, rather than being mere victims of the school system.

When they do this very necessary act, however, we will resent their non-acceptance of our victimization of them. We may deem them as not applying themselves (ever seen that on a kid's school report?). Yet all they are doing is refusing to succumb to our ministrations. Their instincts may tell them what few adults would be prepared to admit, that the bulk of the education system has two purposes, neither of which benefit the kids. One purpose is to give the adults somewhere to dump the kids so that we can get on with going to work and building the economy. The other is to indoctrinate them into the ethos we believe in so that when they take over the world, they'll run it the way we did so our future will be secure and unchallenging. But that's why they rebel – because the way we run things isn't perfect, and they believe they can do it better. We should be thankful for that evolutionary instinct – without it, there would be no progress.

In their mid-teens, we declare the children ready for the world. Suddenly, one day in a September, the child has to behave like an adult. He must make choices and take the consequences of those. Yesterday he was a child. Today he is an adult. He looks at the French, Geography and English Lit., with which we have filled his head, and perhaps does not realize that none of that has the slightest relevance to the huge question of personal responsibility. But if he does not deal with that issue, he is in effect, still a child. And it is with this mental state that he enters the world of work. We should not be surprised then if some of our employees behave as though they were still at school, seeing the workplace, as they did their place of education, as something to which they are victim. Work looks like something done unto them and they may fail to comprehend it as a personal responsibility that as adults, they have undertaken.

Our workers have to understand what I call the 'contract of professionalism'. This is not the piece of paper the new employee signs, it is the psychological truth of the undertaking she makes in accepting a job offer. If we look at the process of starting a new job, we will see a candidate behave in such a way as to convince the potential employer that she is the right person for the job, can get along well with anybody, is hard-working and conscientious, has appropriate skills and is willing to improve on them, is flexible and committed. She will put this across with deft and smiling enthusiasm in her curriculum vitae and then again at the interview. We'll be convinced and we'll give her the job.

The contract of professionalism says that she needs the job because she requires money to live and to pursue her own priorities. Everybody has the right to do this. However, in exchange for that money, she must accept that the entity providing it also has priorities – and that she must subjugate some of her own to those of the company. While she is in our employ, she must put our goals before at least some of her own. She accepts this. She knows it means that to us, she will be an economic resource, and that as a commercial organization we will treat her as such while simultaneously and dutifully catering for her humanity – but first of all, she is an employee, a corporate asset.

Come the Monday morning she starts the job, she'll be fired with enthusiasm and eager to impress. She will marshal all her professionalism and aim it at her function with precision and application. She will show promise. She has understood the contract of professionalism and will conduct herself and her job within its auspices.

Over time, things change. She gets so good at the job that it begins to bore her or fail to challenge her sufficiently. She begins to find the limitations in both her work and the company. Her growth curve starts to flatten. The company makes some changes in the way it does things and this may mean life was not so sweet as it was that Monday morning long ago. And so her enthusiasm begins to wane and her motivation takes a dip. It happens to the best of us.

But it has absolutely no right to. We have no right whatsoever to decrease our professionalism one jot below the level it was on the Monday morning we first took up this job. We made a choice. We promised our commitment. We made a contract of professionalism with our employer. So what if things have changed, or if the job is no longer as exciting or secure as it was? What reason is that to decrease our motivation and along with it our professionalism? *We made a contract.*

The adult makes choices and once made, lives with them. In the workplace, 'living with them' means that the employee's professionalism must be the same from the day he starts the job, to the day he leaves it. The contract of professionalism meant that he accepted some of the company's priorities as being more important than his own and nevertheless would be fully motivated and committed to being the best he could be at all times. To do otherwise is churlish or even childish. Look at the soap opera actor who knows from his script that he will be bumped off in the next scene. He is a professional – he will determine to make this the best soap opera demise ever, even though he is acting his way into unemployment. He will not go onto the set and refuse to act, as his motivation is decreased because he is leaving the show. He will not allow this reality to affect his performance *because he is a professional*.

The problem of low motivation in some IT services groups is exacerbated by the nature of the work as a career option. Speaking frankly, IT services is pretty much a non-vocational job. One does not go to university to learn how to be a procurement clerk or a computer installer. Unlike engineering, law, the priesthood, town planning, music and so on, the work of IT services is generalist, rather than the specific expression of an innate talent. It is the kind of work our employees can and do drift into rather than choose out of a sense of mission or purpose. By and large, most IT services employees are not the type to have been driven from an early age with a burning desire to revolutionize the world of helpdesk technicianship. They are not impassioned visionaries who take the job of computer procurement because their genius for it left them with no other choice. They are people, who for example liked playing with computers when they were younger, so when they found they could do it for a living, it was an easy route. There are exceptions of course – there always are – but even if these exceptions do end up on the helpdesk, they won't be there long. For the rest, the majority, motivation is an emotion more relevant to some other facet of their lives rather than the nine-to-five.

So this is what managers are faced with when it comes to getting the best out of their staff. Our people are likely to be of mediocre motivation, and may well labour under some miscomprehension of the true meaning of personal responsibility. Consequently, they have a flawed application of that truth to professionalism. The result is that the professionalism itself may be fragile. And while the manager may be held responsible for their individual and collective performance, he cannot be accountable for their professionalism and motivation for these are choices that only his staff can make. We can attempt to 'motivate' them as much as we like. But if they choose not to accept that, then all we have done is led the horse to water. We cannot make it drink.

So if you have agreed with my argument on that topic, by now you may be wondering what is the point in trying? There is every point, because their performance is so important. The question is how we manage that performance, and cause our charges to desire to keep their performance consistently high. The way to do that is to get them to focus on their future, rather than on their unsatisfactory present or on the ways their relationship with the company has given them what they feel to be cause for disappointment in the past.

The first thing to do is to make it clear, ideally by example of our own actions, that we understand and live by the contract of professionalism. It may also be appropriate to explain to some of our workers what that contract means, namely that the only acceptable level of enthusiasm and professionalism is the one they demonstrated on their first day because of the promise they made during their job interview.

The reason the horse did not drink the water is that it saw no benefit to itself in doing so. The secret to motivation is this issue of benefit. Our job as a motivator is to place before our staff the opportunity to be motivated. They must see a benefit to themselves of being motivated. Many companies think they can do this with remuneration or job benefits, but I see this as too material and shallow. In any case, once the material benefits have been handed out, then this increases people's comfort levels and in some way this works contrary to real motivation – for why change anything if everything is already hunky-dory?

To motivate our people, we need to understand them as closely as possible to realize what each of them would see as a real benefit to them. That benefit must not exist now. It must remain as a future prospect, only attainable by certain behaviours. The behaviours themselves will of course be the high levels of performance we need our people to produce. This will mean that they have to change their behaviour in order to gain the benefit. If they don't want the benefit, then we have misunderstood what drives them. If the benefit they want is not available from this workplace, then perhaps they should be working where they are more likely to attain it.

Motivation is a form of negotiation – 'if you do *this*, then you will receive *that*', and it must produce a change. If it does not produce a change, then it is not motivation – it is merely morale.

This explains why one of the most powerful forms of staff motivation is leadership. People follow a leader because it is clear that he knows where he is going, and he is prepared to take others with him – and wherever it is, it is bound to be better for the followers than here. So as managers, we must always have a vision of how things in this IT services department will have improved in a given amount of time, provided that the staff behave in a certain way. And that improvement must be one that the individual members of staff see as a benefit to them, and they can also clearly see the link between the necessary behaviours and the acquisition of that benefit.

6.7 Managing skillsets

In my previous book, *How to Manage the IT Helpdesk*, I offer an idea for a matrix to measure the gap between skills needed and skills acquired. There is more about the use of the technique in that book, but it is worth revisiting it here. Whereas in that book, I use what I call there the 'knowledge matrix' to manage technical skillsets, in principle, it could also be applied to any area of knowledge or ability in any technical or administrative function.

Consider any skill, ability or topic of knowledge as though it would have five levels of attainment from ignorance through to absolute expertise. My five preferred levels are:

1. Don't know (novice)
2. Can field, but not resolve issues in this area of knowledge/ ability (beginner)
3. Can resolve most issues in this area (competent)
4. Understand the area well enough to train others in it (trainer)
5. Understand the area well enough to invent new techniques or methods (designer, leader)

These could then constitute the scores a person could attain as a measurement of their proficiency in the area. We have the beginnings of a table, with one axis representing the areas of competence and the other our staff members. In the cells where these axes meet, we have a number between one and five for each skill, for each individual.

Such a matrix could be used to measure any skill. For technical expertise, the areas would probably be little more than a list of products. For non-technical ones, for example customer-facing or numeracy performance, the areas would perhaps be levels of behaviour or performance.

I suggest it would be a job for the line managers or team leaders of each section of IT services to manage the skillsets of their charges. Using such a matrix as this, they would in particular be looking for gaps in the matrix where necessary skillsets are under-represented. In my view, skills redundancy is always a desirable goal – having a useful level of competence in each skillset represented by at least two members of staff. This means there is no single point of failure and all critical facets of service provision can always be covered in the event of typical staff absences. There is not just one person who knows how the equipment procurement database works – there are always at least two, so part of a critical service does not grind to a halt just because someone goes on vacation.

6.8 How many people?

The issue of skills redundancy becomes particularly important when considering how many people we need. Because we have built this IT services department from a quasi-greenfield position, this is relatively straightforward. Prior to each of the processes being defined, we drew up a list of services, which we realized we needed having done a market analysis of likely demand.

The likely demand dictates the amount of work, in all services, but that alone is incomplete. We also need to know how much activity each unit of work is likely to generate. This ultimately leads to the unfashionable issue of time and motion. How long does it take to solve the average computer problem, process the average procurement request, write the average training course, book the average videoconference or re-route the average telephone hunt-group? The staff may not like it, but without measurement of actual reality, we cannot manage it. There will always be a need for absolute science in the running of a production line, even though the people may not like having their productivity measured.

But neither will that be the whole story. In all corporations, there is a consumption of man-hours due to the fact that we work for a corporation. Incidentals erode time. Before we can know exactly how many man-hours (and hence how much headcount) we will need to commit to the production of any service, we need to know how much of our staff's working day is actually dedicated to real production and how much is wasted by unfortunately necessary trivia and consequential activity. As an example, there is scuttlebutt going around at the moment that a large company in the UK has decided to divest itself of the delights of universal electronic mail – the time saved as a result is allegedly equivalent to three hours per head per day. Factor in a few meetings that go on a little too long and the odd unscheduled and unplanned interruption, and this means that resource is being consumed that for the sake of headcount planning must be accounted for.

In recent years, in order to maintain competitiveness and decrease financial liabilities, companies have been reducing headcount. Of course productivity has increased, but to my mind, so has vulnerability. It has in some cases got to ridiculous levels. The train that does not run because no driver is available would have made more money in that day than a train driver's salary for a year. The hospital treatment waiting queue that lengthens for want of a doctor, costs the government more in sick pay and lost tax revenue due to the sick not being available for work than it would have cost to train and employ another doctor.

So it is in IT services. We myopically reduce our headcount because not hiring people is apparently cheaper than hiring them – at least on paper and only so far as the IT service budget goes. But out there in the company, several users are suffering reduced productivity because of the consequent inadequacy of service levels, and that saving in IT results in a much larger cost to the company in lost productivity and therefore revenue that would have been made if those users had not been thus impeded. We need to get some real perspective on the cost of service provision. We must also consider the cost of service unavailability.

I hereby state my heresy. We should always hire more people than we need, even if that means paying for staff to be idle. When the department is not under pressure, that spare resource or 'idleness' can be converted into a higher quality service on average. When urgent and therefore financially risky work needs to be done, the company is grateful that the resource is there so that the risk is minimized. IT services is like a fire station – we can afford to have people playing pool and drinking coffee, because if and when the flag goes up, they will save a lot more money than would have been lost if they had not been available.

The matrix of skills outlined above may suggest where some of this 'idle' resource may be and what it should be doing for a living – covering for potential absences. Another is in the area of where skillsets do not mix and thus people cannot double up on jobs they do and work responsibilities they have.

6.9 Mixing responsibilities

Most employees come in units of one – a single person does a single job. With the exception of part-timers, staff do not usually come in fractions of heads. You can't hire half a person – well you can, but only for part of the day – which does not help if your workload peaks do not happen to match the hours that part-timers are employed for. One way round this is to mix responsibilities. Those jobs that require less than one head per day are shared out among the team, or one full head is given a multiple of part-head responsibilities to keep a head fully occupied. It is an efficient use of resource. As we do this, we may have to be careful that the mix of responsibilities taken by any one individual does not demand too wide a scope of skills or too big a gap between interesting and boring bits of the job, or overall work output quality may suffer.

We must keep a track of these mixed responsibilities so that we can see precisely how much headcount resource each of them consumes. One of the ways to do this is with a 'resource allocation' matrix of staff commitment to service production. These various responsibilities are actually bits of service production and can be notated as such. A worker spent this much time producing service X, this much working on Y and so on. On one axis of our matrix we have the staff members. On the other, the various services. Then using a timesheet, we ask each member of staff to register the approximate amount of their time they committed in the production of each service over a given period of time, say a week. When all these data are collected, the completed matrices will aggregate for us exactly how much resource is committed to the production of each service. These will not be full heads, but also fractions. We may have four people on the helpdesk, but if one of them spent half her time over the measured period on a side-project or in a training seminar, then we actually only had three and a half. The resource allocation matrix tells us much more about the work done than can the traditional measurements out of the call management system and other tools. As such we can know the precise amount of risk to any service of even the smallest drop in resource availability.

6.10 The extended day

As companies offer services in multiple time zones, as corporate employees increase their working hours, the call for extended hours service is getting louder. The phrase 'twenty-four-seven' has entered the English language. Often, but not always, there is a genuine need for round-the-clock working. However, I believe we should be careful that we do not provide the service just because it is requested, but for more commercial reasons. This means measuring the impact – again in terms of lost user productivity – of IT services' working day being too short. The equation is simple – if the user having need of IT services outside the normal working day would have produced more had IT services staff been available, then it makes financial sense to put the staff in place.

As to what the user produces, this too is straightforward – we divide the annual revenue of the corporation by the total number of hours worked by all employees in a year. That gives the average financial productivity per hour per employee. We then run a pilot scheme to see how many enquiries are likely to come in outside normal working hours and whether those enquiries imply that the user is losing productivity. Then we compare the cost of the lost productivity in hours with the cost of making IT services staff available at new times of the day. On a purely commercial basis, the lowest cost wins.

On the other hand, there may be political reasons for extending the working day even though these reasons may be commercially unviable. But that is a separate issue. The corporation ordained the original need for IT services. They will ultimately pay for any extension to that service. It is the corporation's prerogative to spend more on IT services than it actually needs to. So if they want an out-of-hours service, and they are willing to pay for it, so be it.

It is always useful to have a map of time over demand. In my experience, IT services is more heavily used at the beginning of the week and the beginning of the day than at the end. There will typically be a peak of demand around mid morning, a lull around lunchtime and another, smaller and narrower peak around mid afternoon. Of course if we have the same number of staff dedicated to all services at all times of the day, there will be a mismatch. The users may well see this 'mismatch' rather more negatively – the service is bad in the morning when it is most crucially necessary, and fine in the afternoon when it matters less.

One answer is part-time working – have part-time staff work mornings only. Unfortunately, the type of work in demand often requires skilled technicians, who demographically are less likely to be in the part-time employment market, which tends to contain mostly non-technically skilled workers. Unfortunately these natural peaks and troughs of demand tend towards technical rather than non-technical issues – administrative demand usually has a lower urgency than technical problems. So the market tends to force us to hire technical people for a full working day, knowing that they will be less occupied in the afternoon, which can look like a waste.

So another, ultimately more tenable answer is to hire technical staff who are flexible about the type of work they will do. We need more numerous and more technically skilled people on the telephone in the morning, both to deal with the peak of enquiries and to achieve more first-time fixes so the users go back to productivity. Then in the afternoon, or perhaps in the later hours of the extended day, when the telephone lines are quieter, the technicians may revert to other tasks of diagnosing complex problems, performing installations or conducting projects. I believe this form of staff flexibility, particularly among technicians, is crucial to the successful organization of the extended working day.

6.11 Managing small-scale projects

On the question of small-scale projects, often conducted as an ancillary activity by technicians but also in several sectors of IT services, I believe there are issues too over the management of this. It is still the case that in many IT services departments, projects are conducted on a 'by the way' basis, in between other work, 'when you have time'. My view is that these too constitute the provision of a service. As such, they should be subject to the same considerations of financial viability and resource consumption as we would make with any other service. As such, they should be present on the services axis of the resource allocation matrix described above.

These tend not to be projects on the same scale as might be conducted in the development department. They are likely to be short and the responsibility of an individual rather than subject to the integrated and co-dependent activities of, and consequent critical paths through, the work of a team.

Technicians like doing projects. Building something new and increasing knowledge along the way are much more interesting than solving repeated technical problems. Projects have their own motivation built into them. This can mean that if activity in these areas is not properly managed, the conductor can mistakenly spend a disproportionate amount of time on his project to the detriment of other, perhaps more urgent work.

Where the manager does not know how much resource is being consumed by project work, he must by extraction be unaware of how much resource he has to commit to routine service output. Similarly, if there is no predicted completion date of a project or project stage, neither can he know when the resource the project is consuming will revert to general availability. So while small-scale projects usually do not need the sophistication of formal planning and detail of Gantt charts, they nevertheless need some form of management so as to predict completion and account for resource consumption.

To deal with this, I advocate a task-level description of all projects, no matter how small, at the outset. To each project, an owner. The project breaks down into tasks, with some estimate of the work and time effort to complete each task, and a date when that task will be tackled. The aggregate of these tasks and dates produces the target completion date for the project as a whole. Then for each working day, the manager knows which of his staff will be available, for how much time, to complete other, non-project work. Resource planning thus becomes a more complete picture.

7.1 Who is the IT services client?

The most straightforward way to define who are the clients of IT services is just to include 'anybody in the userbase'. In other words, this means anybody who is a direct and obvious consumer of our products and services as we have declared them. But like the obvious often turns out to be, this is too simplistic on a number of levels.

First, we cannot assume that those who demand and pay for our services will necessarily use them. Take for example the board of directors – clearly they will expect IT services to deliver against contract or expectation, but are they actually users? Maybe – but maybe too they get their secretaries to deal with anything that would involve the practical use of a keyboard or a mouse. So their views of the quality of user support services are at best second-hand and based on a premise of real, operational use of computers, to which the director is in fact unaccustomed. The director, or indeed anybody else who needs the output of a computer but not the actual use of one, is a user by proxy. Yet that does not stop such a (usually powerful) individual forming an opinion about the efficacy of IT services.

The implications of 'customerhood'

This brings us to the first complication of who our client actually is. Those paying for the services (the clients) may not actually be the ones using them (the customers). Even further, our customers may not actually be consuming something as we intended them to – but that does not prevent them from judging how well they are being served. We cannot simply assume that the definition of a customer is somebody who consumes our offerings as we have defined them, in the way that we expect them to be consumed.

People can become customers of IT services in the most imaginative and mind-boggling ways. To illustrate – imagine for a moment that there is a group of people somewhere in the corporation who have decided among themselves that the longevity of the corporation stems from the fact that most of the employees have accepted the corporate value system, and as long as this cultural situation maintains, so shall the corporation prevail. Never mind for now if their thinking has merit – as far as they are concerned, it does. And it is on the basis of that thinking by which they will measure IT services. They will observe our behaviour and judge it to be evidential of the level of our compliance with the corporate value system. We probably don't even know that we are being judged in this way, so we certainly cannot do anything about it. Nowhere in our service level statement does it say that we will adhere stringently to corporate culture. There is no formal measurement of this. Yet somewhere, we are judged on it.

So 'corporate cultural adherence' now comes to be expected as one of the things IT services produces and a judgement is made on whether we do it sufficiently well regardless of the fact that it is not one of our published strivings. But the judgement of the customer is the final declaration of success or failure. This brings me to my favoured definition of a customer, who is in my view, **'anybody who consumes anything he perceives us to have produced – whether or not he's right and whether or not we intended to produce it'**.

The implications for this are huge – not least in how we cause our success to be judged. We cannot assume that just because we meet our service level and productivity targets that our customers will accept us as entirely successful – for how they measure us comes from their imagination as often as it does from the service level contract.

Who consumes what

The variety of the take-up of our various offerings adds another dimension of complexity to defining just who exactly is the IT services client. We have designed a range of products that are to be offered to a market. Just as if we were manufacturing a range of shoes or music recorded onto CD or in fact anything, we cannot assume that all our clients will need all our products to the same service level and delivered the same way. In order to ensure that our customers extract the maximum benefit out of our services, we must assure both them and ourselves that we are delivering the right product set in the most appropriate fashion.

141

So just as it was important to identify our services so that we could thereafter define the processes and skills necessary to produce them, we must also define our client base as closely as possible so that our offerings can be delivered as productively as possible. This may sound more like marketing than IT – and that's because it is. We are actively sectoring the market so that we can design products and services from which those consumer sectors will see themselves as having derived most benefit (otherwise known as 'give 'em what they want').

Looking at the users on a broader scale, some patterns may emerge. The company is divided into departments, each with a different business mission or responsibility for a given part of the corporate mission. These structural differences will imply use of different systems and applications. The varying levels of business criticality of these departments will suggest different service levels.

One of my preferred ways of providing an overview of this complexity is to use a table. Our various services form one axis. Identified groups of users, however we define them ('finance', 'the second floor', 'the Belgian office', 'the grade fours'), form the other. In the cells where points on the axes meet is a service level. For example: the human resources, factory and facilities users have all signed up for out-of-hours service after 6 p.m. and before 8 a.m. – but facilities gets an email address (level 1), human resources gets a mobile number to call (level 2) but the factory gets a technician onsite within twenty minutes even at 3 a.m. (level 5). So perhaps we have two other levels, namely three and four, but nobody has taken us up on those yet.

7.2 Corporate responsibility

There is another reason for this close definition, and that stems from our role as a horizontal corporate support service. We look after anybody who may use any IT provision – which in most modern companies, means everybody. This implies that we have a corporate responsibility. The meaning of that responsibility is a function of the fact that for IT to be effective, it must be used effectively. Consequently, we cannot divorce the technology from its usage. If the users are unable to properly exploit the computer systems, then the systems have failed.

Such a failure could be born of design faults, compatibility with business processes or ergonomic shortcomings. To rectify these, we would surely look to the IT architects or business systems analysts who created the systems, or to IT development who cut the code and implemented the software. The question is whether this is where IT's responsibility for systems use ends, for where the failure lies ostensibly outside IT – say in the competence of the user – then that must surely be an issue for the user's line management to resolve. When the problem falls outside IT jurisdiction in this way, surely IT should not be held accountable.

7.3 User competence

I contend that this is an abdication on the part of the IT department. For us to declare that user competence is a business rather than an IT issue opens a dangerous door. Taken to extremes, it would give us license to produce any old rubbish in terms of hardware, software, systems and services and blame its failure on the users. The effectiveness of any communication can only be judged on how that communication is received, not how it is delivered. So it is with IT services. The effectiveness of what we offer to our users can only be judged on how usable they find it. If the users cannot make full use of the products we have given them, then the fault is ours for designing it inappropriately, not theirs for not understanding it. To blame it on the users is akin to the Victorian view of the comprehensibility of the English language, which was often summed up as 'all foreigners can understand English if one shouts'. It is an inescapable necessity of our IT delivery that we must take usability into account, even to the extent of the IT department playing an active role in managing user competence.

In this case, IT services must think the same way as IT development. If the users cannot make the best use of our services because the fit of provision to need is not correct, then we must change the provision. And to do that, we have to know as much about our clientele as possible. The level of competence of individual users is just one element of that. Computing knowledge in users' heads is a corporate IT asset.

7.4 The user as a corporate asset

The level of competence in the use of a computer is in my view a part of the computer system. Without that knowledge, ability, experience etc. among the users, the computers would be at best the subject of numerous technical enquiries and at worst an under-utilized asset from which, therefore, insufficient return on investment was being extracted. The users' level of knowledge has a direct impact on their productivity. The more skilled they are with the computer, the more they can exploit it as a tool rather than serve it as a corporate control imposition. The more confidence they have with the applications, the freer are they to conceive of new ways of using the systems, and with more innovation may come more competitive edge in the corporation's chosen market, or new ways of saving costs by automating.

We happily acknowledge on a broad scale that employees constitute a corporate asset. We must also therefore acknowledge that at the more detailed level of IT services, user computing competence is an IT services asset. Of course it reduces the cost of providing helpdesk services – but more deeply, it allows the users to join in the systems design and selection process, which means the systems will ultimately be more meaningful in terms of the work of the corporation.

We in IT services can play our part in managing that asset. We have, as one of our tools, a database of the IT assets in the company. Typically stored in that catalogue will be the type and location of hardware and software products we have brought in from vendors. But we have also acquired user competence, in the shape of experienced employees joining the company and training courses attended by the less experienced.

The users are assets in terms of their knowledge. We can record this, at least in terms of completed training, against a record of each user. At its most simple level, such a record could tell us about the effectiveness of the training itself, because somebody having attended training on a topic should not, in theory, be asking for technical assistance on that topic thereafter. We could use this to help select training vendors or advise them on topics we need covered in courses.

But it offers us bigger pictures too. From it, we can map training attendance against use of support services, to plot whether increasing user training does actually reduce IT costs. We could measure whether it is indeed cheaper in terms of user productivity to have a less knowledgeable workforce in favour of a highly skilled and extremely effective helpdesk. There is the bare comparison of costs of training against costs of helpdesk – but when user productivity comes into the equation, the picture becomes more highly resolved. The decision would look something like this:

- Training costs up, helpdesk costs down – but the users are less productive because they spend their time solving their own computer problems instead of producing for the company.

- Training costs down, helpdesk costs up – but because the help-desk is so efficient, most enquiries are answered immediately, so the user is straight back to full productivity that much more quickly.

7.5 The question of affordability

Your IT services budget is not limitless and thus demand cannot be unlimited. But as we saw in Chapter 6, there will be a tendency among users to abuse the provision of what appears to be a 'free' service simply because it is free. One way to curb this abuse would of course be to ensure that all users individually understand the cost of their use of a service. This is impractical. In any case we would not want a user to decline the offer of IT service just because it has an associated cost, as not using the service might damage their productivity and thus the company's profitability. What is needed is an ultimate point of reference for the level of service we may offer. If a user then expects a higher level of service, then it would be to that point that he would refer, to see of it could be made available.

This is the question of affordability of IT services. We do not declare our budget in isolation. It is the result of a careful calculation, starting back in Chapter 2, where we identified the services we would provide based on a market study of need. But despite the cold hard science of that process, we must allow for the possibility that we made a mistake, that we didn't think of everything, that we perhaps did not fully understand the true needs of a given group of users. Nevertheless, once we knew what the services were going to be, we then approached the corporation's decision-makers with a bid for budget to acquire the resources necessary to manufacture those services. The budget was declared, we hired the staff and away we went following the strict provisions of our service delivery plan. Hopefully, we would have built in some flexibility, but we're not omniscient and maybe we missed something.

Those things that we missed will come to light sooner or later. They may appear in the form of a user complaining that our service level is not high enough, our response too slow, our menu of equipment provision too rigid and so on. New technologies will emerge, of which the users may wish to take immediate advantage, even though that may push our potential expenditure outside existing constraints. External competition may drive the users to look for new ways of exploiting existing IT and services in attempts to close competitive gaps – and as these happen outside the company, IT services may not even be aware of their occurrence.

I've used the word 'complaining' deliberately. These 'complaints' may be just the user being irrational, having an expectation of a service level or equipment provision beyond what the company can reasonably afford to offer. In other words, just somebody whinging and trying to blame IT for his negativity.

In fact these may be legitimate entreaties to IT services, even though they may emerge as criticisms of our offerings. But when they come, we should not react to them negatively. Even on those occasions where the criticisms are emotionally rather than scientifically expressed, these may still be pertinent indications of how IT services need to be changed, and it should rarely be our reaction to refuse to address the issue just because it goes outside the current limitations of affordability. What we need is a mechanism by which both the users and ourselves can challenge not just the definitions of our provision, but also the question of affordability itself. Which means in turn, that the final point of arbitration regarding levels and quality of IT services should not be the department that offers them, i.e. *us* – but the authority from whom we extracted the budget, i.e. the board of directors.

For this to work of course, we have to presuppose that the IT services department is already doing the best it possibly could with the resources and financing currently at its disposal. If it is not, the point is moot – the service is not good enough, it is wasting money, so do better and make better use of what you have. But if all service level targets are being met, if all IT services staff are working at capacity, if all vendor contracts are as favourable as possible, if all pigs have closed their departure gates and are heading for the taxiway, then any incoming request for further improvement needs somewhere to go where it can be dealt with seriously.

In fact, we already have a way of dealing with this – it is the 'non-standard change' process we looked at in Chapter 4. The only difference is that what we are proposing to change is not one of the IT department's products, it is the IT department itself. IT is great at what it does, but due to changing business circumstances, it needs to be better still. What we have to address is whether to invest more money in it, in other words to change the way the corporation thinks about the affordability of IT. In terms of the non-standard change process, all we are doing is replacing the IT steering committee as the ultimate authority with the company boardroom. We still have to go through the same feasibility exercises of course, but the report goes to a different group, that's all. And the question of affordability can be addressed clearly, because of those 'changing business circumstances' – there is more money to be made out there, or competition has dictated that we need to increase the priority we place on the defence of our business viability. And of course these are board decisions.

Despite the fact that affordability needs consideration at such high levels, the fact that it is in place means that we can use that authority at the more detailed level of day-to-day service delivery. Back in the annals of time, we addressed affordability as part of our service identification and design process. That brought us service level targets, which we routinely meet, so we have by that default justified our expenditure. A complaint from a user therefore has no real place. If he feels the service is not good enough, then that is a matter of opinion rather than fact. There is no point in bringing that issue up with a member of IT services staff – say a lowly helpdesk person – unless his conviction is great enough that he would be prepared to put his complaint in the form of a proposal to go through the non-standard change process. Therefore, under the auspices of how we built the affordability issue into our service design, in fact his complaint is not with IT, but with the board for confining the level of service IT was able to offer. We can change – but only if the user is ready to go through the process of scientifically reassessing the question of how much the company can afford to spend on IT and associated services.

So now, when a complaint arrives, we must assess its true nature. If it is a pure indication that IT services has breached its existing contractual commitments, then it is a *service management* issue, internal to IT services. If on the other hand it can be seen as a legitimate request to improve an already successful IT services provision, then it is an *affordability* issue, and should go through the non-standard change process with the boardroom as the ultimate deciding authority.

7.6 The decline of customer service

Back in the late 1980s and early 1990s, a new watchword emerged in IT user support. The key to our relationships with our users was to be 'customer service'. This was not just an IT movement, it had come from business as a whole. Companies were differentiating themselves from one another on the basis of service. The concept spawned television programmes, magazines, books and countless conferences. Some companies were remarketed on the basis that with better service, market share could be stolen from established players and competitors. Some made such a great job of this transformation that they are still around today and their reputation for service maintains (stand up and be counted, Virgin Atlantic, Richer Sounds and Tesco Supermarkets – some of my favourite brands). The 1990s were the age of service, and how we hoped it would last.

Customer service was about adding value to the offering, and doing so without adding too much cost, so the customer would see this as getting more for his money. To achieve this, the point of focus would have to be the actual service staff themselves. 'Customer service' was a matter of service staff behaviour, such that the encounter between customer and provider would be one that left the customer smiling, having made not just a successful, but also humanly pleasurable transaction. Front-line staff were taught to smile while they were on the telephone. They were selected for their charming personalities. We spoke at length about 'employee empowerment', by which we would give our customer-facing people a broader jurisdiction in their actions when dealing with our customers. We taught them negotiating skills and how to handle complaints. We're still doing it now, and that's good in itself.

While we were so keen to improve our service, we started to do ever more for the customer in order to improve his satisfaction with our provision. This makes business sense. The more he enjoys our interaction with him, the more likely he will be to return. When you are building market share, the repeat business generated by a loyal customer base is a very powerful asset. It provides a guaranteed income, or in the case of IT services, assured and appreciated relevance and usefulness. It bodes well for the future and takes some of the desperation out of our job, because we can relax into our future rather than worry about it. So it reduces stress, and our success builds the self-esteem of our staff. This gives us more confidence to do even more for the customer.

But sooner or later, the more we do, the more we increase our cost base. Slowly, our price begins to rise compared with the competition, and our customers realize that they are paying for us to be nice to them. They start to make decisions about the relative priorities of price and service. Those who can afford it will go with 'service' – others will start to wonder if they really need all this service, or whether what they actually need is to get the same product without the added value and thus save money.

And as our customers begin actively to take these decisions, the market begins to polarize, between those who want the product plus and will pay more for the service and those who want the product only and pay less for it.

This polarization happened in the commercial sector as a whole (note the rise of Ryanair and easyJet and any number of retail websites). It is happening in IT services also. I could call the helpdesk to discuss my problem, but if I do I'll have to carry the additional cost to my time of waiting in the call queue, describing the problem to a first-line operative, wait until somebody comes round to fix it and then have to describe the problem again. Or I could get on the corporate Intranet or the Internet and look up the answer. It may or may not be quicker, but at least I'd be doing something rather than sitting and waiting.

The world has changed since the service age. Markets have polarized. Users have become more sophisticated. They are also busier, which means they need quick resolution of their issues – but their increased 'busy-ness' means they also have narrower attention spans and less time to devote to understanding what it is we offer. So they will take the shortest route to the solution rather than take the convoluted paths of fill-in-a-form, call-the-helpdesk, write-down-this-job-number that we have given them. Customer service is not the panacea it once was. It's no longer the obvious way of producing customer satisfaction, because that added value's consequential added cost has become a matter of choice rather than default for our users.

Depending on your point of view, the change either threatens the emphasis on customer service, or adds a new and even tighter string to our business bow. The new concept is 'productization'. At its most strategic level, it has allowed us to 'unbundle' the purely 'customer service' element from our service offerings, and offer only that as an additional choice. At a tactical level, it has allowed us to take greater control over both the customer relationship and our costs of service production.

Once, the IT services department (or its fragmented forerunners) would make itself available to do anything the user wanted, and it would receive the request with fawning respect, diligence and enthusiasm in the name of customer service. This often resulted in haphazard delivery and unreasonable customer expectations along with some pretty hectic and stressful IT services offices. Now, we have 'productized' our services. We're not just simply available – we market/sell a range of distinct and designed services, which the users can choose to take (or not). They know exactly what they're getting – we know exactly what we're making. They can go for high-cost, added value or low-cost, 'no frills'.

Because we've productized our work, we can measure the take-up of each of these services, which makes planning (and therefore staffing, skill management and workload planning) so much easier.

Having so many products suggests that the manufacture of our services will be extremely complicated. But that's OK too, because we've taken a leaf out of the book written by the chef at our local Indian restaurant. Despite the fact that we have fifty dishes on the menu (fifty services in the service catalogue), we have only three flavours of sauces which we keep hot on the stove at all times. By adding different meats and vegetables and perhaps an extra dash of chilli powder or garam masala on the plate just before serving, we can have a very simple manufacturing process and still turn out what the diners (users) see as a huge variety of dishes (services).

In Chapter 4, we looked at the various procedures of the IT services department and saw how they can be distilled down into very few processes. Maybe your three basic sauces are 'user support', 'change management' and 'moves'. But from 'user support' we get the services of self-help, helpdesk, problem solving, escalation, training and so on. From 'change management' we get development requests, procurement, software upgrades, equipment enhancement etc. From 'moves' we get installations, equipment transfer, loans, project support et al.

And by the way, we also do 'customer service'. But now, it is only an element of, or an adjunct to, the range of services we provide. It is not the be-all-and-end-all it was touted as back in the 1990s. The new relationship with our customers is based around a catalogue of distinct services. 'Customer service' is now nothing more than the expression of our professionalism and is a trivial addendum deserving of little more than to be taken for granted.

7.7 Client roles in the service process

Up to now, this book has looked at our customers, the end users of our service, simply as one of several factors we must take into account in our service product design strategy. We have considered their nature, their business needs and locations. The first six chapters of this book have therefore been a very one-sided consideration of what we shall do to them in the name of IT service.

Once the services are published, however, the clients will come to depend upon them. Our output will become a critical factor in the success or otherwise of their labours. We will anticipate their taking more than a little interest in what we do on their behalf. It is reasonable for us to expect that our clients will have a part to play in the service relationship, not just as passive recipients but also as demanding consumers. It is a truism of IT service provision that users will make demands upon IT services. Not all of those demands will be within what we see as our remit of delivery and some of them may even border on irrationality. Nevertheless, those demands will come. Thus, the first part of the role played by the client in the service relationship is apparently that of the eager consumer.

That gives rise to another element – he who pays the piper calls the tune, and as the consumer is directly or indirectly the ultimate source of funding for our activities, he may feel he has a right to exert an influence on our priorities. That influence puts him in a position of superiority over us. Apparently, the user is our financier and ergo our commander.

The user may also be seen as our judge. Because the efficacy of our service provision has such a bearing on the ultimate success of the user, we may expect that he will pay close attention to whether or not the service meets his need at whatever point he may call upon it. If it does not, he may well vociferously advertise his dissatisfaction, not just to IT services personnel, but also to colleagues, his own manager, perhaps even to the corporate directorate. His judgement about us will add weight to the overall balance of whether we in IT services can justify our activities, priorities, offerings, expenditure and even our very existence.

The default roles played by the client then are consumer, financier, commander and judge. The client is He Who Must Be Satisfied. We hang posters on our office walls to remind us that the Customer is King and that we must treat him with absolute respect and deference. 'Customer service' has become a byword even in IT. We send our staff on service behaviour training courses and carefully select those who must present the face of IT to the outside world.

We encourage ourselves to be intimidated by the customer relationship and the roles that necessitates. No wonder all hell breaks loose in IT when somebody complains. We have made fear of the customer into an intrinsic part of our behaviour. In my view, we've gone way over the top – because the role played by the customer is more often not the one we imagine. It is almost certainly not as active as all that.

In the past few years, there has been an almost relentless industry drive to see the role of the IT end user as the same as that of the active consumer, with all the critical involvement and participation that might go with it. It seems that we might see the users' relationship to us more like that of the theatre critic to London's West End. In truth, the relationship is more like that between the man shaving in his bathroom and the local water company. Rather than playing an active part in the process of and his role in water provision, the man has forgotten the water company exists and takes its products for granted. As service providers keen to make the best possible impression, we in IT services are wont from time to time to overestimate the interest of the user in our output. My favourite way of putting the users' view of IT into perspective is to return to the bathroom. When you turn on the faucet/tap, water either comes out or it does not. If it does, you are not likely to spring back from the basin in amazement at the slickness and professionalism of the service offered by the water company. You take water in the bathroom absolutely for granted. Your relationship with it is passive to the point of ignorance. In fact, if the water did not come, your first thought would probably not be to the water company, but to whether you yourself had done something wrong or your water installation was at fault.

It is the same in IT services. Most users do not even notice us. We are as ubiquitous as the furniture, as irrelevant as the wallpaper. We're just *there*, that's all. No need to think about it further.

In a way, it is almost arrogant of us to believe that our customers would hold any other attitude. Why should we think that we are so important to them that they would invest time and effort in paying any attention to our existence? The company's employees are busy people. They do not clutter their heads with insignificant trivia and background material. They have work to do in finance, personnel, sales, accounting, production, despatch, invoicing, the boardroom and so on. They have home lives, hobbies, families, friends, aspirations and anxieties. With all that on their minds, there simply isn't room for thinking about some distant corporate department whose services, well, just sort of happen to be there.

Despite the facts that some users complain about IT services and that we have to explain our occasional failures, in the greater perspective, those complaints and user involvement tend to come from an identifiable minority of our customer base. The issue is not that the users are too involved in the service relationship. The truth is that the majority of them could not care less, and our frustration should be that they are not enough involved rather than too much. Our challenge is to get them more involved, not less.

There are two levels to the role the user may play in service provision. The first is the psychological one we give them as part of our inferiority to them. Because they are in a position to influence our remuneration, our existence and the acceptability of our services, we assume that they would care to do so. So we may assume a subservient position in anticipation that they may exert an authority only granted to them by our subservience. This is a vicious circle and it is in nobody's interests. In the IT services relationship, we are one department of the corporation providing services to another. Both of these fall under the same corporate structure, mission and commercial priorities – in other words, both of us serve the same higher goals. The relationship is not one of IT services being slightly lower down the totem pole – it is that we are business equals and that the roles in the relationship played by both IT services and the user base should reflect that.

So the role we need the users to play is on the second level of service provision. We need their input in a formal, structured, dispassionate fashion so that we may gauge the realities of our provision and adjust it to increase its appropriateness.

We also need the users to adopt the role of formal recipients of our communications. This is because of the very nature of our work, which hampers rather than assists constructive communication. The usual way IT services comes into contact with its customers is that of reactively dealing with an enquiry, which of course we will do perhaps hundreds of times a day. The enquiry might be concerning a failure of the computer or the customer's ability to make the best use of it, to request a change or installation or to invoke one of our numerous other, published services. In other words, the communication tends to be one of making a demand, i.e. a form of insistence by the user that IT services deliver something to which he believes he has the right.

The very nature of this form of communication highlights the customer's superiority over us – it is the antithesis of partnership. Should the enquiry be to report a system fault, this communications channel becomes even more problematical. This is because the failed system was designed, installed and its use insisted upon by IT. In other words, we are the ultimate origin of the fault. While the fault maintains, the user is under pressure because he cannot complete the work he was hired to do and that is all down to IT. Given that reality, it is only a short step for the user to go from reporting a fault to berating the IT department for causing the fault in the first place. In other words, the default channel of communication between IT and the users is one-way and essentially negative and thus detrimental to the relationship.

That form of negative communication is also the easiest. It requires little to no effort on the user's part. However, the end result of it is that the responsibility for the issue passes from the user's shoulders to ours. This question of responsibility is important in any surface relationship. Humans avoid responsibility wherever possible, for reasons that range from good (shed the responsibility so as to have time to deal with something more important) to bad (pass the buck along with the blame). Because we provide a service, without management we will make no distinction between the quality or morality of the reason – we will offer not just our assistance, but our capacity to take responsibility.

But the user incurs no real cost in abdicating that responsibility, and so it is easy for him to abdicate as much of it as he wishes. And for some people, that will mean all responsibility. We have all heard a service client try to blame their own failure on the service provider, when in fact blame should be a redundant concept and the responsibility for eradicating this and future problems should be shared by both parties and worked out between them.

On this idea of cost to the user, I cite the maxim of 'that which has no cost has no value'. If pushing all responsibility onto IT services comes with no price, the channel will be abused. After all, it's free at the point of delivery as far as the individual user is concerned.

So the passive form of communication between the users and IT is negative by default and detrimental to the relationship in many ways by its very nature. We have to make the communication two-way – which means we have to play a more proactive role in it and we must encourage the user to do the same.

It is perhaps notable that in spite of all our professionalism, our organization and our skill and cleverness in building complex service delivery structures, when the whole edifice starts to crumble, it is usually human spiritual weakness that is the root cause. While IT services departments suffer from inferiority complexes and users try to evade responsibility, the whole machine will start to wobble. But people are people, bless them, and they will continue to misbehave. Fortunately, history has taught us that there are ways to curb that corrosive misbehaviour. These ways are *society* and *legislation* – and just as we have used them since time immemorial to build nations, alliances, ideologies, philosophies and religions, we can also use them to build better IT services departments. In other words, if the users do not play an active part in the service relationship, we can use society and legislation to encourage – force? – them to do so.

Thou shalt behave better towards the IT services department. Broadly speaking, I'm not a great believer in too much legislation. It has always been the classic governmental reaction to perceived misbehaviour among populations. It is a slippery slope – once begun, it is seen as a panacea to all the ills of society and so accelerates. Some people felt threatened by the noise and boisterousness of others drinking beer in parks – so it was made illegal to drink beer in a park. A few dogs of a certain breed bit a few people – so under threat of official extermination, dogs of that breed had to be registered as deadly weapons. To solicit acceptable behaviour from the miscreant few, we legislatively impact the lives of all, including the innocent. In other words, weak-minded bureaucrats and politicians will often use legislation as an attempt to control all others, even those that need no such control and even to the point of silliness. The reality is lost, that those they wish to control have as much right to freedom of action as they do. Rules beget rules beget rules. Authoritarians patronize their fellow society members. The freedom of all is eroded. Sooner or later, prohibition begets rebellion as resentment grows between those who would act freely and those who would impose control. It's all very unhealthy. Make rules if you must, but consider the consequences of overdoing it.

A better way to do it is to encourage mutuality between IT services and its customers. Turn the relationship into a form of society where each member benefits the other. Why is the concept of benefit so important here? There are those in the human race, and by extraction in the corporations we work for who will act to assist those around them purely because a need has been spotted. There are those who will take that a stage further and encourage their departments to help other departments. But such corporate philanthropy cannot be assumed to exist in all companies, because most of us are too busy responding to daily pressures to worry about the pressures of others. Users will not enjoin in the service relationship because it is the right thing to do – they will take part because it benefits them.

The default relationship between IT services and its users is that we provide, they consume and then ask for more. The users benefit from this relationship and increase that benefit steadily by asking for more. They need no other form of relationship with us. The obvious one, the one they have now is beneficial enough, thank you very much and they do not really have the time to make any other relationship a priority, seeing as there is no obvious benefit to them in making the time for it.

As to what these benefits should be – we could go for the standard ones 'with improved communication between provider and consumer, we can improve services in a targeted fashion'. First that is a promise of nothing today but probably jam tomorrow and second, it's a cliché[1] that professional people accept but rarely believe. How can a user group that plays an active part in the service relationship gain a real benefit? Of course it depends on the user, but the benefit must be real. What can IT services offer beyond the standard service portfolio? We must know the user to divine the answer, but it will probably be some form of special treatment. An elevated service level for user groups most active in the service relationship, training for users, statistical reports, advance knowledge of new software releases, opportunity to take part in product tests, pro-active support from floor-walking technicians, etc.

7.8 Formal user roles

The 'key user'

Probably the most common role played by a user in the service relationship is a form of local computer support. It would probably occur informally any way – among any group of users there are always some who are more expert than others, and these may find themselves becoming a kind of unofficial first stop for enquiries concerning computer usage. Common terms for these are 'local support' and 'key user'.

---

[1] It falls into the same category as that classic 'For our customers' convenience ...' A hotel I used frequently decided to cut the number of ice machines from one on each floor to two in the whole building. The sign read 'For our customers' convenience, the ice machines are now located on the fourth and eighth floors.' Another one of my favourites is the magnificently contradictory 'Thank you for waiting. Your call is important to us.'

Where the types of enquiry are purely technical, they are in effect taking some workload that should perhaps have gone to the IT services helpdesk. This is a problem because it disguises from IT services management the true nature of, and demand for, IT support services in the corporation.

There is a legitimate use for the key user in a support context, and that is to take the sort of enquiry that is not directly computer related, but more associated with the business use of the computer rather than the technical detail of it. The key user would answer the question 'Which screen-based form do I use to make such-and-such a business transaction?' He would probably pass straight to IT services an enquiry such as 'I cannot get access to the application that provides this form.'

Key users are also regularly used in the procurement process – for example to verify that an order about to be placed is within departmental standards and budget. But where IT services does the actual procurement, once that process has been started, the key user will probably step out of the loop.

Another use of the key user is as a communications channel, to whom IT services can formally announce scheduled downtimes or report on user performance.

IT co-ordinator

The 'key user' is more a clerical post, dealing with the operational details of day-to-day user interaction with the computer. The IT co-ordinator or IT representative is a position I have seen filled in various versions by both user and IT staff. Its main function is to represent the IT interests of the user group and as such it has a political duty to the users, but a need for considerable IT knowledge.

Where a service level agreement is in place, it would be this individual who would negotiate the service demand side of the relationship. This post also often appears as…

Client-side manager

This representative of the users' interests is more often found in an outsourcing contract, where the IT support services are provided as a managed offering by an external party and governed by a strict service contract.

While the role is clearly to handle the relationship, it is also to carry the customers' complaints to the supplier, to attend the performance review meetings as part of a responsibility to ensure the users are getting what they paid for, and to act generally as the counterpart to the service provider's **supplier-side manager**. It is a policing as well as a liaison function, looking after the customer's interests.

7.9 The service level agreement

For an increasing number of companies, the formal relationship between IT services and its customers is a document known as the 'service level agreement' (SLA).

In effect, this is a contract. It sets out the demands of the customers, the provisions of the service supplier and the duties of each in the mechanics of the relationship. It describes the service levels – how much of what to be provided how quickly, to whom and how.

It formalizes the information flow – the content and format of the statistical reports at the end of the month, supplier performance review meetings, document exchanges. It lays out the processes. It sets the budget. It describes how it can change to keep itself relevant in the face of business and IT developments. It deals with everything important about the supplier–consumer relationship. Very senior people sign it.

But that does not necessarily make the SLA the solution for all IT services departments. Where IT services is an outsourced provision, the SLA is a crucial management principle. Where IT is just another part of the corporation, the SLA may become irrelevant within weeks of being signed.

The most common reason for this is the SLA does not serve the interests of the users but those of the crucial management interaction between IT and the business. It frames the nature of the relationship and probably sets fiscal parameters – but it is probably never read by anybody below a senior rank, and not even the IT technicians are aware of how quickly the SLA says they should be working.

As a matter of routine, the users ignore IT and anything to do with it (including the SLA) until they need it. At that point, any document is irrelevant because the need is now. So some document the user has never read says that IT doesn't have to do anything about the user's contact for four hours – who cares? That just means that IT is dragging its feet.

I must emphasize here that the SLA is a useful document that provides a general management framework for service provision. But don't be surprised if it is paid but scant attention outside of that.

A full study of the SLA is outside the scope of this book – it is a work in its own right that others have covered in the past. I offer below an outline design for an SLA, which I have found useful in drafting contracts for clients. It's not new – I've taken it from my book *How to Manage the IT Helpdesk*.

SERVICE LEVEL AGREEMENT

1. INTRODUCTION
Outline description of contents.

1.1 Purpose of this agreement
E.g. to set client expectations, define mutual responsibilities, describe service catalogue etc.

1.2 Scope of the agreement
E.g. what's included, what's excluded – covers the helpdesk but not network support and so on.

1.3 Terminology
Glossary of any special jargon or terminology used in the document.

1.4 Authorities
Description of role and duties of signing authorities; client-side manager; supplier-side manager; review body, etc.

2. SERVICE PROVISION

2.1 Supplier services and responsibilities
List the services here, what they do, how they work, what purpose they serve, how the customers obtain them. Note: do NOT describe the actual service levels – they appear later in the Schedule. This part is your catalogue, so you can offer the same SLA to several clients but differentiate the actual services delivered by only making the schedule specific to a given client. This may mean that not all clients get all services – but from the SLA,

they then know what's available and can come back and ask for more services if they need them.

2.2   Client responsibilities
All the things the customer has to do as part of the service relationship. So if they have to attain a given level of technical competence, use only the helpdesk for reporting problems or be available when your second-line technician comes to fix their machine, say so here.

3.   SLA MANAGEMENT

3.1   SLA administration
Who ultimately owns the SLA; who administrates it, produces the reports etc.

3.2   Review process
E.g. how frequently the reports are compiled, who they go to and what happens with them. How the 'performance review meeting' is constituted; what should be the output of that meeting and what actions may be taken as a result. Who signs off the reports and meeting minutes.

3.3   SLA change management
E.g. how the agreement may be suspended in the light of any external circumstances affecting either party; how that suspension is documented and what effect that has. How the agreement itself may be changed in the light of any significant alteration in demand, how that alteration is authorized and how it links into the change management process.

3.4   Performance reporting
E.g. processes, names and purposes of various reports coming out of the SLA process.

3.5   Breach of agreement
E.g. process invoked as a result of any breach by either participant. How the breach is measured, acknowledged, recorded and actions to be taken.

3.6   Termination
How the agreement should be terminated (but not when – that's in the schedule).

4.   FORMAT OF DOCUMENTS
Copies of (or references to) templates of all the documents pertaining to or produced by the SLA relationship, e.g. reports, sign-off sheets, change documents, meeting minute formats, change request forms, project initiation documents, equipment procurement forms etc.

SCHEDULE OF SERVICE PROVISION

S1   SCHEDULE ADMINISTRATION

S1.1   Client details
S1.2   Period of validity

S2   SERVICE LEVELS

A table like the one below. Remember to allow for changes to service levels based on increase or reduction in demand.

Service Name	Service Level	Exceptions	Comments
As per the list in 'supplier responsibilities' but this time only for this client	*How much of it they get, how quickly – response and fix times, etc.*	*Any particular exceptions, e.g. user departments that do their own thing and don't want this service*	*Anything relevant*

S3   Anticipated demand level

E.g. number of users, pace of growth in user population, expected number of moves, installations, training course requests etc.

S4   Supported products list

Table: it may be handy to put a note here to refer reader back to the third section for instructions on how to add or remove products to or from this list.

S5   Agreement acceptance

We the undersigned ...

APPENDIX

GENERAL TERMS AND CONDITIONS

Where the legal bit goes. Useful if you have general T's & C's pertaining to all intra-company agreements or all client contracts.

8 Managing service delivery

So we've examined our market and designed services to meet the needs we saw there. We engineered processes to produce those services. We worked out what sort of human skills would be needed for those processes to run properly and then acquired those skills by hiring, training and motivating the right sort of people. In acknowledging that our own people would be dealing with other people out there in our customer base, we gave ourselves some strategies for those human interactions. But we're not finished yet. There are still a couple more steps before we can switch our IT services machine on, before we can truly say it is complete and ready to work. One of those is deciding how we will manage the actual service delivery. This opens up questions like:

- How will our current and potential customers know what they can get from us and how we will go about providing it?
- How do we finance this IT services factory of ours?
- Who pays us and how?

8.1 The service level agreement (revisited)

A service level agreement (SLA) is a formal document acknowledged by a service provider and a service consumer stating the duties of both parties to the agreement in terms of delivered services and service levels and customer reciprocation or remuneration.

Each service is described in detail, including, where appropriate, the descriptions of the duties of both parties in the service provision. In a 'schedule' attached to the SLA is a list of the precise levels to which the service will be delivered – how often, how quickly, during what period and so on.

On the face of it, the SLA is the IT services department's formal announcement of how it treats requests, be these for support, change or equipment, with a given set of priorities, and that it will respond to and resolve problems within stated target times. It guarantees a certain level of system availability.

The SLA also includes a description of how the SLA process itself should be managed. It is only a document and thus is a snapshot in time. Business and technology are both subject to change, and without some built-in adaptability, the document can tend to become irrelevant. So there will be a process for changing the SLA to reflect service alterations in the light of external change.

The SLA is a contract between two parties, each of whom have expectations of the other. There needs to be a way of monitoring that the parties are keeping to their side of the bargain – that the service provider is adhering to the agreed service level targets, that the customer is paying the bill, using the proper channels to invoke services and so on. So the SLA will usually contain a description of one or more processes for monitoring and managing the service relationship. These may include the appointments of client-side and supplier-side managers, to act as the formal conduit between the two parties. Where the users are divided into groups for the purposes of service delivery, there would be a client-side manager for each user group. This distinction might also be reflected in IT services, if that department has enough people of the right skills to commit to service relationship management roles. Some larger organizations have staff dedicated to the role. Others share the responsibility out among senior IT managers.

Other aspects to relationship management, also covered in the SLA, will be the format of performance reports; and description of an SLA review process, which normally takes the form of a regular meeting between the client- and supplier-side managers to discuss service performance.

There are other volumes around that will describe the SLA in much more detail. In here, I cover it because it is part of the IT service process. It looks like a fairly simple and logical way of managing a mutual relationship. It's also idealistic, flawed, commonly disrespected, widely misunderstood and often disregarded. The SLA process is a veritable steeplechase, with refusals at every hurdle. And despite the size of the field (in terms of the numbers of IT departments operating in the belief that an SLA is in charge) there are surprisingly few finishers, and some of those are riderless – the SLA may be running, but there may no longer be anybody holding the reins.

Given agreed quantities of demand and defined acceptable service levels, the service manager can effectively plan his processes and staffing to produce service as required. In theory, this should ensure a constant match of demand with ability to supply, so everybody's happy.

In practice, however, there is often another governing rule, not mentioned in the SLA, which precludes this reciprocation. That rule is set by financiers who, regardless of the SLA's provisions, may limit the expenditure on IT services resources. The provider therefore cannot control its ability to deliver, so it cannot succeed and in effect, the SLA is meaningless because it is stymied by a force outwith the SLA process. This can frustrate the planning effort because the authority to implement the plan can be removed or adjusted for reasons that have nothing to do with user service. We must of course acknowledge that business and finance take precedence. But for service planning to make sense, we must allow for the eventuality of a change in finance priorities. My view is that the SLA should also contain some description of why the IT services expenditure is important. Below I look at cost justification for IT services.

One of the benefits of a published SLA is that service level expectations are set on both sides. The customers understand what level of service the company has acknowledged it can afford, and so knows what to expect. So they do not make unreasonable demands, and they are neither surprised nor disappointed by the service level they ultimately receive. This means that adequate customer satisfaction is actually built into the service process. The provider will always succeed, because it always delivers what the SLA has told the customers they can reasonably expect.

Except that this is more often than not little more than a fantastic ideal. In truth, very few of IT's actual clients are likely even to know that the SLA exists, let alone the details of its provisions. The SLA is a management document. The user on the Clapham omnibus has not read it and so its existence will have no impact whatsoever on his expectations. The average user with a computer problem is probably completely unaware that the SLA promises a response in one hour and a fix within two working days. All he knows is that without a functioning computer, he cannot work at all, and that his boss is breathing down his neck, so anything less than immediacy of reaction is no use to him. The acceptability of a delivered service level is two-dimensional by nature – there is no sliding scale – it's either good enough or it's not.

The users are too numerous for them all to be consulted in the design of the SLA, which is negotiated at the highest level in the organization by people who may not fully understand precisely how the employees use the computer and thus what their exact service needs are. This is why the design of the SLA must be a by-product of the original market analysis when we define the services, because that is the closest we will get to understanding what the user actually needs. In other words, writing the SLA is ideally not a separate process from service design.

The point of any agreement is that it must be mutual – beneficial to both parties. But the typical SLA tends to be a demand-only document. The IT services department is expected to deliver a raft of service levels. But what does the IT department get in return? It gets to avoid being outsourced for a little while longer, perhaps. It gets to keep its job, maybe. What role does the user community take in the service delivery process? Usually a passive one, of demanding services but having no other responsibility. The users are not expected to attain a certain level of technical competence, to acknowledge that the service provision can only be guaranteed against a known level of demand or to undertake to be at their desk when the technician arrives to make the repair.

That is one of the bases for SLA failure. If the IT services process and staff quantity are static and governed, then so must be the level of demand or else the whole company suffers. If the level of demand may be flexible, then so must be the ability and authority of the IT services department to meet it.

The SLA probably has provisions for reporting the performance of the service providers. However, the purpose of this policing and review process is often lost. The reports may say how bad things are, but do they offer a vehicle for what must be done about it? I've seen too many SLA review meetings that serve as little more than an additional opportunity to reiterate and even amplify the complaints about the service. Complaints don't fix anything. Often, they do little more than erode an already fragile relationship. The ideal SLA gets beyond the complaints to embody rectification by prescribing standard actions in the event of service failure – and because the SLA is mutual, the actions should include responsibilities and duties for both supplier and client.

In practice, most organizations know instinctively when their SLA is flawed. But instead of fixing the SLA, they may just ignore it and allow it to slip into disuse. On one hand, this can lead to a relaxed atmosphere – especially, say, where the service is adequate, but could be better, but not so much that the users need to actively enjoin in forcing improvements. But on the other hand, the disused SLA constitutes the waste of a valuable opportunity to govern service costs and provision, along with the effort in composing the SLA in the first place.

8.2 The service catalogue

This term is often used to describe two very different forms of communication. In one form, it is an abridged description of IT's services for consumption by the actual users, as opposed to their managers. It tells the users precisely what the IT services department does for them, gives instructions for invoking the service ('call this number', 'fill in this form', 'speak to your IT representative', etc.). It will also describe the nature and speed of response the user can expect. The user's own responsibilities will be detailed ('don't store company information on your local hard disk', 'what to do if you suspect a virus attack', etc.). In short, this is a computer user's User Manual for his IT services. It presumes that the user's managers have already decided to accept IT services as the provider of this assistance.

In its other form, the service catalogue is a precursor to the SLA. It is IT services setting out its stall, making an offer of or proposal to supply certain services. Its audience is limited to the same high corporate levels as the SLA.

8.3 Financing IT services

Everything has to be paid for. There is no universally accepted way of covering the costs of IT services. In some companies, the market approach prevails – charge for everything, user community decides whether to buy it or not. In others, the company behaves a little like a nation state, with a government subsidizing IT as a necessary infrastructure.

'Market approach'

In deciding how to charge for services, on the one hand, there is the principle that nothing is free of charge, and thus every expense ultimately must be recouped from the customer by whom or on whose behalf the expense is incurred. I call this the 'market approach' to service pricing. In effect the IT department becomes (usually) the sole supplier of IT equipment and related services to the captive market that is its user base. For the purposes of recouping costs, IT looks and behaves as though it were a separate company.

The user pays for everything he uses. This includes the computers and printers on his desk, the network point he plugs into, the number of bytes he sends across the network and how many helpdesk enquiries he makes. Where IT is also in charge of telephones, the user is charged for his handsets and fax machines, his connection to the corporate telephone exchange (private automatic branch exchange or PABX) and the calls he makes.

Infrastructure is managed on a project basis. When the IT department wants to change to a more powerful business applications suite or increase the size and reach of the network, the capacity of central processors, it must specify costs and benefits and then approach the users to bid for the money to carry out the project. In theory then, the users know exactly what they are paying for.

The strongest feature of the 'market approach', namely that all costs are identified, recharged and thus covered, may also be its greatest weakness. Charging for everything carries with it tremendous administrative overheads. Invoices or cross-charging follow every transaction and intra-company activity. The change process can become clunky and slow, as authorities are pursued for signatures. Every department has a charge code. Internal budgets are credited and debited as services and products change hands. Of course, this keeps the accountants very busy, but this raises the question of whether keeping accountants busy, in and of itself, produces a benefit for the company. In improving the recording and recouping of the costs, the administration of all that recording and recouping actually adds to the costs. The question is whether that improvement in cost control is worth the money it costs to control the costs.

In this approach, the usual means of collecting the money is 'transfer pricing'. Every department in the company has a cost code. This is effectively a current account held at the bank of corporate central finance. When a user makes a purchase from IT, he gives his authority for IT to make a charge against his cost code. A price list has to be consulted, which is why a catalogue of provided services and their associated costs is a prerequisite for this kind of IT financing. In effect, IT (and every other department in the company) is acting as though it were an independent supplier of computer services to the corporation's userbase.

This has security implications – IT will have to verify that the individual making the request has the authority to spend the money. There also has to be an assessment of whether the user department has sufficient funds remaining in its current account.

Of course much of this can be automated. Budget levels are recorded in ITS's procurement system, along with a catalogue of equipment or services available and their respective prices. For common purchases, such as computers, printers, office software and so on, the procurement system can reflect these as 'standard' items. In this way, the procurement system is linked to the change management process. A procurement request is seen as a form of change request. The new equipment will constitute a change to the corporate computing platform, but this is a 'standard change'. In other words, the need for it has been anticipated in the budget round, so when the request is made, it goes through without impediment.

With IT operating as a separate entity within the company but providing services to it, the question of outsourcing usually arises at some point. The price of everything is known, and so the question of value for money has to be answered. The company opens itself up to approaches from external service providers, ready to compete with the internal IT services department. Where the IT is not strategic – i.e. it does not require specialist understanding of the business operating principles – these approaches may be freely received. Outsourcing is rarely straightforward. It would appear that bringing a specialist IT service provider should mean better and more cost-effective services. It can, but not always. In every instance of IT services outsourcing I have encountered, costs have been higher. Service levels may be slightly better. What can suffer even more, however, is user freedom – mindful that an external company provides the service, the user gets careful with his use. My research suggests that the outsourced IT services provider tends to attract fewer contacts from the users than did the incumbent IT department it replaced.

'Micro-economy approach'

There is something to be said for what I call the 'micro-economy approach'. This is to see the corporation almost as though it were a nation state, with a self-sufficient economy. This begs the need for a government – and if this were a macro-economy, one of the duties of the government would be to provide the infrastructure upon which the rest of the economy would run. The government builds or instigates the building of the roads, the drains, maybe even the railways and the airports. It finances these apparently from its own coffers, but in fact from a fund created by compulsory contributions (i.e. taxes) from all members of the economy. The infrastructure built, the members themselves then directly and privately provide the vehicles and services running on that infrastructure.

The British government took taxes from me and from those who came before me and used those taxes to contribute to the building and maintenance of the M4, the main highway between London and South Wales. I don't even see my taxes paying for the motorway, because those taxes contribute to hundreds of other things as well. In other words, how the motorway got there is totally transparent to me. I am not given the detail of precisely how much of my personal tax contributions went into the M4.

The end result is that the government provided the infrastructure that is the M4. To make use of it, however, I must either obtain my own car, or 'outsource' my use of the M4 to a bus company, who will take me to London on one of their vehicles. At this stage, I can opt between levels of economy, depending on my own priorities for speed, comfort, efficiency, economy, traffic avoidance etc. weighed against the expenditure options I have due to my level of wealth and the proportion of my income I am willing to dedicate to travel. I may choose a motorcycle, an inexpensive runabout, a workaday motorway muncher or a luxury cruiser.

A company could take a similar approach to providing IT. The 'central government' of the company, the board, takes advice from a building contractor, namely the IT department, about what sort of computer and communications infrastructure is needed and how much it will cost. The government then finances the building of the infrastructure from levies placed against all the corporation's budgetary profit centres. It commissions the IT department to perform the proposed construction.

With the infrastructure in place, now the services are created to run on it. The individual user departments purchase these services privately, according to their specific requirements.

The users would be oblivious of how the corporate computer network was financed and came into being. They can take it for granted, just as I do the M4. The infrastructure appears to be free of charge at the point of provision, but incurs private costs at the point of use.

If as a user of the M4 I deem it in my business interests get to my meetings more quickly and comfortably, I may thereby choose to incur the higher costs of reduced miles per gallon and leather seats, so I make specific choices when I purchase the principle resource I will use by which to exploit the infrastructure of the M4, namely my car.

Similarly, if as a user of the corporate computer infrastructure I choose for my own business reasons to have a faster response to my technical enquiries and computer hardware failures, I may choose especially to pay for a higher service level than do the other user departments around me. I may also choose to take higher specification machines, use services outside normal office hours and so on.

8.4 Cost justification

In Chapter 9 we will look at how cost justification is used in a statistical context. First, however, it is important to establish a few principles.

IT services operates within a business. At the core of business is money, whether in the private sector, where the purpose is to make the stuff, or in the public sector, where the purpose is to spend it in order to foster the stability of the state. It all comes down to money sooner or later. However, those who control money are not necessarily single-minded about it – Ebenezer Scrooge is an extreme figure. Financiers are open to an argument, at least one they can understand.

IT services needs money – so to varying degrees, it has to justify its expenditure to those who would provide the finance. But it must word that justification carefully. The goal is to ensure that as a result of that justification exercise, the financier does not see himself as *spending* money on IT services but *investing* in it.

Where the decision the financier has to make is 'Shall I spend money on IT services or not?' – then the answer is likely to be 'not' because it appears to have no negative consequence. The ideal decision for the financier is 'Shall I invest in IT services or by not doing so, incur costs elsewhere; and which of those two cost options would be the most advantageous?'

The financier is not an IT services expert. He cannot be expected to be fully aware of the consequences of investing or failing to adequately invest in IT services. On the other hand, we IT people are not financial experts. So how can the two come together? Simple. He talks money, so it's his game, so we learn to talk his language. IT only exists because business does. Finance is the cause. IT is the effect.

The difficulty comes from the fact that IT does not actually make any money by doing what it does. But there must be a reason why finance people tolerate the existence of IT services. I would doubt that the reason is one of an aesthetic appreciation of our cultural contribution to corporate life – so the reason must be financial. It is a safe conclusion then that IT is deemed to merit having money invested in it. So we are not arguing about whether to have an IT services expenditure – only about how big that spend should be.

While IT remains a cost- rather than a profit-centre, this must be a debate over intangibles. All we can go on is what has become common practice in some economies, which is the adoption of 'accounting assumptions' – in other words, we apply a nominal financial benefit to those company operations that do not contribute directly to corporate revenue. With that principle established, there are numerous premises to start from, all of which are in some way unsatisfactory, because they do not really quantify hard cash. But we need something, even if it's not perfect.

One such premise is that the company simply could not do what it does without IT and the accompanying services, so IT makes up a necessary part of the cost of sale. We decide on the size of the proportion in a board-level meeting. We then ring-fence that proportion and thus would all corporate revenue then provide for the IT budget.

Another is the total cost of ownership (TCO) model, much researched and cited by organizations such as the Gartner Group. In this, a benchmark figure can be taken from a comparison between one's own IT costs and those of peer organizations. This can be used as a basis upon which to decide upon a corporately acceptable level of expenditure. The temptation may be to go for the simplistic 'lower than all our peers because they are also our competitors and lower costs mean higher margins', but life is never that straightforward, except perhaps in state-monopoly economies. Because the TCO model shows us our peers, we may also decide to compete with them on the quality of our IT, rather than just on its costs.

Yet another way is my preferred 'lost user-productivity' model. This works on the basis that the total corporate revenue over a given period (say a fiscal year) is the product of the aggregate effort of the corporation's employees. That whole revenue figure had to be made in order to cover costs and make profits. So it all had to be earned.

171

That figure can then be broken down into something more usable – my favourite unit is the currency contribution to revenue, per man-hour of employee time. In other words – if a thousand employees produce an annual $100 000 000 turnover, then each employee produces $100 000 per annum and since they are at work for about 1725 hours a year, they generate about $58 per hour. And when their computer isn't working, or they haven't bought it yet, or they're waiting to go on the training course, they are less productive than usual. We agree with corporate finance a figure of how much less productive computer users are when they are waiting for an IT services intervention – say 40 per cent – and multiply that by the time in hours it takes for the problem to be resolved. Because the longer that is, the less money they are making for the company, at a rate of 40 per cent of $58 per hour.

That 'percentage less productive' figure I call the 'computer dependency factor' (CDF), because that is what it means. It can be adjusted for different types of services – waiting for training will make the user less dependent than suddenly finding the computer is down and nothing is possible. So in IT services, I would set a different CDF for different services. The higher the impact, the higher the percentage.

How big does the CDF need to be? For most white-collar organizations, it will be high – start at 40 per cent and negotiate up or down from there.

Measuring IT services

9.1 Tactical view of measurement

In any services department, there are two tactical areas of measurement.

One is service level measurement and this is the most common and the one that usually gets the greatest level of attention. It is the measurement of our performance as a service deliverer. It is the measure of whether we met our stated objectives, did the job we said we would do, are worth the money we are charging to do the job, are any good at what we do and so on. It is part of the way the outside world sees us. This is not just measurement – it is judgement.

The other is operational measurement. This one tells us how well our process is behaving, if everything is happening as it should within the department, if cause produces effect as efficiently as it should within our designed process. It also looks at the performance not of the department as a whole, but of the individuals within it. As a form of measurement, it is profoundly and routinely neglected. It is actively shunned in some IT services groups, sometimes because it is difficult to measure the productivity of white collar workers, sometimes because doing so is discouraged by industrial agreement (e.g. in some parts of mainland Europe), sometimes simply because the staff would complain and we wish to avoid conflict.

My position on measurement is very plain. If you do not measure it, you are not controlling it.

A lack of measurement is therefore a loss of a management opportunity. At its worst, it is letting the department do as it wishes, which is the opposite of designed process. Certain things have to happen – they have to happen at the hands of individuals – if they do not happen, then nor can other things dependent upon them. Maybe it's just me, but if I design a machine to work a certain way, I do not then want it to ignore me and work the way it wants to work. If I could countenance that, I would not have designed the machine in the first place, I would have let it design itself. But if I as manager am being held accountable for the performance of my machine, I will manage and that means measure that performance. If the machine fails, I have to know where, so I can fix either the failure or the flaw in my original design.

'Service level' and 'operational' management are inextricably linked. A failure to make that link results in the following scenario. The IT services department has targets imposed on it by a user population expecting support for its computer usage and a finance department wondering where the money goes. The service level targets are thus set. So, at the beginning of the measurement period – typically a calendar month – the workers of the IT department attend their stations and get stuck in. They are busy, busy, busy until the end of the month, when an administrator runs the performance reporting routine, by which we are assessed in the harsh, cold light of service levels. We done good here, we done not so good there. Passable overall. Smiles from the manager because we got away with it again, frowns from the users because it's not quite good enough. The problem is that whether we succeeded or failed, it is irrelevant. We made no link between all that activity and the end result. So if we fail, we don't know why. And if we succeed, it is at best a fluke. Where operational measurement is not linked to service level measurement, the attainment of service level targets is not achievement, it is fortunate happenstance, it came about despite the fact that it was not being managed. And as to all that activity – without operational measurement, we have no idea how much of it was actually dedicated to producing the service level result. For all we know, we could be fifty per cent overstaffed, or have a department that could hugely improve its self respect and job satisfaction by blowing the service level targets away every month if we wanted.

Without operational management, we don't know why what happened, happened. And it is a braver manager than I who is happy to be able routinely to say, 'I don't know how that happened' about everything for which he is accountable. If I'm in charge, then I'm *in charge* – not just happening to be there while it all goes on around me. It happens because of my managerial design, not despite my accidental presence.

To meet a service level target, a certain outcome has to be achieved in a certain period of time. The problem is that we tend to get lost in the scale of that stipulation. It is rarely as plain as that – it is often covered by caveats, maybes and proportions of cases. So the service-level stipulation of 'complete installations within one week' is modified by something along the lines of 'in eighty-five per cent of cases'. We're not just doing a handful of installations, we are doing dozens a month, so the whole function of installation – from request receipt through budgetary check through purchase order through goods receipt through commissioning through environmental check through porterage through installation through user acquaintance – has to happen within a week in eighty-five per cent of cases.

If we then miss the target, it is very difficult to find out why, because there are so many people involved in the process, it is not straightforward to figure out precisely where the flaw is. There is no one person responsible for that end-to-end delivery cycle because it is a sequence of events in separate areas of responsibility[1]. And if it is only right eighty-four per cent of the time, then it is probably not worth the effort of finding out why to make one per cent difference.

To look at some of the issues with this common service-level experience:

First – why a week? Where did that come from? Why not a half a year, a month, a working day, sometime between now and next Easter or twenty-seven and a quarter minutes? The answer is that it was arrived at without science. It was plucked at random out of the 'Oh, that'll do' cloud (probably by a consensus, group or committee decision).

Second – why eighty-five per cent of the time? Why not sixty-five or seventeen or even a hundred? The answer is because there has to be some allowance for service department failure due to circumstances beyond their control. But surely if such an occurrence took place, it would be an exception from the routine, one that all parties involved in measurement could recognize. This is just a statistical gimmick with little real meaning.

Third – there are co-dependencies here. If the machine has to be installed within a week, that means it has to be commissioned within six days. So it has to be onsite within five. For that to

---

[1] Ah, the ubiquitous human excuse. 'Don't blame me, there were lots of people involved.' It's right up there with 'it was a group/committee/cabinet/senate decision.' We try so hard to avoid responsibility that we even invent systems to do the avoiding for us.

happen, it has to leave the warehouse within four. So the order has to be there within three. So the budgetary verification has to be done no later than the day after the request.

All of those co-dependencies can be measured. If one of them does not happen on target, then it will not matter if the others do. The service level target will still be missed, at least in this case. That is an operational, rather than service level measurement.

The person making the budgetary verification has to do it within a day. That's an operational target. From the number of arriving requests, there is a quantity target also. We can do the same right the way up the line. Performance targets to measure not necessarily the people, but the efficacy of the process. We can pinpoint exactly where it goes right and how it goes wrong.

But there is a people issue also. Take a simple service level target – say, that for all escalated helpdesk calls, the second-line technician must respond within thirty minutes (I know that's tight, but I'll come back to it) and that you have four second-line technicians, one of whom is called Tom. What a service level target says is that over the range of escalated helpdesk calls, a certain proportion of them met the stipulation of a thirty-minute response time. What an operational target says is 'Tom, pick the phone up and call that user in the next half hour. If you don't, then you personally will have to explain why you personally failed.' A service level target suggests that the department as a whole must perform to a certain level. An operational target is the embodiment of the realization that departments only 'perform' when people do.

What an operational target does is force the issue of all this busy-busy activity in the IT services department. That activity – all of it – has a meaning. It all contributes directly and consciously to the overall targets, against which our customers measure us. There has to be operational measurement. Without it, the fact that we worked and we made our service level targets is just coincidence.

9.2 Strategic view of measurement

In looking at service level measurement above, I posed the question as how we arrive at so many apparently arbitrary service level targets. I used the example of an 85 per cent achievement of installations within a week of request, challenging the scientific basis of numbers like this.

It is not just in installations where this happens. Some IT services helpdesks have what is termed an 'abandonment rate', which is the number of incoming calls at a given length of time in the queue. Some of the common targets set for this also bring one cause for wonder. There are two aspects to abandonment rate – one is the number of abandoned calls, the other is the length of time in the queue prior to abandonment. This second factor can say a lot about the type of customers IT services must deal with. At its extreme, I have seen IT services desks berate themselves for having a five per cent abandonment rate, but no target on how long a caller may reasonably queue for. In polite society, one might wait several minutes to engage a colleague who was already in conversation with another. When contacting IT services, it appears to be reasonable to put the phone down after queuing for only a few seconds.

A call abandoned after a short time is akin to the caller realizing two things; one, that the person or service they wished to address was already otherwise engaged and two, that their intended enquiry was not so pressing that it needed immediate attention. An abandonment rate alone is just a meaningless number. We have to allow for the fact that some callers will simply come back later, and if they abandon their call, that action may mean only that they have decided that now is not the best time to continue the call. An abandoned call, especially if it happens quickly, does not necessarily mean that the service is inadequate. It may also mean that the caller is unreasonably impatient or that his need was not really so great that it could not wait a little.

> ### Case study:
> ### Why queue for seconds when one can waste whole minutes elsewhere?
>
> A client of my consultancy service is a manufacturing company with a separate executive management building and factories dotted around the continent. Few of the executive block's inhabitants see much more of the company than these few corridors of power. While interviewing some of these people as clients of the IT services department I was analysing, I was more than a little concerned by some of the attitudes I encountered. At the time, the average telephone wait time upon contacting IT services was twenty-two seconds from end of dialling to hearing a human voice, with a 75 per cent chance that the issue would be resolved during that telephone conversation, typically in less than five minutes. The most extreme response, but not by far, was along the lines that the IT services

support offering was dreadful – 'can never get through' – a clear misappraisal. Can never get through *immediately* would have been more accurate.

It appeared that these users were unwilling to wait twenty-two seconds. 'Far too long for somebody in my position' was one comment. When I asked what alternative these people used for getting an IT support service, the most common answer was that they each run around the building interrupting each other instead. So twenty-two seconds of waiting was too long, so instead they used what they considered to be the far less wasteful several minutes chasing colleagues and interrupting their productivity also – thus at least doubling the cost to the company of the issue with which they had attempted to contact IT services.

To the outsider, it appeared that while it was unacceptable for IT services to provide a service that was superior to many in the industry, it was perfectly acceptable for corporate managers to have unreasonable expectations, ignore truth, react aggressively, behave petulantly and blatantly squander some of the most expensive resources in the company. It was not in my project's terms of reference to report on whether such behaviours and attitudes were appropriate among senior strategists and decision-makers – yet I could not help but wonder.

My recommendations did however include a greater focus on improving public relations and marketing of IT services. Clearly, there were some users out there whose view of what IT services should be providing in terms of service levels was based on their own, not necessarily well-considered ideas and imaginings. A dose of truth was needed.

Measurement alone is meaningless. Before plucking statistics out of the air and chaining ourselves to them as commitments, we must establish a strategic view of them. We can see that service level targets such as installation dates need science so that our striving to meet them constitutes neither inadequacy nor profligacy – and so that we can break them down into operational targets.

We have also seen that a statistic used without context, such as the abandonment rate, just puts pressure on a service team to defer to what may be no more than an unreasonable customer expectation or to a fear that our customers may judge us more harshly than is really the case.

The strategic view is one that puts the statistics into a background context. One such context is what I call the 'big four'.

9.3 The 'big four' statistics

In my view, there are four types of statistics, all of which must be measured, because all of them are necessary for any one of them to make sense. These are:

- Quantity – how many we did, in how much time
- Performance – the quantity compared with a predetermined target
- Quality – whether our customers liked what we did
- Value – whether it made business sense to do what we did.

The **'quantity'** is the purely numeric part. This is the result of a query against data, and results in more data. It gives us a number of how many of what, or how much time was consumed in doing what and so on. The most common type of statistic to come out of, say a telephone system or helpdesk management software or a typical timesheet. Raw and not much use on its own, but often interesting. When we know how many or how much of something exists or has happened, at least we know more than nothing. But not a lot more. Facts are not wisdom and it is not always possible to make tactical or strategic decisions based on a single quantity statistic. More quantity statistics increase the scope, however, and some decisions can be taken on the back of quantities alone.

How many support enquiries show a low user competence level? Say it's 50 per cent – so does that mean we need to send the users on training? Maybe – but not if another statistic tells us that most of those calls came from users who had already been on the training course. A lone statistic can suggest diametrically opposed conclusions unless it is countered by another, such as how many people had been on the training. Without that second statistic, a high first result can suggest we increase the business we give to the training company. The second, qualifying statistic says we never let that training company near the place again.

The **'performance'** part is typically what appears in the schedule at the back of a service level agreement or in an employee's list of objectives for the employment period (where these are numerical). This is where the questions arise most starkly over whether the targets are real, arbitrary, generated by scientific study, plucked from the air or used because everybody else seems to be using them. To raise the issue, we looked earlier at examples from installations and call abandonment. Another, which serves to clarify the 'science' aspect, could be taken from hardware maintenance.

If we use an external company to repair hardware faults, that company will undoubtedly offer a range of service levels. The shorter the guaranteed time limit between a fault being reported and repaired, the more the engineering company will charge. In the absence of anything to tell us otherwise, we may allow ourselves to fall into the trap of thinking that 'the more the engineering company will charge' directly equates to and means the same as 'the more expensive the quicker repair is'. So we set our service levels at targets, which if they were any shorter, apparently would be more expensive to provide. I use the word 'apparently' deliberately. For the moment, with only quantity and performance statistics gathered, the only thing we can use to decide whether that target is too long or too short is the maintenance company's price list. But that is the world as they see it. It looks different from in here – so different that with another couple of statistical types, we may actually discover that the quicker repair service is a long way more financially advantageous than the slower one. It could just be that the target is completely the wrong one caused by an incomplete perspective.

The simplest form of **'quality'** statistic is a customer satisfaction metric. This tells us whether the customers liked what we did, numerously, quickly and within target. Let us say that we have been 'improving' the service recently. Call times are shortened, so we use fewer staff taking calls, thus delighting the financiers. But what do the users think? Put it another way – suppose we have really improved the service, beating service targets routinely, accelerating deliveries, improving network resilience, in fact all the classic service level agreement statistics – and the customers don't even notice, as is shown by their unflinching customer satisfaction responses. If that is the case, then what exactly was the point of all that service improvement? What may have happened is that we've invested time and effort improving all the sort of things the customers regard as unimportant and not enough on the customers' own top priorities. Customer satisfaction brings us even closer to the point.

The traditional way of collecting satisfaction data, the formal survey, is too cumbersome, slow and inaccurate for our purposes here. The object is to collect statistics of all 'big four' types simultaneously and with the same frequency as each other. So if we measure performance monthly, so too must that be the case with quality, quantity and value. My preferred way of collecting snapshot customer satisfaction information is a telephone survey, to a specified small number (say one or two dozen) of very recent clients of IT services asking them to rate their satisfaction with various aspects of their recent experience. Random and limited may be unrepresentative in the short term, but it allows surveys to be conducted more frequently, making the information over the longer term much more usable because trends can be examined at much higher resolution.

Most important of course is the **'value'** statistic. This type tells us whether it made business sense to produce those services at that pace to those customers, requiring that much investment in those resources. For this, we need to know the cost of everything and everybody.

The quantity and performance statistics tell us that we achieved such and such a service level. The value statistic will know that over that period, we expended so many man-hours of effort. Now we can compare one with the other – are we getting more or less efficient, delivering a higher or lower quantity and/or service level for a higher or lower cost?

What is the typical cost of a change request, an installation request, a helpdesk enquiry, a virus attack, a software upgrade? These all consume people and facilities, all of which have costs.

Beyond that however, is a concept crucial to the value statistic, namely the 'cost–benefit analysis'. This assumes that there is a business reason for the existence and thus a justification for the costs of every part of IT services. Everything we do produces a benefit of some financial consequence for if it did not, the company probably wouldn't want to do it anyway. So we are not questioning the basic promise that there is a benefit to our costs – the debate centres round how the cost and the benefit compare, which is greater by how much, and whether increased service levels produce greater financial benefits or just higher costs.

As I stated in Chapter 8, my favourite statistic is the lost productivity figure. Because IT services keeps the user producing, and IT services provides and maintains the end-user portion of IT, then IT services is thus a direct contributor to that productivity and is the one who restores it to optimum when it is impeded by computer failure. As a value statistic, it cannot be said to be all encompassing, because it really only kicks in when the computers fail or are ordered and remain undelivered. Along with the man-hours statistic, it is perhaps the most pragmatic of the assumptions. And given that we need an assumption, lost productivity is for me the strongest candidate.

9.4 Quantifying the unquantifiable

In Chapter 11, we will look at the tools – for which read forms of computer application – we can use for running IT services. Wherever there are computers there are data, which can sometimes be output in a report. These data can often look like they are numbers we could refer to as measurement, but they may not be any use in practice. The main reasons for this stem from the nature of the tool, how faithful was its implementation to the design of the IT services process and how assiduously it is used.

On the other hand – garbage in, garbage out. There may be megabytes of numbers in there, but they may be incomplete because not everybody fills in all the fields in all the forms as uniformly as they are supposed to with the same diligence as all their colleagues. That's all right – we're not dead yet, because we may be able to garner some estimate of how inaccurate the data are. Perhaps we can survey a sample of the work done, and so test its accuracy and veracity. If we then create a measure of that inaccuracy – say 20 per cent – then we can allow for that by building in as an error factor every time we extract a statistical output[2].

That is an inadequate method. It is guess based on an assumption gleaned from claims made by IT services operational people who may have an agenda of their own.

Measurement is necessary, but data collection carries with it an overhead. There is a trade-off between how much resource in terms of people time we commit to measuring service production.

We may also expect some resistance from staff too – especially as is so often the case, that they see no benefit to the data collection. The best way to get somebody to do something is for their actions to be seen to directly benefit them. Where measurement is sloppily implemented, such that it seems to produce no benefit either to IT services or the people who work in it, it can be little surprise if not everybody puts their heart and soul into the measurement side of their work. There simply has to be a feedback loop of any measurement. Possible feedback loops include:

- Offer incentives for high productivity – be sure to have a quality standard that all work must pass before the reward can be presented, otherwise quantity will take over, so tell people what they are being measured on.

---

[2] Years ago, my doctor asked me how many cigarettes I smoked in a day. 'Twenty', I replied. 'Right, twenty-five then', he concluded, adding, 'I find they always underestimate by about 20 per cent.' The error factor strikes again.

- Feed back all statistics to the whole group – if it is legal to do so in your part of the world, break that down by individual performance. They won't like it at first, seeing it as a league table and so on, but over time, in my experience, people warm to a little fair competition.
- Make it clear that the individual is responsible for their bit of the work and for their own output. Collective responsibility is an oxymoron.
- Build productivity targets into the staff appraisal process and make sure people know these are measured.
- Report back to the group on matters arising from the measurement process, which suggest ways in which the department could improve and how this could concurrently improve workplace quality and job satisfaction.
- Show that the measurement matters.

These may look like motivation techniques, but they are more than that. We are trying to improve the depth and quality of management information and to do that we need our people to play an active role in statistical data gathering. If they get feedback on how many of this and that they did and how well they did it, they can see that not just the activity but also the measurement of the activity is in their interests.

The computerized systems will give us some statistics and hopefully by using feedback loops we will improve the quality of the data going in to them. But no matter how much we may insist or spin the importance of good quality data, good habits thereby fostered may still not maintain. By and large, IT services is not a compelling dramatic and hard-driving place to work. Boredom is never far away, and people will slip. To get round this, I like to change the method of measurement from time to time, away from our usually incomplete computerized systems[3] and back towards a form of survey project of how much work we're actually doing.

This method is a little onerous, so it is one I prefer to do on a snapshot, rather than routine basis.

This consists of two forms, both based on a type of timesheet. The first, the 'enquiry type sheet' measures the types of enquiries arriving at any part of IT services, at any time of the day, whether or not these were logged officially and whether or not they came through the official channels (see Figure 9.1).

---

[3] 'Usually incomplete computerized systems' – a contention I explore in more depth in Chapter 11.

What enquiries you took:
Count enquiries – one tick per call

Bruton Consultancy Project Number 1794/PR01   **Enquiry Type Sheet**

Please give one sheet to every member of the IT services team for each day for the week of 6th to 10th December 2004. This is **five sheets per operative**. This sheet is **only for people who take calls**, but it is for **anybody** who may take a support call. That includes managers, second-line support staff, network engineers, everybody – I'm trying to count users using back doors, too.

Instructions for use: PLEASE READ CAREFULLY   *FILL THIS IN AS YOU GO – DON'T WAIT UNTIL LATER OR THE FIGURES WON'T BE ACCURATE*

- This looks like a timesheet: IT IS NOT. This is NOT a time and motion exercise. It is a study of **what types of enquiries you get at what time of the day.**
- To use the sheet, simply **put a tick in the cell** that corresponds to the type of enquiry you had at what time. So if you had five forgotten passwords before 08:15, there will be five ticks in the 'Forgotten password'/'08:15' cell.
- Don't forget to enter your name and the date at the bottom of the sheet.
- For background information on who is doing this to you, see www.noelbruton.com. Thanks for your help. *Noel Bruton.*

To time:	08:15	08:30	08:45	09:00	09:15	09:30	09:45	10:00	10:15	10:30	10:45	11:00	11:15	11:30	11:45	12:00	12:15	12:30	12:45	13:00	13:15
Login issues																					
Software failure																					
Hardware failure																					
'How do I…?'																					
Printer problem																					
User error																					
Query status																					
Is Fred there?																					
Change control																					
Purchase request																					
Other																					

To time:	13:30	13:45	14:00	14:15	14:30	14:45	15:00	15:15	15:30	15:45	16:00	16:15	16:30	16:45	17:00	17:15	17:30	17:45	18:00	18:15	18:30	Later
Login issues																						
Software failure																						
Hardware failure																						
'How do I…?'																						
Printer problem																						
User error																						
Query status																						
Is Fred there?																						
Change control																						
Purchase request																						
Other																						

YOUR NAME: **DATE:**

Figure 9.1 Enquiry type sheet

What you were working on when:
Mark out boxes

Bruton Consultancy Project Number 1794/PR01

Resource Commitment Sheet

Please give one sheet to everybody in IT services for each day for the week of 6th to 10th December 2004. This is five sheets per operative.

Instructions for use: READ CAREFULLY FILL THIS IN AS YOU GO – DON'T WAIT UNTIL LATER OR THE FIGURES WON'T BE ACCURATE

- This looks like a timesheet: IT IS NOT. This is NOT a time and motion exercise. I'm not measuring you, but your workload. It is a study of how much real resource is allocated to each IT services function.
- To use the sheet, simply blank out the cell that approximately describes the time you spent. at what time of the day, working in what IT service or other activity.
- Don't forget to enter your name and the date at the bottom of the sheet.
- For background information on who is doing this to you, see www.noelbruton.com. Thanks for your help. *Noel Bruton.*

To time:	08:15	08:30	08:45	09:00	09:15	09:30	09:45	10:00	10:15	10:30	10:45	11:00	11:15	11:30	11:45	12:00	12:15	12:30	12:45	13:00	13:15	13:30
Helpdesk																						
Deskside fixes																						
Self-training																						
Administration																						
Absent																						
User problems																						
Projects																						
System maintenance																						
Installs/moves/configs																						
Meetings																						
Other																						

To time:	13:45	14:00	14:15	14:30	14:45	15:00	15:15	15:30	15:45	16:00	16:15	16:30	16:45	17:00	17:15	17:30	17:45	18:00	18:15	18:30	18:45	19:00
Helpdesk																						
Deskside fixes																						
Self-training																						
Administration																						
Absent																						
User problems																						
Projects																						
System maintenance																						
Installs/moves/configs																						
Meetings																						
Other																						

YOUR NAME:

DATE:

Figure 9.2 Resource commitment sheet

From it, we can see the peaks and troughs of the day (and the week if we do it for five days). We can see what route the enquiries take to arrive at and pass through the IT services process – because this system catches all enquiries, even those not officially recorded in any call-log. This is a recognition that not all enquiries will be logged because the majority of IT services are not required to log all their calls, even those from customers, whether they should have arrived by that route or not. Other reasons for calls not being logged include the complexity and appropriateness of the call-log form, meaning that it would take longer to log the enquiry than to resolve it; or repeat contacts on a previously logged enquiry.

But all these contacts consume resources, and for proper management information, we need to know exactly how much resource and where in the department that loss is being encountered.

The second type of sheet is the resource commitment sheet (Figure 9.2). This acknowledges that during the course of a working period (day, week, month), IT services staff may not always be working on producing the same service. But as they move around between services, this means that the resource committed to the production of each service is in a state of flux. So we cannot know, for example, precisely how much resource is being consumed by the generation of each service.

The object with the resource commitment sheets, when they return, is to add together the results to calculate the headcount overall in each activity area of IT services. This is where we find that there are actually fractions of people producing some services. We may also find by comparing call quantities on the enquiry sheets with resource commitment to call handling on the resource sheets, whether or not we put the right number of people in the right place to do what is required in the peaks and troughs of the day.

Note that the categories on both the sheets are generic. You would of course use your own categories, based on the services you had designed.

Reporting

A business report is a formal method of communication of business information. There is really only one reason to produce a report, and that is to be able to draw an informed conclusion resulting either in action or in an active decision not to act.

10.1 Data for data's sake?

We collect data and measure our activities not just to record what we did, but also to be able to look back upon our past to see what it can tell us about how to prepare for our future. In other words, the very existence of collected data implies that a report must come from them so that we can use the information. In fact one of the key difficulties in IT services reporting is not how we should go about it, but that we don't do enough of it at all.

IT services is blessed with some of the most sophisticated, operationally dedicated software tools in business. We have tens of vendors offering hundreds of products, which purport to collect data on every aspect of our interaction with our customers. All enquiries, diagnoses, installations, changes and requests can be logged in complex databases. Vendors compete with one another to produce systems that collect the most data, citing the benefit to IT services as the system owner that we can extract the most detailed and decision-assisting reports. The problem is that when it is possible to capture every item of information about every interaction, the temptation is to attempt to do just that. If we succumb to that temptation, the result from a measurement and reporting point of view is often – no, usually – a shambles. The following story is not about one company – I've lost count of the number of companies who have found themselves in this situation.

A company changing its support enquiry handling software decided to raise the quality of its reporting, so that it could potentially increase the range of feedback it could offer to its customers about their use of the service. In theory, for all incoming calls, an onscreen form would be completed. The first-line operative would select from a drop down list, a basic category in which to place this call. For each item in that category, there was another drop down list, to further define the nature of the enquiry. From this second selection, another drop down list was summoned. The result would be that rather than logging the details of the enquiry in free text, the content of the enquiry could be distilled into key words selected from predefined lists, which themselves were so designed to anticipate as many as possible different types of enquiry.

As well as gathering precise information on the technical details of the enquiry, the form also dealt with various aspects of the actual delivery of the service. This would include looking up the user to verify the service level this user and the enquiry would attract. The enquiry might have to be reassigned to one of several second-line resolving agencies, and the options for doing this were also presented on the form. The space required to gather and display all this information meant that the enquiry form was actually larger than the computer screen. As the service level could not be calculated and the enquiry not reassigned unless the enquiry had been placed in the appropriate category, the form would have to be completely filled in for every enquiry where reassignment was necessary.

The data collected by this form meant that the company could produce profoundly detailed reports on the real-life behaviour of every IT product and service.

Except that no such reports were ever produced. The attempt to collect so much data meant that the enquiry log form was quite complex and thus time-consuming to complete – in fact, most telephone conversations with users took less time than the form. At the end of each call, there was another in the queue, waiting to be answered. The first-liner's dilemma was whether to make the next caller wait even longer, or not log the previous call. The helpdesk was there first and foremost to serve the users – the call did not get logged.

The first-line staff commented that filling the form in did not really seem to matter anyway, as management never made any use of the information. Management rarely bothered to run detailed reports because they knew not all calls were logged, so the data could never provide a complete picture – and because they could not be sure of the extent of the incompleteness, they could not build in an error factor. So the end result was that for management information purposes, the call log data were as close to useless as makes little difference.

10.2 Data-centric and decision-centric reporting

This is the paradox of the over-developed measurement system. It is designed to gather data to produce reports and thereby prevents itself from doing what it was designed to do.

Invariably, the problem is this – we capture data because we can, not because we should. We start from a point of view of measurement – our system can tell us so much – rather than from a view of the use to which we will put the data. The ideal way to decide how to collect data is to design the report first.

Don't collect statistics just because you can, because if you do the collections will compete with one another and gaps will ensue.

Design the form from the point of view of the people who will be using it, because if you don't, they will invent their own way of using it the instant your form starts to impede them and your intended data will be incomplete.

I advocate a decision-centric way of deciding what statistics to collect. This means we design the report first, based on how people involved in the service interaction are likely to act in

Order	Data-centric	Decision-centric
1	Collect data on various aspects of IT services provision	Hypothesize what actions will be likely to maintain service standards
2	Run reports to see what they tell us	Consider who will be involved in the decision to take that action and what they will need to know for that decision to be well informed
3	Make decisions	Work out what data will be needed and how they will have to be presented so that they become information rather than just data
4	Take action	Collect those data

Figure 10.1
Data-centric and decision-centric reporting

189

certain circumstances. These can be hypothesized from experience. What service circumstances occur regularly that service managers, operatives and customers need to understand well so as to act appropriately? What is the nature of that understanding in terms of numerical data that could aid it? We then collect regularly only the data that we will need to report on regularly.

The decision-centric way of designing reports can be seen as an insult to the magnificent sophistication of the data-gathering tool. These software packages are not cheap, and when properly implemented, will usually require expensive programming to make them match the processes of the IT services department they serve. And it may appear that I am proposing minimal use of one of the greatest strengths of such products. My view is pragmatic, based on experience. Allowing a tool to do something just because it can is in effect creating a new process – for we will then have to allow for the tool's action in the way we work. We saw it above, when the first line could not adapt its way of working to the tool's demands, and as a result, the reports were ruined. IT services software applications have huge capability, far in excess of what is commonly needed. We should not feel we have to exploit that capability just because we paid so much money for it, or invested so much effort in it.

10.3 Snapshot reporting

This minimalism does not preclude gathering other data to make other decisions. These can be done on a snapshot basis. For example, we are considering the replacement of a major application. We need to know what service issues that application generates. So for now, we will pay particular attention to non-standard change requests, support enquiries and training course bookings for that application. We advise the first line that for the next few weeks, we are particularly interested in all enquiries associated with that application, and we have the call-log software display a brightly coloured reminder on the support staff's screens.

The reports we run as a result will have real meaning. We can incorporate those findings into the new design and the first-line staff will see the cause and effect of the data gathered for that specific purpose. When we have all the data we need for that decision, we switch the feature off in the enquiry handling software and revert to the minimalist gathering of data needed for regular report-based decisions.

10.4 Reporting in isolation

Wherever statistics are found, it is simple to produce a report. The most basic of these is the summary or total of an isolated statistic:

- 'What's happening?' or
- 'How many such incidents took place?' or
- 'How much time elapsed?'

The problem with any such number in isolation is that a conclusion based on it alone may not be safe. A number is an item of data – it can provide interest but it may not enable a decision to be made. For example – the number of incoming calls is increasing steeply. Conclusion – we need more call-taking staff so as to maintain first-line service levels. But add to that another statistic – that the recent increase in calls matches the proportion of all calls where the user is ringing up for a progress report, and a very different conclusion is reached – namely that the second line is not keeping clients sufficiently well apprised of the progress of their enquiry. So in fact, we don't need more staff, we just need to insist that the existing staff become more communicative.

What is needed is a bigger view of statistics than just isolated statistics. The other questions we have to ask include:

- 'Does it really matter?'
- 'What's causing it?'
- 'What other factors influence it?'
- 'Are we sure we have taken everything into account?'
- 'What other statistics could we gather that could make this answer more complete?'
- 'How do we interpret the result?'
- 'What exactly do we do about it?'

Very few if any statistics have meaning in isolation. Events do not occur in isolation, but among circumstances. Statistics need other statistics to put them in a context. A report has to enable a decision. For that decision to be informed, there has to be a complete context.

> ## Case study:
> ## Management reporting: the ITS departmental review meeting
>
> The meeting took place every Thursday. It was chaired by the IT services manager and every line manager in the IT services department

was expected to be there – so the section heads of first line, second line, infrastructure, administration and procurement, operations and the supplier-side manager for the moves and changes team were all seated round the table. The meeting always started at ten in the morning and the catering department had a standing instruction to bring coffee at that time, a buffet lunch at twelve-thirty and further coffee at two-thirty. So it was more accurate to say, not that the meeting happened on Thursdays, but that it took all day Thursday to conduct it.

The format of the meeting was fairly simple. The ITS manager addressed each attendee in turn and asked them to report how work was going on in their department, what issues were outstanding, what new events were anticipated, and what other sections might be impacted by those events.

The ITS manager had all the right reasons for this meeting. His goal had been to create an executive layer below him, so that the section heads could run the department even in his absence. But to do that, they each had to know what was happening elsewhere in ITS, and an open forum such as this meeting seemed an effective way of doing that. It also showed all the section heads that their peers were indeed pulling their weight. So as well as just being a reporting meeting, it was also a team-building exercise. The peer pressure intrinsic to the meeting was also important – a section head may rue the possibility of being publicly identified as the head of a department that was apparently not pulling its weight – so the attendee was potentially motivated by this pressure to produce results and demonstrate them.

Unfortunately, that was not how the section heads' staff saw it. It started when the staff began to resent the fact that their manager was unavailable for twenty per cent of the working week (month, year) just because of this meeting. It impeded the staff – because of course this was not the only meeting their manager attended. The section heads found themselves having to apologize to their teams for their unavailability, and this need to apologize began to undermine their authority. They came to feel that the meeting was not for reporting at all – but designed with the main purpose of cementing the ITS manager's control over his immediate reportees.

During the meeting itself, the ITS manager was hard-pressed to keep things on track. Each attendee came with a large agenda, as dictated by the purpose and structure of the meeting. This meant that much of what each attendee had to say was irrelevant to most of the other attendees. So attention wandered, boredom would be frequent – and some of the meeting members would attempt to alleviate that boredom by interrupting the flow to make comments or attempt to bring the meeting round to something more interesting, namely back to their own agenda. This meant that digression was almost always the order of the day.

The benefit of this long meeting was also questionable by another yardstick. The staff noticed that even though their manager had been absent for five hours, when he returned from the meeting, nothing changed. After all the meeting was a form of reporting, and not one to make decisions. So the staff never saw any benefit. The revolution came with the arrival of the corporate intranet. The technicians had created a sub-page for themselves to exchange technical information. Realizing that the main purpose of the weekly meeting was an exchange of information, some of the line managers began to wonder if the intranet could not handle information distribution. The next step was a well-worded proposal to the ITS manager. Each of the section heads defined their own key statistics and posted these on a secure page of the intranet, along with the key issues affecting their section, highlighting those requiring action by other sections.

Each section head was now expected to keep abreast of this regularly updated page – better still, all the ITS staff could see it too, if they wished. Information distribution was now a routine activity, and the brevity of each of the pages gave some to wonder why they had ever needed a five-hour meeting to impart such a relatively small amount of information.

After that, whenever the meeting took place, it was no longer for the purposes of communication, but to decide what actions to take on any exceptions or special cases described on the intranet report, and only where those exceptions affected the whole department.

And with all the section heads reading this report, they and the ITS manager found themselves going direct to one another to deal with issues that would normally have had to wait until Thursday.

The long meeting shortened to less than an hour and the standing order to the catering department was cancelled.

10.5 Reporting as a customer interaction

SLA reviews

In Chapter 8, we looked at the service level agreement (SLA) as a way of defining the relationship between IT services as the supplier and the user community or the company as customer. From the customer's point of view, the SLA is a contractual stipulation of the services and service levels to be provided. So SLA's always necessitate reports, because the users want to be assured that they are getting the service level they paid for. The format of the report and the statistics it will need to contain are usually described in the SLA. What may not be so well described, however, are the actions that should ensue given that the report describes a certain set of circumstances.

This is where the SLA reporting process tends to break down. The report is necessary to police contract compliance – but it should also be a vehicle by which both parties can resolve difficulties and shortcomings the report identifies. If it cannot, then the report can become little more than an opportunity for one side or the other to complain about the inadequacies of the part taken by the other side. If that happens, then doubt can descend over the integrity of the report itself.

It is usually IT services that produces the SLA performance report as IT services own the data from which the report will be extracted. In extreme cases of failure to meet contract stipulations, there may be a temptation to adjust statistical interpretation to produce the most favourable report and thus avoid complaints. Everybody wants an easy life.

This doesn't help either side. The report does not depict the actuality, so the real nature of the problem cannot be defined. Misunderstanding the problem takes us even further away from a solution, meaning that the situation will probably be just as bad in the next reporting period.

There are really only two ways round this. One is for the customer side to gather and report on its own version of service statistics. This is clearly impractical because the users are unlikely to have the tools to gather the data and they are so spread, geographically as well as hierarchically, that they could never be sure of the uniformity or completeness of their version. In any case, it is a duplication of effort, which is a waste. But worst, it is a defensive position, more likely to set the two sides more firmly at loggerheads than to come to a resolution. The other way is to decide what the reports mean and what responsibilities **both** parties must take in resolving the problem. If IT services is already failing, then somebody else has to get involved to assist them – their failure indicates they cannot resolve the situation alone. When IT services reports failure to provide a service in a routine relationship, there is something wrong with the relationship, not simply with IT services. Perhaps more investment is required, perhaps a decrease in demand or a change to its nature. There has to be a customer involvement and the SLA reporting process must reflect that.

Reporting as a service

Reporting of any kind consumes resources. If that report is produced for the benefit of an external party such as a customer or user representative, then it becomes a service. This means that report production must be treated in the same way as any other IT service – its market assessed, the necessity defined, the service designed, associated process created, staff recruited and trained, costs budgeted and so on. We will of course provide some information to the customer as a matter of goodwill – but regular reports must become part of due process. The consumption of resource means that if a customer-oriented report does not ultimately benefit the customer, then maybe we stop providing it so that we can use the resources elsewhere. In other words, we take reporting to customers as seriously as we take everything else we do for them.

In the routine of service provision, we will gather data about customer interactions; how and why they use us and what that tells us about how they need us. Of course we could use those data to redesign our services to improve their appropriateness, but there is another potential use for the customers themselves. User line managers can see how their staff cope with business computing. This may suggest changes to the computer systems, but also to the users' ability to cope. While I have stated elsewhere in this book that IT services should play an active role in managing users' technical competence, this does not detract from the fact that a line manager has a duty to ensure that his staff can do the job. The data we gather about user behaviour can show line managers how their staff are developing and suggest future opportunities and potential pitfalls in the deployment of user computing advances.

Reporting as public relations

SLA reports are often associated with shortfall or failure – there is a negativity about them. That can never be the whole story, for if IT services really were a failure, the company would find an alternative solution. If you were that bad, they'd fire you. The fact that you are still here means you're not that bad. And there's nothing wrong with pointing that fact out to people who need to know.

The reports we issue can be used not just to highlight exceptions and shortcomings but also to put those difficulties into perspective. Things are better than they are bad. We have a duty to manage our reputation so that it is seen in a positive light.

195

A relationship based on negativity will decay, which services the interests of neither party. The users need to see the benefits they accrue from their business relationship with us. This is not a cheap selling exercise – using statistical reports as a public relations output is a worthy contribution to the smooth continuation of the service relationship.

10.6 Operational reporting

In the midst of all this reporting to customers, we must also report to ourselves. Along the length of the IT services production line, there are events taking place as a result of other events successfully preceding them. Cause and effect, everywhere we look. That installation could only take place because the machine had been commissioned in an area where space had been planned and staff were available, because the need for those resources had been anticipated right back when the procurement section placed the order, which they were able to do because the administration manager expected a certain number of equipment requests that day and had staffed the desk to cope. In other words, there are statistics coming out of every part of the production line. We monitor and report to ourselves on these for the purpose of ensuring the line is operating as it should.

On any production line, there is a potential for a bottleneck, a spot where the input workload exceeds the output. The result is a backlog, which if not dealt with quickly enough, can bring the whole line to a halt.

This is why the operational managers across IT services are paying close attention to the critical statistical reports, which tell them about the capacity of their part of the line. They keep records of all significant events and capabilities, including the presences and absence of staff, their skillsets and their productivity.

This is operational reporting – looking after the internal-use only statistics that tell us everything is behaving as it was designed to do.

11.1 Outline of IT services tools

If we consider the numerous administrative functions in IT services, it becomes clear that we can use tools, in the form of computer automation or assistance, to help with our governance of our workload. We may have various specialized systems to look after various aspects of our work. The following is a list of the most common of these:

- telephone queuing/call distribution system
- enquiry logging, assignment and prioritization software
- remote control over users' computers
- hardware inventory
- knowledge base of previously resolved problems
- project management tool
- order book of procurement requests
- list of pending installations.

Less common, but useful especially in larger service departments may be:

- software license management
- end-to-end change request processing
- small-scale project tasks assignment and prioritization
- time recording
- resource allocation, staff to workload.

Case study:
'Users! Who'd have them?'

A computer manager alongside whom I worked for a while spoke these words. He went on to say 'And my staff are no better.' He was referring to an issue one may encounter in drawing up speculative lists of processes such as these.

These lists are not exhaustive. As is this whole book, the list is only one set of views of how IT services works or should work, and your version of reality may have fewer or more processes and thus fewer or more tools. I presume, however, that we have this in common – each member of IT services staff has a computer.

Wherever computers appear, people will invent ways of using them to assist in their work, which is of course the main benefit touted for computerization – it allegedly increases productivity, as people exploit its power to manage a process and store its output. The problem with that, however, as some IT managers see it, is that it can cause process automation and data to abound without central management – so what may be mission-critical systems are left in the hands of users rather than computer professionals.

There are consequential risks to that. They may include a less than perfect backup regime, imperfections and inaccuracies in the user-written program, an increased need for user support as these incidences of private computerization increase. It happens in our own departments – our staff may have invented sub-processes and are managing them through computer software, about neither of which we as their managers are aware. Thus any process we may design, and any subsequent list of tools we may draw up, may not be entirely accurate because our staff and other users have had the temerity to take responsibility for their job and do it their way, using the computer we gave them in innovative ways without consulting us. How dare they?

My colleague's answer to this was to declare that if he had his way, the corporation would uninstall and then ban all instances of a copy of a certain office software package, which usually contains a spread-sheet and powerful database-handling tool. This would reduce the need for user support in those areas, because as he reasoned, any form of computerization ultimately belongs to the whole company and thereby carries with it risk for the whole company – as such, any form of computerization should always be solely through the auspices of the IT department. But this was in a place where any request for IT development would take weeks and cost thousands as project management and programming resources were brought to bear.

In the end, my colleague had to accept reality. Users will invent ways of using computers to solve problems, the very existence of which we could never conceive. They have their own areas of expertise, so they see the world in a different way. As he came to modify his view, he took three significant steps:

● Insist that users store all mission-critical data and that systems were stored centrally rather than on local media. A word with the

> human resources department made it a corporate disciplinary offence to do otherwise.
>
> - Increase the scope and capability of the user training and support services.
> - Formally offer a service to support user-written programs, to include a published and version-controlled central registry so that other users could see what had been written elsewhere and would be less likely to reinvent.
>
> His worst fears were realized. Hundreds of mission-critical systems appeared. He thought his services would never cope – but they did. And he had a new way of justifying user computing, as the whole exercise showed that people were using computers to benefit the company in ways of which the company had been ignorant until now.

Within those two lists, I have included the tools in what I see as a rough order of how likely there is to be a commercially offered product for the job. That order also reflects how likely, in my experience, the issue is to have had any form of mechanization applied to it. So for example:

- Every company has a telephone system, and most commercial private automatic branch exchanges have some form of call distribution, even if it is only hunt groups.
- Surveys suggest that over 60 per cent of IT departments have installed a program for logging helpdesk enquiries.
- Remote control over users' computers is becoming increasingly popular, given how it often produces a rapid return on investment by improving technicians' productivity – the technology enables them to spend more time resolving problems and less time on their way to the user's desk to examine the problem at first hand. Users see it as a way of getting a problem solved more quickly. 'How do I...?' calls are simplified because the remote technician can illustrate rather than merely describe the solution[1].

But after that, the use of formal computerized tools usually begins to get a little sketchy...

---

[1] Remote control software is wonderful stuff. The problem is in using it for the first time – it makes for a major shift in ways of working and some IT support groups may be structurally or psychologically not ready for change on that scale. Staff who are used to visiting users may have reasons for wanting things to stay the way they are. But users too may bemoan the decrease in first hand contact with IT support that necessarily accompanies the technology.

- We all had to get our hardware inventory up to date in readiness for the millennium bug, but we may have let it slip a little since.
- There may well be a knowledge base built into the helpdesk software, but if your IT department is typical, no real use is made of the facility.
- Some people in the development department make some use of the project management tool for some projects.
- The order book is a spreadsheet written by somebody in the department but not many use it.
- The installation engineers have a whiteboard on the office wall that shows which big installations still need to be done and also has the telephone number of the pizza delivery place.
- Change requests are just different categories of enquiries in the helpdesk system.
- The technician doing the small project looks after his own task prioritization – some have to-do lists on their computers.
- We don't record time routinely, so there's never been a need to computerize it.

Everybody is busy. Good reasons for using a purpose-designed tool are the same as those alleged for any form of computerization:

- reduce that 'being-busy' – i.e. productivity as opposed to just activity
- improve efficiency and consistency in the face of a complex and demanding workload
- increase user productivity.

In the absence of a commercially available tool, providing one will often be left to the IT department. They in turn may be already too busy to set about writing software programs, spreadsheets or databases for which there may not be a regular use. The process requiring automation may simply be too specialist to be written by a generalist programmer or the eventual user may not be fully able to describe the process, so between them they simply do not have the knowledge to produce an appropriate system. Where there is no specialist vendor, there may be no tool, simply because nobody knows how to write it.

The use of a formal tool to manage a process will probably depend upon how often and by how many people that process is undergone. The more often and the more people affected, the more likely is mechanization. The less often, or the more specific the process, the less likely people may be to get around to buying or creating a tool.

The list also shows how different and purpose-specific these tools often are. It would appear that the work is so complex, with so many different processes producing so many different outputs, to mechanize it all would require a dozen or more tools. The software vendors seem to agree – at the time of writing, I have come across no tool to manage all aspects of delivering IT services. Where such offerings appear to exist, they are usually different systems linked together by a similar interface or perhaps little more than similar branding. The market for the more esoteric tools at the lower end of the list above is by and large seen as simply not strong enough for a vendor to justify investing the programming effort.

The vendors know their business, and seeing the market in that way would make that a reasonable conclusion – but perhaps there is another reason. It may also be because too many vendors still labour under the misapprehension that IT services is primarily about handling enquiries and requests from users. It isn't – it just looks like that.

11.2 Why no purpose-built IT services tools?

To see the true nature of the tools we require in IT services, we have to look at not just what the processes do, but why they exist at all. For example, helpdesk enquiry-logging systems are everywhere. But handling enquiries is merely an effect of our existence – it is not our actual purpose, it's just something we do as a by-product of our purpose. The same can be said of all those other tools that show little or no integration with one another. We have separate tools because the processes themselves are taken to separate by their very nature. Even though helpdesk and procurement and network administration all come under IT services, they use different tools because they exist for different reasons, have different cultures and objectives and do things differently. So preaches the received wisdom.

But base instinct suggests that cannot be right. IT services is a business, delivering defined services to a largely identified market. We know what we do, how we do it and for whom we do it. We are structured and organized. We have put mechanisms in place. We may be a grouping of various functions, but that is just detail. We have an overall purpose, to which that variety ultimately defers.

That overall purpose dictates that there must be a point of commonality in everything IT services does. If that were not the case, then neither this book, nor the esteemed Information Technology Infrastructure Library (ITIL)[2] nor the Information Technology Service Managers Forum (ITSMF)[3] could exist in their present form. All three of those entities presume a type of commonality across IT services, and then go on to base business strategies on that presumption. So the practitioners of our industry know that there is a point of commonality, which philosophically links all of IT services, albeit that we may debate what that point is. Given that, could it just be that the vendors and software designers have simply not yet caught up or spotted the industry-in-the-making that is IT services? And is this the actual reason why they persist in offering us reductionist tools? There is a need and a market for properly, fully integrated, joined-up tools in IT services. And if the vendors cannot provide it, perhaps we ought to consider doing it for ourselves.

Whatever interaction takes place between any point in IT services and either the user or equipment base, has ramifications at all other points in IT services. A newly arrived computer obviously affects the procurement and installation sections, because those two sections have a cause-and-effect mutuality in fetching the machine in, paying for it and getting it working. But that incident also affects the training section because the user may need new instruction. It affects user support, because this new user may increase the loading on the helpdesk or change the nature of the enquiries that group has to be able to cope with. It affects network administration because there may be a need to increase the number of ports on the switch/hub, the capacity of a router, the very presence of a cable. Server administration may need to create a new user ID, increase server capacity because of the implied storage and usage changes or change backup routines because this rash of new users means we'll have to start the backups earlier. And so it goes on. A helpdesk enquiry can have consequences that go right back to the way the applications software is designed.

Pass me that soapbox. Right. Now hear ye!

We in IT services need decent, integrated, joined up tools to match our integrated philosophy. Can we all finally cease messing

---

[2] A methodology or framework for running an IT department – originally created by the UK Civil Service, now widely used in the commercial sector also. Your author cautiously appreciates it but is wary of its flaws. See 'A few words about ITIL' in this book's preface.

[3] A body of IT professionals, strong supporters of ITIL, who meet to discuss and improve IT services management. Has representation in the UK, USA and elsewhere.

about with all these isolated spreadsheets, desktop databases, Web-logged knowledge bases and shrink-wrapped agglomerations with only a vendor's badge to integrate them? Can we do IT services management software properly now please? One tool with one core data item. It's about time – as a concept, IT services has been around for nearly a decade – but our tools remain primitive.

11.3 The 'point of commonality'

The absence of integration is in my view because we may not yet have identified that 'point of commonality' between all these different processes and procedures with their various tools. If there were such a point, then perhaps we could design tools that would cover many more aspects of running and administrating IT services in a more integrated fashion. We don't yet know what the 'one core data item' is.

Some vendors seem to think it is a hardware or software asset, so they base their software around that. They end up limiting their market then, because they miss out on managing other aspects of IT services that have nothing to do with hardware and software. Others seem to think it is a helpdesk enquiry, which means their program needs an add-on or a tweak to make it handle change requests, implying inadequacy in its natural state. So separate programs with separate modules.

Of course there may be genuine commercial reasons for this. Why offer only one big program when not everybody will need all of it? That would limit sales opportunities. Better to sell modules. But then customers will make judgements about which modules they want or are able to pay for, picking and choosing on the basis of cost as well as need. Inevitably, some modules will be left out of the buying decision – and so we're back to people writing spreadsheets to fill the gap. But the gap will still be there and through it will fall missed business opportunities, lost helpdesk enquiries, slipped projects, forgotten users, repeat occurrences of problems, illegal software installations, untrained users, inaccurate statistics leading to false management decisions, staff absent in times of emergency and all the other hundreds of things that can go wrong when one process or part of a process does not communicate effectively with another.

11.4 One concept to link all IT services operations

Fundamentally, IT services is about one thing. The whole of what we do can be summarized in one simple concept – which is that **all we ever do is change an asset from one state to another**. That's all. So the tool has to be able to register any kind of asset and record a change to it. Of course there are associated actions, like prioritization, statistical reporting and so on, but they are just gadgets on top. Know of an asset. Change it. End of story. A software program built around that idea could run the whole of the IT services department. But we will have to change what we usually mean when we talk of an 'asset'.

It's not just about lumps of hardware with barcodes stuck to them, although that's as good a place as any to start. If we expand that idea, we can apply it to the whole of the IT services world. It's about everything we own or for which we have a responsibility. That includes physical, virtual, humanoid or intellectual entities. So whether it has the latest processor chipset, occupies two gigabytes of disc space, likes to go out for a beer on a Saturday night or took four years of hard study to master, it is still an asset. We change that asset in an ordered fashion, and thereby produce a benefit. All we need is a tool to record how that asset changed state – and remember that one of those changes can be from 'absence' to 'presence'. So even if we don't yet own that asset, we can still account for it and all we do to get to own it is change it.

The only real difficulty is the record structure. Admittedly, it may take a little imagination to encompass in one database every type of change to every type of entity IT services may encounter in a professional sense. But the way round that is to stop thinking of an asset as a separate item and realize that assets can have assets of their own.

A user is an employee, and therefore a corporate asset. He will need a computer – another asset. He will acquire skills to use that computer – these too are assets the corporation may exploit. The same goes for the staff, equipment and skills within IT services. Everything is an asset and an asset must or may be:

- identified – what is it?
- sourced – where can we get it from? Who sells or makes them?
- correlated – what dependencies does it have, and what depends on it?
- placed/installed – where shall we put it?
- paid for – from whose budget are the costs of acquisition to come?
- owned – who owns it?
- repaired/upgraded – when and why? What spare parts were used and where did we get them?

- changed – where have we moved it, who is the new owner, over what period is it depreciating?
- performance assessed – how reliable or efficient has it been? What support enquiries have been associated with it?

In that list of impacts, I have implied that I am looking at a hardware asset. But as Figure 11.1 below shows, it does not need to be a lump of metal or plastic to conform to that sequence of definitions. What makes an asset what it is, namely its attributes, apply to any form of asset, be it structural, mechanical, virtual, human, intellectual or otherwise.

I contended earlier that some assets will have assets of their own. In the following chart, I highlight occurrences such as this by showing them in *italics*. If this table were a design for a database, these italics would make a direct reference, perhaps quoting the ID of one or more records of a given type. So for example, where we have a software asset on the horizontal axis, to be subjected to a change on the vertical axis, that process may begin with a helpdesk enquiry, which can be specifically referenced.

The only limit, to how many of IT services' responsibilities could be accounted for in this approach, is imagination. I have used only the 'assets' of hardware, software, user, IT staff, vendor, training course and helpdesk enquiry. You may choose to use more, fewer or others.

My contention is that tools based on a uniform structure such as this would lead to greater integration of the information within IT services. That would reduce the risk of confusion, gaps and delays in ownership changes and enable managers to think more clearly about the department as a whole rather than as a loose conglomeration of distinct processes.

11.5 Projects and tasks

In many IT services departments, there is a natural split in the kind of work. The main purpose of IT services is to support the day-by-day use of user computing. In other words, it is a maintenance function, rather than a development one. We deal with the glitches, the impediments to user productivity, the routine of keeping the user working and producing on the company's behalf. We operate, not develop.

We tend not to produce anything new, because we leave that to development. Except that that's simply not true. As part of our function, people will ask us to perform maintenance functions

Asset type & attributes	Hardware	Software	User	IT Staff	Vendor	Training course	Helpdesk enquiry
Identification	ID, name, model manufacturer, *IT staff* creating record	Name, version number, *IT staff* creating record	Name	Name	Name, type, specialization	Name of course, date of iteration	ID, date and time
Source	*Vendor* record	*Vendor* record (including where vendor is internal to IT dept)	(HR dept eyes only)	(HR dept eyes only)	Market sector, known competitors, recommended by …	*Vendor*	*User* or *IT staff* ID or *hardware* IT for automated lags
Correlations and dependencies	Project association, bandwidth/connectivity requirement, required *training courses*	Backup regime, space required, bandwidth/connectivity required, required *training courses*	Standard of equipment to be assigned, special duties requiring specialist support, service level targets, *hardware*, *software*	Standard of equipment to be issued, *hardware*, *software*	Contract stipulations, service levels offered, standards and methods of relationship	Topics covered, attendee prerequisites, limitations	Availability of *user*, specialist skills or *training course* attendance required of *IT staff*, service level target
Placement	Location installing *IT staff*	ID of storing *hardware*, installing *IT staff*	Location Record opened by *technician*	Section of IT, name of recruiting	Location, contact details	Course location	*IT staff* dealing with this issue
Financing	Budget, discount	Budget, discount	Service level category to be applied	IT management eyes only	IT spend to date	Fees, budget, discount	Currency value of user productivity lost thus far

Owner	User	User/department	Department	IT staff to whom reports	User/department (e.g. for specialist suppliers)	User/department	Name of IT staff to whom placement reports
Repairs upgrades	Date, reason, hardware parts used, helpdesk enquiry number	License renewal date, maintenance updates applied	Helpdesk enquiry numbers, training courses a-tended	Helpdesk enquiry numbers, training courses attended	Contract modifications, minutes of meetings	Improvements made to course	Progress, diagnosis
Changes	Date, reason, helpdesk enquiry number	Date, reason, helpdesk enquiry number	Date and details of move	Date and details of move	Date of and reason for choosing this supplier; reason for getting rid of previous one	Date of and reason for choosing this course, reason for getting rid of previous alternative	Changes to ownership or level of escalation
Performance assessed	Associated helpdesk enquiries	Associated helpdesk enquiries	Associated helpdesk enquiries	Performance against service level targets	Compliance with delivery dates, alacrity at dealing with passed-on helpdesk enquiries	Number of helpdesk enquiries on this topic	Against contracted service level

Figure 11.1 Asset types and attributes

that are in fact part research projects, part changes. To a certain extent, the installation of a new computer or the education of a new user is a change. And changes need planning.

Wherever there is a coming together of knowledge workers with high levels of technical skill, there will be experiment at the boundaries of those skills. Wherever there are humans, there will be exploration.

Technical ability will always be exploited, and so there will probably be a spill of work from development into services, just because the skills are available. These will be smaller scale projects than is common over in development, where they are set up to invent the new, but they will need managing nonetheless.

In IT services, we need clever people to deal with the complex systems we are asked to maintain. Then we give those clever people routine maintenance jobs to do in a system designed to make work look similar so that we can do it quickly, efficiently and often. We have made IT services a production line, because mass production is fast, manageable and cheap. Then we staff the production line with highly skilled people. They are going to get bored.

If you don't give them projects, they'll invent them anyway. And if you then don't govern that reality, it will rob time from your resource plans, because you will not know how much of their time they are dedicating to the designed routine of IT services and how much they are conversely squirreling away to their side projects. That project activity will happen, whether it is official or not. If it is unofficial, it will go underground. And you can't manage what you can't see. So get it above ground, where you can spot it. You will have happier workers as a result.

But the problem often is that there is no tool to manage the type of projects done in IT services. These are short developments – e.g. little databases, templates, helping the users by creating small software systems for them. Or they are typical IT services work but on a larger scale, thus requiring a little more planning than is normally necessary.

However, they tend not to need the absolute project management associated with building new systems from the ground up. So the typical 'project management' tool will not match – it tends to seem too big, and preparing it to manage a little project often requires an effort out of proportion to the project itself. In fact few tools actually do offer this match – which again leaves the smaller scale projects at risk of not being managed at all.

Nor do these projects fit precisely into the model described earlier in this chapter in the table of 'asset types and attributes'. The reason they do not fit is because they are simply a list of sequentially dependent tasks – and this is the clue to managing them.

There are milestones in any project. There are things to be done before other things can be started. The problem is when the project is seen as a whole, there is nothing by which to measure it except the final outcome. But on the way to that outcome, there will always be stages of progress. We determine these – and treat each one as a little 'asset' in its own right, where that 'asset' does comply with the definitions in the attributes table.

In effect, arriving at each of these milestones or stages is the completion of a task. So the project is broken down into tasks. To each task is an owner, even if it is the same individual throughout the project. And to each task, there must be a target completion date, which itself denotes a proportion of the end completion date for the whole project.

A stipulation must be made – that no project, no matter how small, can begin without management (or at least team leader) approval not just of the project but also of the tasks and associated target dates within it. That approval in place, work can begin – but more importantly from a management point of view, these individual tasks can now become part of resource planning. Because we know what project tasks an individual worker is due to complete today, we know also how free he is to do the routine work of IT services.

11.6 Match the tool to the process

A common mistake with tools deployed to govern workflow – and this is especially the case when such systems are commercially available – is that the tool is acquired in order to *provide* rather than *reflect* the process. Put more simply, the situation goes like this: process does not exist, or it is so incomplete that it is more or less left to the instincts of the employees. A vendor offers a tool that reflects a common way of running a department in roughly the same situation. So the tool is acquired and implemented in the desperate hope that it will provide 'organization in a box'.

It rarely does, and it is a common complaint of system vendors, that their products are bought and used by services departments that are badly organized at the beginning. They buy a software system which just shows up the gaps in their organization, and so blame the tool.

The process should always come before the tool. The process itself is a result of the design of the services, which themselves only look like they do because of a market assessment. So in other words, the tool is one of the last steps in the chain. When the tool is chosen, it must reflect the process.

We should not expect to buy a tool in a box. That can never work. Systems vendors are business people. They will tend, within their chosen market, to design their product to appeal to the maximum number of potential customers – so to everybody and therefore, by extraction, to nobody in particular. One thing that can be sure – one thing to be sure about – any tool designed to govern process that claims to work without customization will describe a generic process only. It cannot anticipate the idiosyncrasy of any one IT services department of a particular size, at any one point in its development lifecycle, with a certain portfolio of services, working in any one company, in any one sector of any one industry working under any one legal and taxation system. It cannot look like you. And the vendor should not be blamed when it does not.

One thing the tool must deal with precisely is the concept of **ownership**. Wherever a human being must be involved in order for a required result to be produced, the workflow and any tool governing it must state that human's name or designation. Without ownership there cannot be responsibility, without responsibility there is nobody to perform the act. Never assign a job simply to a group, because groups don't do things, individuals do. A project does not get assigned to the development department, it gets assigned to a project manager, or at least to somebody who will influence the decision of which project manager will eventually take charge of delivering the result. The tool must reflect this.

Conclusions

12.1 Greenfield site?

In this book, I am offering a means of designing an IT services organization from scratch. But perhaps your design won't be from scratch, because it's already established. People who came before you designed it and now its methods, relationships, perceived benefits and personalities are deeply rooted. In which case, the 'greenfield' approach I have advocated in these pages would appear to have limited applicability.

Not so. My career has shown me that in business and industry, establishment is no guarantee of absolute permanence. If it's not good enough, it can be changed, no matter how deep the roots. Furthermore, I encourage the reader not to assume that his predecessors 'designed' IT services or its components in the way this book advocates. I would contend that the structures and methods of most IT services departments owe more to reactive, survivalist, organic growth than they do to architecture and engineering.

When you are building the IT services operation you know your company needs, nod in the direction of the past – but don't pay too much homage to it, as much of it is an illusion created by conservatism for its own sake.

12.2 Subsuming the helpdesk

I acknowledge that very few of the readers of this book will be designing an IT function from scratch. What they may be doing, however, as is a current industry trend at the time of writing, is maturing an existing IT service around an established helpdesk, formalizing the service ethos in a once development-dominated IT department, taking the customer bias of the helpdesk and spreading it across IT to create a more complete service platform.

From about 1985 to about the turn of the century, the helpdesk was all there was to provide a service alongside the hardware and software. 'IT services' began to appear as a department in its own right in about the mid-1990s and would eventually encompass the helpdesk as one of its services. Given that the job of the helpdesk is to keep users producing, day by day, it is probably the most important of the IT services, but nevertheless it has been subsumed.

The helpdesk was the pioneer of IT services. For the world of information technology, the service culture was born there. It still continues to be for most organizations IT's principal point of contact with both the business and the user community. IT services as we know it could not have existed without the helpdesk having been invented and professionalized itself first. To impose a service ethos on the desktop support technicians and network administrators as we have done across the industry, we first had to experience the success of such a concept, and this was another of the helpdesk's achievements.

But for all that the helpdesk has done, for all the paths it pioneered, for all the magnificent change it wrought in the mindsets of technologists, we have to accept that its days are numbered. A new business culture has overtaken the helpdesk from without. First, it has already been subsumed into IT services, meaning that it now has become part of a bigger perspective. The replacement of the helpdesk with a larger IT services function was inevitable. We have made use of the helpdesk's methods in new ways – we can use it not just to solve problems, but to take any form of enquiry. Change starts there, where once it used to start between users and business analysts. Procurement goes through there, where once it may have gone through the users' own administrators or through a specialist buying department. All these new functions add to the enquiry quantity, so we find ourselves using call-centre technologies.

In fact we are expecting so much versatility from this thing that used to be the helpdesk that we simply cannot call it 'the helpdesk' any more. It is something new – at once the mechanical core of and representative gateway to IT services. It is not just one function in the IT services department, next to network administration, user training, procurement, administration, change management, telecoms section and desktop support. It is the hub of all these. And because of this new role, the helpdesk is dead. Long live IT services.

12.3 Taking mature IT services back to basics

Even if the IT services function is well-established, there is still scope for a more complete consideration of what it does and how it does it. You could go through the whole process as I have described it up to now, an exercise commonly known as 'business process re-engineering' (BPR). It does one good to have a complete rethink once in a while, not least to bring back into a fuller context all the cobbling together and rush jobs we've found ourselves having to do in the past, which have meant that some parts of our installation have drifted away from the standards and we're no longer entirely sure what is connected to or dependent on what.

The examples of process and service design I have described in this volume are largely the results of projects I've conducted for mature organizations, with established service patterns and delivery mechanisms who felt that their service catalogue and process documentation needed something a little bit more than a spring clean. They could have gone on for much longer without the rethink, but they had begun to realize that management information was not as complete as it could have been.

They had noticed, for example, that some jobs were disappearing into black holes or adding to the height of private 'too difficult' piles dotted around the department. The managers of those departments had begun to concern themselves with the professionalism of the service. In some cases, they were being faced with the dreaded 'corporate growth' – often by merger, acquisition or globalization. Others had found themselves in the fortunate position of being a major player in a market and having a short-term opportunity to exploit that position, which meant the company was going to grow anyway because of the pull from the market. There are lots of reasons for change.

To do this book's proposed exercise completely, in a typical IT services department, would probably take a number of months – more than two, probably less than six. That may seem daunting – but because the impact runs throughout IT services, no one person has to shoulder the burden alone. There will be functional managers in each of the main services departments – operations, helpdesk, infrastructure, administration and so on, each of whom could take their part in the service and process design. Or perhaps IT services management is structured around the service groups I mentioned in Chapter 3, namely response & resolution, production, consequential and administrative. Give them the job. Let them design their own production lines, thus giving them increased ownership of their product lines and the processes they undergo. You never know – encouraging them to think that big may suggest to them that they can take a bit more responsibility for their sub-departments, widen their perspective and hint to them that they can apply for your job when you get your voting directorship (if you're not on the board already).

12.4 Power and authority to act

Until that directorship arrives, however, there will always be the issue of authority and power. Do you have the right to consider and enact such sweeping changes in your department? Surely some upper sanction is required. Maybe. Maybe not. In business, power is a strange commodity. Learning about its true nature was something I did the hard way.

In the late 1980s, I got a job as a helpdesk manager. This was my first management job and the company that hired me knew it. So I was a tad surprised to find out that nobody in the company knew any more about running helpdesks than I did.

Coming from the rank-and-file, I naïvely assumed people above me in the hierarchy were more experienced, knowledgeable, skilled, knew better than I. There must be somebody up there who could give me a little guidance on delivering the visions I had for how helpdesks should be run. But no – that's what they'd hired me for. I was on my own. It was up to me.

This was the classic surprise realization of the first-time manager, slowly coming to terms with the fact that one really is the boss. Not all managers make that leap of understanding – there are still a lot of so-called managers out there who are leaving the real decisions and authority to those hierarchically above them. Some of these are indeed labouring under restrictive regimes so have no other choice – but many if not most of these are in that position because either they have chosen to abdicate power or because they have not realized the nature of power in the organization.

The lesson I had to learn, and it took a while in my case, is that in any corporation, power is not necessarily a conferred commodity but in fact a created one. The illusion of hierarchy is that all power starts at the top and is then apportioned by delegation through the subsequently lower ranks. This is wrong. For a start, it falsely attributes to the most senior entity in the corporation some kind of omniscience, a universal and prior knowledge of all the forms and ways in which power will have to be exercised throughout the life of the corporation. For power and authority to be delegated, they must have existed and been identified prior to the delegation in order for them to be conferred on the lower ranks. But the chief executive officer is not an omniscient god. He also lives, as we do, in a day that contains only twenty-four hours and has a brain that is biologically similar to our own. He has neither the time nor the capacity to consider all ways of exerting power and authority and if he cannot do that, then neither can he confer them to the lower ranks.

There is also the question of his motivation to conceive of and delegate power – I would also suggest that as he is a senior director, he probably also has not the slightest interest in the relative triviality of how power is exerted in the company's various operating departments.

So if power and authority are not conferred, where then do they come from? It is probably more accurate to see them as commodities to be invented and manufactured in a free market that has yet to spot a need for them. If the CEO could not know or care enough to create and delegate all forms of power, then it is safe to assume that this is a pattern repeated at all ranks. My boss does not necessarily know how to run the department he has hired me to run, because he has bigger fish to fry and that's why he hired me in the first place – to look after the relative triviality of the department he's given me. He has not even conceived of all the areas where I could exercise power, so he could never be in a position to delegate it to me. If I need power, I look around to see where it is needed because it is not yet currently being exercised, and I then go ahead and create it. Coming to that understanding was one of the most liberating things that ever happened to me. I sincerely hope it has happened to you.

I looked around at the staff and the space I had been given and examined both the spoken and unspoken expectations. With all this stuff already in place, I had mistakenly presumed, what they wanted me to do was to just continue running it the way it had been run hitherto. I was wrong about that, too. What I was looking at was a greenfield site and nobody had told me that in the interview – I later realized that they probably did not even know it themselves. Even though the department appeared to be established, in fact it was not. The possibilities, instead of being confined by senior constriction and corporate expectation, were in fact endless.

It was one of the biggest surprises of my career. Anything truly is possible. Things don't have to be done the way they always have been. It sounds trite, I know, but it has real meaning. It took me a little while to work out that the only real confinements were in my head, stemming from my lack of knowledge and my naïveté about the real capabilities of people in management positions. It meant so much to me that I have carried the idea throughout my management career. It culminates in this book's argument that even though the institution may be well-established, the methods practised, the personalities well entrenched, there is still somewhere an angle from which the whole edifice can be seen as a greenfield site. No matter what the legacy, the history, the distribution of power, there is always scope for change at the hands of whatever individual chooses to manufacture the power and authority to pursue a vision.

12.5 IT industry events encourage service change

So the helpdesk, the bastion of IT service provision up to recent past, is being absorbed into the IT services department as a whole. This alone makes re-engineering IT service delivery inevitable. There are other pressures in the IT industry that have already brought some companies to the point of completely reassessing the nature of IT support. Take spam email and virus attacks as examples. A few years ago, these were just mild annoyances that could be dealt with by install-and-forget automation. Not now. They take up a major proportion of the bandwidth of the Internet, cost billions and stem from an industry based fundamentally on dishonesty and deception. They have become such a threat to both software vendors and their users that governments have become involved. Operating systems manufacturers quake before the threat that somebody of malicious intent has found yet another gap in their security and so will threaten their reputation in front of billions of their customers. Something will have to be done. The vendors will have to protect their customers and their reputations. They'll close their software's back doors and put bigger bolts on some of the front ones. Computer security is about to become a very big issue.

We should expect that new versions of standard operating systems will become so secure that absolute technical authority will be needed to configure them – authority that will not be granted to the vast majority of users. So the users will be less free to change their computers – and this is bound to lead to a decreased need for user support. The IT industry is already starting to change its nature as companies make their computers more secure. This will bring about a considerable shift in power, away from user freedom and towards IT governance. In the near future, users will be able to use the computer for the purposes determined by the company and only for those purposes. Increased computer security will both demand and enable that.

The new technologies will necessitate a new and ultimately less hands-on kind of computer support. The associated change in what it means to be a user will bring a new ethos to IT services.

12.6 Last words

There is change coming our way. It is cultural, political, structural and technological. We are going to have to react to it, and we have the power, authority and knowledge to do so. This book is not just a way of re-engineering IT services – it is an acknowledgement that we have little choice but to begin that journey.

Index